HOW TO
WRITE IT

HOW TO
WRITE IT

A COMPLETE GUIDE TO EVERYTHING YOU'LL EVER WRITE

Sandra E. Lamb

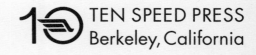
TEN SPEED PRESS
Berkeley, California

To Charles, Christopher, Eric, and Jay

Copyright © 1998 Sandra E. Lamb

Ten Speed Press
P.O. Box 7123
Berkeley, California 94707
www.tenspeed.com

Distributed in Australia by Simon and Schuster Australia, in Canada by Ten Speed Press Canada, in New Zealand by Southern Publishers Group, in South Africa by Real Books, in Southeast Asia by Berkeley Books, and in the United Kingdom and Europe by Airlift Books.

Design by Gary Bernal
Production by Lisa Patrizio

Library of Congress Cataloging-in-Publication Data

Lamb, Sandra E.
     How to write it: A complete guide to everything you'll ever write
over 250 models / Sandra E. Lamb
          p. cm.
     ISBN 1-58008-001-4 (alk. paper)
     1. Commercial correspondence. 2. Business report writing. 3. Technical writing
4. Letter writing I. Title.
HF5720.L36   1998   98-8420
651.7'4–dc21   CIP

First printing, 1998
Printed in Canada

3 4 5 6 7 8 9 10 — 02 01 00

CONTENTS

ILLUSTRATIONS AND EXAMPLES

Two weeks after starting my first job as a technical writer, my boss called me into his office. "Sit down," he commanded. Mr. A. owned a reputation as a hard-bitten, ex-military training manual writer.

He immediately started expounding on the necessity of clear communications in our medical instrumentation manuals. Some forty minutes into this monologue he said, "The military has the right approach. There is a precise test for evaluating the ultimate effectiveness of communications. In the Army we call it 'the fog count.'" He picked up a copy of the first manual draft I had written from his desk and began riffling the pages, a look of deep concern spreading over his face. "Let's apply the fog count method to this, for example," he elevated one eyebrow before continuing. "Starting with the first paragraph."

I started to sputter something about how I felt this introduction with equipment names like gaschromatography, instrumentation, and analyses might skew the results just a bit.

He held up a hand like a traffic cop and began to silently lip numbers.

After five minutes and a number of written calculations on his yellow pad (which he shielded from my view), Mr. A. held up his pad and pointed at his scrawls. Solicitously he explained that he had taken the total number of syllables in the first paragraph and divided by the total number of words. "Your fog count," he announced with a grief-stricken look, "is three." He rolled his lips tightly, making a small tuft of hair on his chin point accusingly at me. "Much too high," he said, shaking his head. His expression darkened and he became so pained, in fact, that I thought he might cry from the sheer magnitude of my transgression.

After several nervous and silent minutes, I suggested we try the test on the final draft of the introduction to a manual that he had just finished. Quickly I pulled two copies from the file on my lap.

"…Well…," Mr. A. cleared his throat, pointed the tuft of chin hair at me, and with a blush began to move his lips in time with his finger. I, of course, did my own count on the second copy. "Fog count," Mr. A. cleared his throat while his face flushed a bright red, "five!"

I learned two important lessons about writing that day:

(1) Make your writing simple, clear, and concise.

(2) There are many aspects to communicating besides the writing, itself, that must be considered.

Know them all. And use them wisely.

That's the reason I wrote *How to Write It*. To provide you with easy-to-use, total answers for creating effective communications.

INTRODUCTION

What will you be putting into writing over the next several months?

Maybe you'll write a personal invitation to a wedding anniversary party, a letter describing why you expect a manufacturer to replace your broken dishwasher, a resume, or a request to the neighborhood architectural committee asking the committee to approve your use of a new siding for your home. You may write an employee newsletter, a production report, a sales forecast for next quarter, a press release announcing a subordinate's promotion, a letter of condolence, a letter of recommendation, or a response to a letter from an attorney concerning your rights in a property line dispute. And maybe you'll want an error on your credit record corrected, or you'll respond to a notice of audit by the IRS.

Even though we are marching toward becoming a paperless society, every day the demands to produce well-written business and personal communications grow in number and complexity. So the ability to write easily and effectively is valuable and will make your life easier.

How to Write It is a complete writing reference. It was designed to equip you to take on all the writing tasks you will face, both personal and professional.

A quick review of the contents pages shows you just how easy this book is to use. The first chapter provides a solid start, focusing on writing principles. Browse through and select a specific written communication you find tough—if not impossible—to write. Turn to that chapter, and note how it is organized. It gives you visual examples—models—you can adapt for your own communication. And each chapter gives you guidelines to successful communication. You may use the lists of sentences and paragraphs to get started or to eliminate stilted words or phrases. Review several chapters, and you'll see that this book is organized to help make all your writing tasks easy and efficient. But more than that, each chapter is designed to help you produce an effective written communication.

Chapter 2 gives you some additional help with layout and design and illustrates how to create show-don't-tell visuals, like tables and charts. For sticky questions about forms of address and spelling, check the appendices.

This book will help take the fear out of any writing project and help you save time and prune your communications down to their essential, effective best. It will help you check what you've written and eliminate lethal, stilted prose. And, as you continue to use it, *How to Write It* will help you develop the skills of clear, powerful writing.

I. PRINCIPLES

GETTING STARTED

Put it in writing!

—ANONYMOUS

Stop. Before you dash off that written communication, it's important that you first think it through from beginning to end. Use the steps in this chapter in all your writing projects. Establishing the habit of using these steps will save you time and effort, and will help make your writing simple, clear, and concise.

WRITE FOR YOUR AUDIENCE

Your reader is your reason for writing. So, ask yourself some basic questions:

- Who is my reader?
- What does my reader know about this subject?
- What does the reader need to know?
- How will the reader respond?
    - Will he or she be receptive?
    - Will he or she object?
    - Will he or she be hostile?
    - Will he or she be indifferent?

Make some notes about your reader, as a guide. This will help you ensure that you have your reader firmly in mind which will, in turn, give your writing the proper focus.

Example: You are going to announce a company open house to department employees and to the general public. For the department employees, the focus and content of your announcement will be very different from the announcement for the general public. Think about who your two groups of readers are, what they already know, and what they each need to know. Your notes about what to include in the announcement to each group might look something like this:

	General Public	Department Employees
What:	Occasion/ Open house	Open house
Why:	New product/ background, development, benefits, etc.	New product launch
Where:	Address and directions	Specific instructions about areas to be open and those to be closed to visitors
When:	Date, time	Date, time, complete schedule of employees on duty for specific time slots
Who:	Open to public	Detailed assignments for each employee

Obviously, since you have two very different groups of readers, the best approach will be to complete two written communications.

Knowing your reader before you begin writing is vital to effective communication.

START WITH A CLEAR, CONCISE MESSAGE STATEMENT

It will help to ask yourself exactly what you want to communicate. Get down to the core of your message. Before you write your message in a single sentence, ask yourself some basic questions:

- What do I need to tell the reader?
- What do I want to accomplish with this message?
- How do I want the reader to respond?
- What do I want the reader to do after reading my communication?

Then crystallize the intent of your message by looking closely at your own motive in writing. Ask yourself what you want your message to accomplish. Do you want to inform the reader? What information do you want to give? Do you want to persuade the reader? Of what? Motivate the reader to take some action? Apologize to the reader? For what? Or, is your purpose to follow up on or confirm a verbal discussion, or to simply create a written record?

Most of your messages will be to inform or persuade; sometimes you will want to motivate.

A little work here will help to ensure that your message hits the bull's-eye. So, be very precise. Here are some examples of well-thought-out message statements written in a single sentence:

- You can save $525 each month if you use our accounting services.
- The meeting is at 10 A.M., Tuesday, in my office.
- Buy our Model 104B Analyzer.
- Please send me complete information on the Model L15 Wicker Whacker.
- We must reorganize our distribution system to be profitable.
- I cannot attend the values seminar.
- I recommend we invest $5.2 million in the new analyzer product line.
- I was so sorry to hear about the loss of your spouse.
- I need twelve volunteers for the dance.
- This plane won't fly!

- I want your suggestions on our lunchtime policy changes.
- We need to hire forty assembly-line workers.
- You overcharged me $376.50.
- Our Model 650B machining station will help your company make $1.4 million next year.

Distilling your message into a single, precise sentence gives you a head start. You'll be taking the next writing step from a secure position. Your message, when complete, will be strong and clear, and undoubtedly, shorter than it would have been without this step.

For practice, read through several communications on your desk. What, in a sentence, is the message statement of each? What should it have been? Is each message clear? Garbled? Off base? Complete?

Now you know (1) who you are communicating with, (2) the exact scope of what you want to say, and (3) what you want to accomplish with your communication.

You should view writing as a two-way conversation. Your job will be easier, and the end result will be better.

It's time to begin to put your thoughts in order.

USE A CLEAR, LOGICAL PROGRESSION

When you began thinking about writing, you had some ideas in mind. Maybe you even made some notes—a very good practice.

Write down the main points, or parts, of your communication in the most logical order. You can do this in the traditional alphanumeric system (I., A., 1., a.) or in a stream-of-consciousness form, often depicted by a series of connected circles, as shown in the two figures. You can put your ideas into your computer, or you can use index cards and write them out by hand. But start to think about organization and form your headings in as logical an order as possible. Then list subpoints: (1) Be consistent with the information and the background of your reader, (2) order your outline the way your reader most likely thinks about the subject, or (3) order it chronologically or developmentally.

By organizing your thoughts on the basis of what the reader needs to know about the subject and what you want the reader to do after reading your communi-

The Alphanumeric Outline

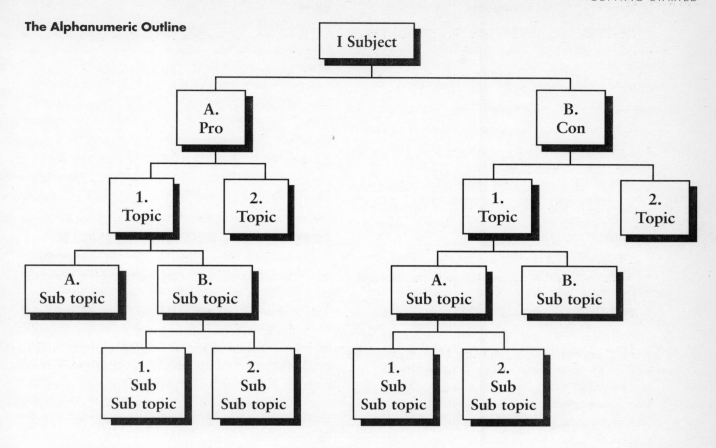

This traditional outlining method works best for material that follows a logical progression.

The Stream of Consciousness Outline

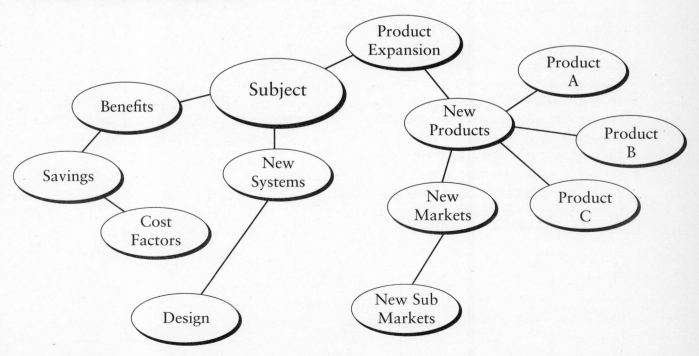

This outlining method works best for material that doesn't follow a logical progression.

cation, you will make your task much easier. And keep going back to your message statement. It will help you stay on track.

Your points should be lining up under these sections:

Introduction/Statement of Purpose
Why you are writing and/or what you are writing about.

Background/Explanation
Outline the body of your communication under the subpoints you have organized, keeping your reader in mind.

Summary/Conclusion
Summarize your points.

Call for Action/Response
Call for action and/or request the reader's response.

As you write down your points, think of them in terms of occurrence or chronology. This will give order to your ideas. If you are going to define a procedure like running laboratory tests, your ideas will need to be sequential. If you are writing about sales growth over the past five years, your order may be chronological. If your subject naturally orders itself in one of these ways, go with it. Your choices for developing your writing are many:

* Chronological
* Sequential
* Spatial
* Comparisons
* Analysis
* Division and classification
* Deduction (general to specific)
* Induction (specific to general)
* Cause and effect
* Increasing order of importance
* Decreasing order of importance

Think while you write, too, about whether illustrations will make your message clearer and more interesting.

FLESH OUT YOUR OUTLINE

Remember, a strong outline frees you to begin writing. The complexity of your message, your reader, and your own work methods will dictate when your outline is complete. And remember, too, that the steps are not all sequential: Some of the important steps in the writing process cross over and cross back. For example, during the outlining process, you will probably write some parts of your message, go on to the next step, and then return to a previously written portion of your communication.

COMPLETE ANY NECESSARY RESEARCH

You may need a number of kinds of research. At a minimum, you will go to the notes you made when outlining. You may also have to interview others for facts and input, research published sources, and read through special unpublished papers and facts. Or, you may have to do a survey or develop a questionnaire to get your facts and information. Make sure your research is thorough, and if you develop a research instrument such as a survey, use care in creating one that will give you valid, objective data (see "Survey and Questionnaire," page 149).

Although often the form of your communication is prescribed by your industry or discipline, you will need to fit your message into one of these general categories:

* Formal report
* Informal report
* Memorandum
* Proposal
* Letter

After selecting the format, follow the instructions given in the correct chapter and the conventions of your own organization, industry, or discipline.

WRITE YOUR DRAFT

Let yourself go. Using your outline, notes, written passages, and gathered information, give yourself over to the act of writing. Most writers should concentrate on getting all the writing done first, without trying to polish. If you have completed all the other steps, you will be clear on your point of view, methodology, and content. For many writers, the draft is written in a very concentrated work session, writing without rereading. Let your ideas flow, and get them all recorded.

REVISE

Although writing is hard work, revising is the most difficult task. Clear, precise writing that appears to have been written with ease usually requires hard, intense labor. Here are a few guidelines:

- Be sure you have written a topic sentence for each paragraph, and then pay off in the paragraph by producing the content this sentence has promised.
- Insert headings and subheadings to keep and direct the reader's attention and to make your message easy to grasp and visually appealing.
- Know that revising is usually a several-times-over process. Be diligent.
- Check for accuracy and completeness. Put on the reader's hat here: What does the reader need to know and in how much detail?
- Go back to your message statement and write your opening and introduction.
- Keep sentences short, between twelve to fifteen words.
- Keep paragraphs at about eight lines.
- Vary sentence length and structure to add interest.
- Think about visual appeal and arrangement as you proceed.
- Check for continuity and create transitions. Does each paragraph build on the one before it?
- Be sure your message is clear. Have others read it and give you input.
- Check for any word or paragraph problems outlined in the following sections.

EDIT, EDIT, EDIT

Writing is really talking on paper, so make your communications talk. Sometimes reading aloud what you've written turns on a light. Listen for stilted words, remoteness, obscurity. You want your communication to sound conversational, more like a face-to-face conversation than a speech. That means, of course, that you should look for any hint of talking down to your reader.

There is a place for formal writing, but formal writing isn't pompous, wordy, remote, stilted, or stuffed with polysyllabic words.

Be Clear and Be Brief

It's very easy to get attached to what you write, but in revising, you must be ruthless. Ask yourself whether each word has real meaning, a necessary function. If the answer is no, cut it. Getting rid of all the deadwood takes a real effort.

Simplify for the General Reader

Use a simple word if it works. Use technical words only when they are the best choice—when their meaning is known to your reader and when technical words are the most direct and precise. This doesn't mean that your writing will be dull or simplistic. It will be clear and easy to understand. Check the examples at the end of this chapter for direct, simple words instead of pompous, stuffy ones to make your meaning clear.

Make Your Communication Reader-Friendly

Reader-friendly writing means clear and direct writing, yes. It also means an overall visual layout and appearance that invites the reader to read. Use white space so your communication looks open and easy to read, and use headings to catch the reader's attention. Lists, graphs, and charts will make your communication visually appealing.

For lists, observe a few rules:

- Start each step with an action verb, but not the same one.
- List each step separately. Don't combine them.
- Make sure each step is in logical sequence.
- Write each step as a full sentence.

- Keep the sentence construction parallel.
- Use an active voice, if possible.

Use Parallel Construction and Consistent Tense

It's amazing how important this principle is. When your ideas are equal, give them equal construction, whether they are items in a list, headings, sentences, or phrases. You can do this by using the same grammatical structure. Like the list statements we just did, each is constructed as a complete sentence, and each begins with an action verb.

Use Powerful Words

Verbs are your friends. They will happily carry your meaning if you select the correct ones. Verbs enliven your writing and turn passive statements into active ones, if you pick them from the active side of the family.

And don't stop at active verbs; select colorful, precise, and vibrant ones. Let's try these comparisons:

The hour passed very slowly.
The hour crept by.
The hour inched by.
The hour crawled by.
Time stood still.

None of these sentences is wrong. Some verbs just do more precise work than others. Some create a more vivid picture, and some are more appealing because they don't suffer from overuse. If you write in an active voice, use active verbs, and select them for their precise meaning, you will enliven your communications. So, put your subjects to work with active verbs.

The most listless verbs, and often worst offenders, are those in the nominals category—verbs turned into nouns by added endings: *-ing, -tion, -ment, -ance, -ing, -al,* or *-ure.* Here are a few of those verbs that usually appear with *to* in front of them:

Verb	Nominal
assess	assessment
attend	attendance
conclude	conclusion
direct	direction
fail	failure
inflate	inflation
provide	provision
submit	submission

You can see how important it is to use active verbs whenever possible.

Now, with these principles in mind, turn to the chapter that features the communication you are writing. Each chapter is set up so you can use these steps to make your writing reader-friendly and bullet-proof. You may want to check the lists in this chapter while writing. The chart that follows provides some more guidelines to help you select simple, powerful words.

To help the flow of your ideas, use words and phrases that work as road signs for your readers.

Use Transition Words

To Help the Reader Understand	Use
sequence	then
	in addition
	to enumerate
	number __
	first, second, third
	next
	the next in this series
	besides these
contrast	unlike
	different
	in spite of
	on the other hand
	on the contrary
	opposite
	opposing
	however
	contrary to
	very different
similarity	like
	the same
	similar
	close
	likewise
	also
	near

To Help the Reader Understand	Use
an explanation	for example
	one such
	for instance
	to illustrate
	also
	too
	to demonstrate
cause and effect	then
	as a result
	for this reason
	the result was
	what followed
	in response
	therefore
	thus
	because of
	consequently
	the reaction

Substitute Simple, Direct Words

Instead of	Use
10 A.M. in the morning	10 A.M.
a substantial segment of the population	many people
above mentioned	these, this, that, those
absolutely complete	complete
absolutely essential	essential
accounted for by the fact that	caused by
achieve purification	purify
activate	begin
actual experience	experience
add the point that	add that
adequate enough	adequate
advise	tell
along the lines of	like
am in receipt of	have
an example of this is the fact that	for example
analyses were made	analyzed
answer in the affirmative	yes
any and all	any, all
are of the opinion that	think that, or believe that
as of this date	today
as to whether	whether
assent	agree
assist	help
at a price of $10	at $10
at the present time	now
at the present writing	now
at this point in time	now
attached hereto	attached

Instead of	Use
attached please find	attached is
attempt	try
attributable	due
basic fundamentals	facts, basics, fundamentals
be desirous of	want
came to the conclusion	concluded
cancel out	cancel
category	class
cease	stop
circle around	circle
coalesce	join
cognizant	aware
collect together	collect
compensate, compensation	pay
components	parts
concede	admit
conceive	think
conception	idea
conclude, conclusion	end
connect to	connect
consensus of opinion	consensus
consequent results	results
considerable	much
constructive	helpful
deemed it necessary to	[eliminate]
deficiency	lack
delete the most insignificant	delete
deliberation	thought
delineate	outline, draw
demonstrate	show

9

GETTING STARTED

Instead of	Use
descend down	descend
despite the fact that	although
determine	find
disappear from sight	disappear
discontinue	stop
during the year of 1999	during 1999
early beginnings	beginnings
effect a change in	change
eliminate	cut out
empty out	empty
enclosed herein	enclosed
encounter	meet
endeavor	try
enter in the program	enter
equitable	fair
establish	set up
evince	show
exactly identical	identical
exemplify	show
exhibits a tendency to	tends
facilitate	help
few in number	few
first and foremost	first
following after	following
for the purpose of	for
for the reason that	because
frequently	often
function	use
give encouragement to	encourage
give an indication of	indicate
give a weakness to	weaken

Instead of	Use
have at hand	have
hold in abeyance	wait
I am of the opinion	I think
it has been recognized that	[eliminate]
illustrate	show
in a satisfactory manner	has
inasmuch as	because
in my opinion I think	in my opinion, or I think
in order of importance	order
in regard to	[eliminate]
in the amount of	for
in the course of	during
in the event that	if
in the interest of time	[eliminate]
in the majority of cases	most, or usually
in the majority of instances	often
in the nature of	like
in the near future	soon
in the neighborhood of	about
in the matter of	about
in the normal course of our procedure	normally
in the opinion of this writer	in my opinion
in the same way as described	as described
in view of the fact that	because
indicate	show
initial	first
initiate	begin or start
institute an improvement in	improve
interpose an objection	object

Instead of	Use
involve the necessity of	require
is corrective of	corrects
is found to be	is
is indicative of	indicates
is suggestive of	suggests
it appears that an oversight has been made	I [or we] overlooked
it has been brought to my attention	I have learned
it is noteworthy that	[eliminate]
it is the intention of this writer to	[eliminate]
illustrate	show
it is apparent that	therefore, or it seems that
it is incumbent on me	I must
it would not be unreasonable to assume	assume
I will endeavor to ascertain	I will try to find out
join together	join
large in size	large
make a decision to	decide to
make the acquaintance of	meet
may I call your attention to	[eliminate]
may or may not	may
the modifications contained herein	these changes
most complete	complete
multitudinous	many
mutual cooperation	cooperation
my personal opinion	my opinion
new innovation	new
objective	aim
obligation	debt
of a confidential nature	confidential
on behalf of	for

Instead of	Use
on the basis of	by
on the few occasions	occasionally
on the grounds that	since
on the part of	by
optimum, optimal	best
owing to the fact that	since
perform an analysis of	analyze
perform an examination of	examine
perhaps I should mention that	[eliminate]
permit me to take this opportunity	I want to
pertaining to	about
preparatory to	before
present a conclusion	conclude
prior to	before
prior to the time of/that	before
proceed	go
proceed to separate	separate
procure	get
prolong the duration	prolong
provided that	if
provide information about	inform
the purpose of this memo	[eliminate]
range all the way from	range from
reached an agreement	agreed
report back	report
secure	get
similar	like
state the point that	state that
still continue	continue
structure our planning pursuant	make plans
subsequent to	after
subsequently	later

Instead of	Use
supplement	add
surrounding circumstances	circumstances
take into consideration	consider
take under advisement	consider
taking this factor into consideration, the committee made an agreement	the committee agreed, or we agreed
tangible	real
terminate	end, stop, dismiss
the committee made the decision	the committee decided, or we decided
the fact that	[eliminate]
the field of photography	photography
the question as to whether	whether
the undersigned	I
the writer	I
there is no doubt that	[eliminate]
this report is an offering	this report offers
to be in agreement with	agree
to have a preference for	prefer
to summarize the above	in summary

Instead of	Use
total effect of	effect of
transact	do
under date of	dated
under no circumstances	never
undertake a study of	study
until such time as	until
utilize, utilization	use
visualize	see
we deem it advisable	I suggest
with a view to	to
with regard to	about
with reference to	[eliminate]
with the result that	so that
with this in mind, it is therefore clear	therefore
within the realm of possibility	possible
what is believed is	[eliminate]
whereas	but
whereby	which
whether or not	whether
you will find attached	attached is, or here is

2

LAYOUT AND DESIGN

One picture is worth a thousand words.

—FRED R. BARNARD

Design and layout can make your communication come alive and make your message immediately apparent. Now, with so much technology at your fingertips, design becomes much simpler, but you must develop the ability to plan and visualize what you want to convey. Then decide what will appeal to your reader and help his or her understanding of the material.

Plan. Use spacing, indenting, underlining, numbering, and different sizes and types of lettering to make your message more understandable and visually appealing. Learn to think in terms of text formats that set off paragraphs; typefaces to denote sections; use of color; and graphs, tables, flowcharts, drawings, and lists that promote your message and reinforce it to your reader.

THINK ABOUT CONTENT

- Know your audience and decide what, precisely, they need to know.
- Decide what you want to emphasize to begin to focus on how you will create special displays.
- Review the options of the system you will use to produce your communication. Desktop publishing and computer capabilities create many possibilities.
- Begin to think in multiple colors if your communication warrants and you have this capability and budget.
- Examine your text for ways to make it visually more appealing:
  1. Use boldface headings in a larger type size to draw the reader's interest and help him or her focus on the subject.
  2. Use white space to create the impression that your communication is easy to read.
  3. Use underlining, indenting, and varied but consistent spacing to break up the density of the text and help the reader scan for specific information.
  4. Decide which elements of your communication should be reinforced in graph or chart form and create these.
  5. Decide if a lot of your information can be distilled into table form for easy, immediate understanding.
- Create tables to display large important groups of data:
  1. Think of general-information tables first, keeping them as simple as possible.
  2. Use specific-information tables as needed, but don't create tables where simple tabulating within the text works as well.

- Design graphics that are understandable at a glance, using these guidelines:
  1. Reduce graphics to their simplest, clearest elements.
  2. Make graphics appropriate to their contents in size and arrangement.
  3. Use complete titles that answer the *who, what, why, when, where,* and *how* questions.
  4. Number graphics consecutively by type.
  5. Locate graphics near the related text.
  6. Refer to graphics in the text.
  7. Use footnotes as needed below the graphics.
- Pay special attention to the layout of text and images. Remember, the eye focuses first on the upper outside corner of a left-hand page and the lower outside corner of a right-hand page.
- Create a communication in which all the parts look like a unified whole.
- Reader-test your communication whenever possible and make any necessary changes.

ELIMINATE WRONG MESSAGES

Remember that graphics supplement your written message; they don't replace it. Don't create visual "noise" by using too many, confusing, or too varied illustrations, charts, or graphs, and don't make the visuals too complex. This defeats the purpose.

Selecting Type Arrangement

Design and layout can make your communication come alive and make your message immediately apparent. Now, with so much technology at your fingertips, design becomes much simpler, but you must develop the ability. Design and layout can make your communication come alive and make your message immediately apparent. Now, with so much technology at your fingertips, design becomes much simpler, but you must develop the ability Design and

Long lines, double-spaced

Design and layout can make your communication come alive and make your message immediately apparent. Now, with so much high your fingertips, design becomes much simpler, but you must develop the ability to plan and visualize what you want to convey. Then decide what will appeal to your reader and help his or her under-

Short single-spaced lines, which make use of white space

Design and layout can make your communication come alive and make your message immediately apparent. Now, with so much technology at your fingertips, design becomes much simpler, but you must develop the style, want to convey. Then decide what will appeal to your reader and help his or her understanding of the material.

Design and layout can make your communication come alive and make your message immediately apparent. Now, with so much technology at your fingertips, design becomes much simpler, but you must develop the style, want to convey. Then decide what will appeal to your reader and help his or her understanding of the material.

Type on facing pages should align at top, left, and bottom

Justified Copy

Design and layout can make your communication come alive and make your message immediately apparent. Now, with so much technology at your fingertips, design becomes much simpler, but you must develop the ability to plan and visualize what you want to convey. Then decide what will appeal to your reader and help his or her understanding of the material.

Design and layout can make your communication come alive and make your message immediately apparent. Now, with so much technology

Left justified
Lines start at the same position at left.

Design and layout can make your communication come alive and make your message immediately apparent. Now, with so much technology at your fingertips, design becomes much simpler, but you must develop the ability to plan and visualize what you want to convey. Then decide what will appeal to your reader and help his or her understanding of the material.

Design and layout can make your communication come alive and make your message immediately apparent. Now, with so much technology

Fully justified
Lines start and end at the same position on the left and right, respectively.

Design and layout can make your communication come alive and make your message immediately apparent. Now, with so much technology at your fingertips, design becomes much simpler, but you must develop the ability to plan and visualize what you want to convey. Then decide what will appeal to your reader and help his or her understanding of the material.

Design and layout can make your communication come alive and make your message immediately apparent. Now, with so much technology

Right justified
Lines end at the same position at right.

Setting Type in Columns

Design and Layout

Design and layout can make your communication come alive and make your message immediately apparent. Now, with so much technology at

your fingertips, design becomes much simpler, but you must develop the ability to plan and visualize what you want to convey.

Then decide what will appeal to your reader and help his or her understanding of the material. Design

Two-column grid

Design and Layout

Graphic design and layout can make your communication come alive and make your message immediately apparent. Design and layout can make your communication come alive and make your message immediately apparent.

Now, with so much technology at your fingertips, design

becomes much simpler, but you must develop the ability to plan and visualize what you want to convey. Then decide what will appeal to your reader and help his or her understanding of the material.

Design and layout can make your communication come alive and make your message immediately apparent. Now, with so much technology at your fingertips, design becomes much simpler, but you

must develop the ability to plan and visualize what you

Design and layout can make your communication come alive and make your message immediately apparent. Now, with so much technology at your fingertips, design becomes much simpler, but you must develop the ability to plan and visualize what you want to convey.

Then decide what will appeal to your reader and help his or

Three-column grid

Design and Layout

Design and layout can make your communication come alive and make your message immediately apparent. Now, with so much technology at your fingertips, design becomes much simpler, but you must develop the ability to plan and visualize what you want to convey. Then decide what will appeal to your reader and help his or her understanding of the material.

Design and layout can make your communication come alive and make your message immediately apparent.

Now, with so much technology at your fingertips, design becomes much simpler, but you must develop the ability to plan and visualize what you want to convey. Then decide what will appeal to your reader and help his or her understanding of all the fantastic material. Design and layout can make your communication come alive and make your message apparent.

Layout

Design and layout can make your communication come alive and make your message immediately apparent.

Now, with so much technology at your fingertips, design becomes much simpler, but you must develop the ability to plan and to visualize exactly what you want to convey.

Six-column grid
This design consists of two text blocks, the first with four columns of space, and the second with two.

Table

Types	Samples		
	Column 1	Column 2	Column 3
A	xxx	xxx	xxx
B	xxx	xxx	xxx
C	xxx	xxx	xxx
D	xxx	xxx	xxx
Total	xxx	xxx	xxx

Use tables to display groups of data.

Flow Chart

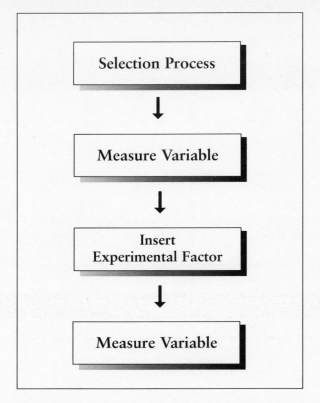

Use flowcharts to show progression or sequential steps.

Line Chart

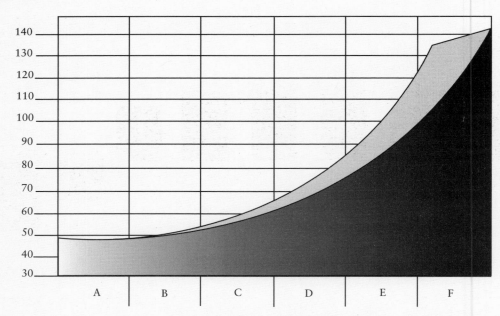

Use a line chart to show quantity change.

Horizontal Bar Chart

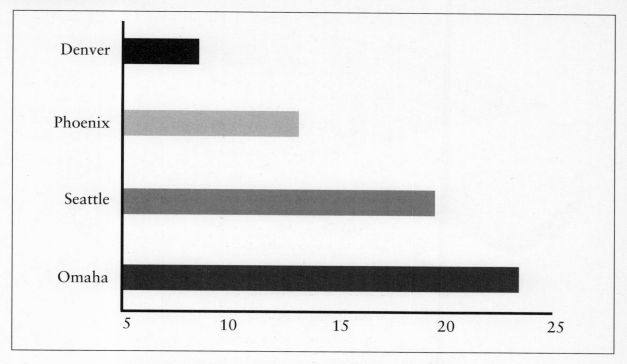

Use simple horizontal bar chart to show quantity change over time or distance.
Use a multiple bar chart to show up to several kinds of quantities. Different colors add visual interest.

Bilateral Bar Chart

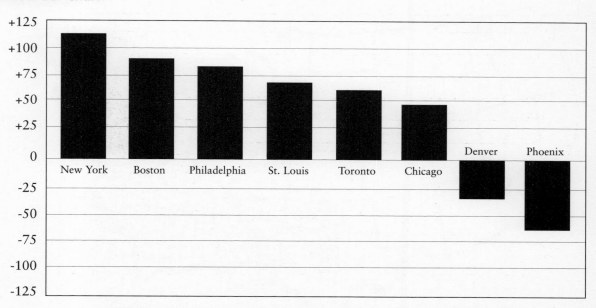

Use the bilateral bar chart to show plus and minus changes and percentage changes.

Pie Chart

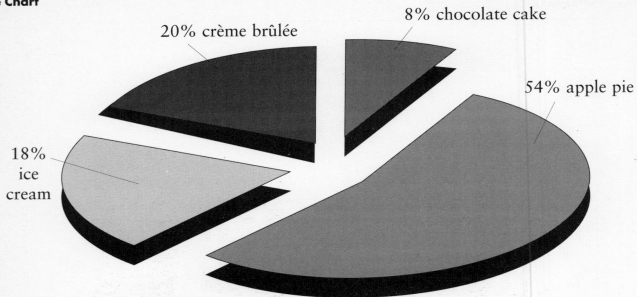

20% crème brûlée

8% chocolate cake

54% apple pie

18% ice cream

Use the pie chart to show how the whole is divided.

Statistical Map

Use a statistical map to illustrate distribution.

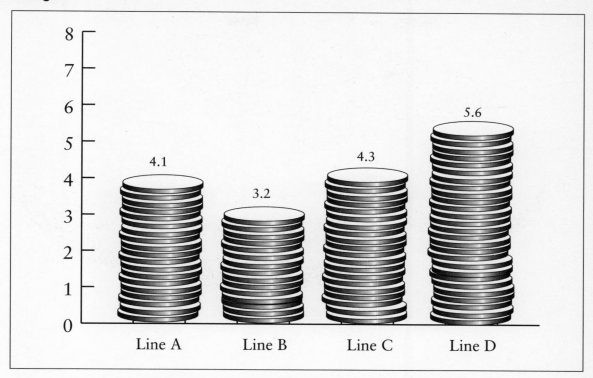

Pictogram

Use the pictogram to show quantitative differences in picture form.

II. SOCIAL

3
ANNOUNCEMENT

The difference between the right word and almost the right word is the difference between lightning and the lightning bug.

—MARK TWAIN

An announcement may be good news or bad news, but the form is consistent: Get the reader's attention, then give him or her the single message you want to communicate. Be direct, focused, and brief.

DECIDE TO WRITE

Announcements are suitable for many of the changes in our lives:

- Change of address
- Anniversary: wedding or business
- Personal life event: graduation, wedding, birth, adoption, marital separation, divorce, retirement, or death
- Employee change: resignation, promotion, transfer, special achievement, new employees, job opening
- Opening a business, branch office, or store
- Business changes: new business name, price changes, product recall, new programs, products, policies, hours, practices, contracts, organization buyout, merger, bankruptcy, expansion, acquisition, company layoff, downsizing, closing, or record sales
- Seminars, workshops, or conferences
- Open house

THINK ABOUT CONTENT

- Ask yourself *who, what, when, where, why,* and *how* to help focus the information you want to communicate.
- State the information in order of importance.
- Be direct, brief, and concise.
- Follow the prescribed format of different kinds of announcements.
- Emphasize the goodwill aspects of your news. If your company is changing working hours, for example, emphasize the greater convenience for employees and customers.
- Use the need-to-know guideline in making your announcement. Who needs to know your news?
- When it's appropriate, emphasize the reasons for your news, to promote understanding and goodwill.

ELIMINATE WRONG MESSAGES

- An announcement should supply complete, basic information. It is not the vehicle for lengthy explanations or extraneous facts. Even when the announcement is a hybrid—combined with a sales message, for example—the format and style should strengthen the single message.

- Don't let employees hear or read your information from an outside source first.
- Don't put off a bad news announcement. It is usually best that your bad news be received directly from you rather than from another source.

CONSIDER ANNOUNCEMENT TYPES

- A personal name change is announced by stating that, as of (date) the person formerly known as (name) will be known as (name). No explanation is needed, but written notes to friends and colleagues are desirable.
- Graduation announcements are usually formal and printed but certainly may be handwritten. This announcement has evolved because space at graduation ceremonies has had to be restricted to only a few invitations per graduate. This announcement may be sent with an invitation to a graduation party. "No gifts, please" may be written in the lower left-hand corner.
- Engagement announcements can be handwritten or printed and should be sent to relatives and friends. Because of the rich tradition of this announcement in our culture, a special section has been devoted to it (see page 31).
- Wedding announcements are often printed in a prescribed format. They may also be personal letters or notes (see "Invitations," page 48).
- Birth or adoption announcements are usually made by both parents to friends and relatives. The announcements may either be selected before the birth, and then the final information phoned in to the printer after the birth, or commercial cards with blanks may be purchased and then filled in and sent out. Include the infant's sex; birth date (and time, if you wish), or age (if adopted); parents' full names; siblings' names (if you like); and an expression of happiness. Parents may also send an announcement to newspapers and other publications that print this information:

Roger and Brenda Dell of 344 South Parker Road, Littleton, are delighted to announce the birth of a son, Jared, on August 12, at Littleton Hospital. They have one daughter, Meredith, age four. Mrs. Dell is the former Miss Brenda Sales.

When the couple has been divorced before the birth, the announcement is made by the mother, in the name she now uses. Widowed women may use "Sally and the late Paul Davidson." A single mother should use her chosen title and name. In all these cases, personal announcements are in the best taste. Personal birth and adoption announcements should also be sent to close colleagues and work associates.

- Retirement announcements are especially important when the retiree is a doctor, dentist, or other professional. These announcements are usually combined with the announcement of the person taking over the practice or any other changing business information. Printed announcements with a good-news emphasis are important here.
- A death in the family is difficult at best. The immediate family must notify other relatives and friends by telephone and ask that they notify others. If funeral arrangements have been made, this information can be given, eliminating the need for another round of calls. The next step is notifying the attorney of the deceased. Written announcements generally take a number of forms:

1. An announcement may be arranged by the funeral home, or a paid newspaper notice may be placed.
2. An obituary may be written by newspaper staff. Usually the information is verified by a close family member. The information usually included is the complete name of the deceased (including the original family name), date of death, date of birth or age at the time of death, address at the time of death, names of immediate family and place of residence, hours and location where friends may call on the family, place and time of the funeral, whether the funeral is private, and frequently

a request that any contributions be given to a charity instead of flowers being sent to the funeral home.

3. A news article describing the achievements and contributions of the deceased may be written by newspaper staff or a family representative.

4. Printed announcements may be sent to colleagues and out-of-town acquaintances.

5. Handwritten notes may be sent to out-of-town relatives, friends, and acquaintances.

- Legal announcements or announcements with legal implications should be made in conjunction with the proper attorney. Plans to remarry where there are legal agreements in place, adoption of children, change in payment of debts incurred, etc., all come under this category.

- Annulments are very private matters and should be handled with the utmost confidentiality. Generally, only immediate family and close friends need be told, and then only on a need-to-know basis, informally, verbally, or in a personal note.

- Divorce is also the private business of the two people involved and a printed announcement is in very poor taste. Informal notes may be sent, as necessary, to those who have a need to know. A statement and no explanation is best.

- A new business (opening a branch, moving to a new location, introducing a new product, etc.) can be an opportunity to stage an open house. Printed announcements or invitations, a newspaper announcement, and perhaps announcements by other media are the best ways to get the word out.

- Good business news is best announced by using a press release. Sending the release to newspapers and other media is a good way to get the word out. Be sure to include a contact person and a telephone number, a fax number, and an e-mail address (see "Press Release," page 256).

- Bad business news—if the news is of major public concern—may best be handled by calling a press conference to make a statement. Letting people hear directly from you first gives the organization points for being forthright, open, and honest. This approach also preempts cover-up rumors, which can follow when a story originates in the media.

- Board of directors meeting announcements should follow corporate bylaws, state requirements, and federal laws. Include the date, time, place, reason for the meeting, and who is invited. A waiver of notice or proxy card is enclosed with a postage-paid, addressed return envelope.

- A change of address, status, or mode of doing business should be announced with only the pertinent information, to the businesses or people who need to know. If this change has legal ramifications, check the particular requirements for making such an announcement or notification.

- A business change should put the information in its best light. State the change; why it's being made; the benefits for employees, customers, clients, etc.; and any expressions of appreciation to those involved.

SELECT A FORMAT

- Formal personal announcements for such things as an engagement (see page 31), open house, new business, retirement, etc., are often printed or engraved on a white or off-white card and mailed directly to the readers in matching envelopes.

- Birth or adoption announcements may be hand-designed, printed, or commercially available blank cards filled in and sent to friends and relatives in matching envelopes.

- Interoffice announcements are usually made in memo format.

- Meetings, changes of address, sales, new business openings, and reminder announcements may certainly be made on postcards.

- Newspaper announcements are best completed after contacting the correct editor and learning exactly how he or she wants the announcement submitted.

- Business letterhead, typewritten, with generous margins all around is the best choice for disseminating information to a general readership, or submitting it to the media. The media announcement (see "Press Release") must include a contact name and telephone number.

WRITE STRONG SENTENCES

Start with a key verb. Then construct information in concise order of importance:

▶ We welcome Brian Lee Turner, born August 20, at 3:36 P.M., weighing 7 pounds and 6 ounces, measuring 22 inches, to the family of James and Janice Turner.

▶ Greg and Alice Albright are proud to announce the adoption of a baby boy, Alexander Lee, age seven months.

▶ Our new sales policy will allow you to extend the billing period fifteen additional days for new orders.

▶ We are pleased to announce that Mr. George F. Frommer has accepted the position of Chairman of the Board of Directors at Chances effective June 1.

▶ We must increase the price of the Model A-455 Diluter from $566 to $625 effective July 1.

▶ John H. Hadley, formerly of Danberry, a physician and program director at St. Mary's Hospital, died August 30 in St. Louis.

▶ The "Race for the Cure" breast cancer benefit 5K run will take place at Washington Park's Pavilion on September 29, at 8:00 A.M.

BUILD EFFECTIVE PARAGRAPHS

▶ We rejoice at the birth of our beautiful new daughter, Kathleen Kate McNeilly, born at 2:34 A.M., Sunday, May 10, 1998, measuring 21 inches and weighing 8 pounds, 4 ounces. Her parents, Ben and Mary McNeilly, and sister, Jennifer, age two, welcome her into their hearts and home.

▶ Baby Boom will open its doors in the Tamarac Square Center (next to Lloyd's Jewelry, main floor) Friday, July 15. Bring in this card for your free T-shirt. Store hours will be 10:00 A.M. till 9:00 P.M Monday through Saturday. Open noon till 6:00 P.M on Sunday. Sign up for our $500 shopping spree!

▶ Cooper's sales grew 33 percent this quarter over last quarter. The growth, said C.E.O. Bradley Sandler, was due to the introduction of the new Model Z-560, which sold over 3,000 units.

▶ Quick Lube offers you a full oil change—including filters—for just $24.95 at our new full-service garage on Evans and Orchard. We'll change your oil in just twenty minutes, while you wait. Bring in this card to receive your free sun visor.

▶ Davis & Company Manufacturing announces the recall of their Model A-7655 air conditioner due to defective gaskets found in some units. Leaks from these units may cause nausea due to gases that are not properly sealed in the compressor. Please return all Model A-7655 air conditioner units to the place of purchase for a replacement.

▶ Barker, Taylor, and McKenzie are pleased to announce that Harold P. Garon has joined the law firm as a partner. Mr. Garon, who has spent the past five years at Yale and Gates, will head the firm's corporate practice.

▶ Jake Walker Pierce, formerly of Denver, a physician and program director at St. Mary's Hospital, died August 23 in St. Louis. He was 35.

▶ The opening of the Burn Unit at St. Joseph's Hospital will take place Thursday, April 10, at 2:00 P.M. The dedication ceremony will include a speech by the governor and music by the Utah Children's Choir.

▶ New production hours for Plant D are 6:00 A.M. to 3:00 P.M. for Shift A, and 3:00 P.M. to 12:00 midnight for Shift B. The Shift C schedules, special assignments, and shift changeover policies will be handled in each department. This new policy has been set in response to employee requests and to coordinate with suppliers' schedules.

▶ Sandra F. Frank, formerly of Schenley Advertising, has joined Marks, Inc., as creative vice president. She will handle all the conceptual aspects of the new Brewer campaign.

▶ Dr. Richard Lewin announces his retirement effective April 30. His practice will be taken over by his associate, Dr. Stanley Dever.

EDIT, EDIT, EDIT

Pay attention to precise details to ensure that your reader gets the message you want to send.

Birth

*Larry and Lucy Melville
welcome a beautiful baby girl,*

Melanie Louise,

*who arrived August 12, at 2:30 P.M.,
weighing 7 pounds, 8 ounces, and
measuring 20 inches.*

State the good news up front.

Use the *who, what, when, why, where,* and *how* words to make sure your message is complete.

Adoption

*Roger, Delores, Jonathan,
and Allyson Carver
are proud and happy to announce
the adoption of*

a daughter	*a son*
and a sister,	*and a brother,*
Jessica Rae,	*Michael Roger,*
born January 12,	*born November 13,*
1996	*1997*

*who arrived from China
December 10, 1997.*

Divorce

[Handwritten]
(Date)

Dear Eleanor,

Regrettably, Dan and I are divorcing.

My temporary address for the next six months will be my parents' home, 144 East Walnut, Detroit, MI 49332. I will stay on at Becker and Becker, and Dan plans to take a position in Los Angeles. I'm sure he will let you know where he settles.

I cherish your friendship and will be in touch again as soon as I get things settled.

With love,

Jennifer

Divorce

[Handwritten]
(Date)

Dear Alice,

For reasons I don't wish to discuss now, Patrick and I are divorcing after five years. Since we both value your friendship, it makes this separation even more difficult. (Who gets the friends in these situations is always a dilemma, but I hope in our case it will be all of us.)

I will be living with Susan Blake for the next six months, 167 Downing Street, Denver, CO 80233. When we get moved in and the telephone is connected, I'll give you a ring.

I'm sure Patrick would welcome a call from you. He will be staying in the house.

Talk to you soon.

Yours truly,

Jennie

Obituary

CALVIN LEIGH HOLMES, of Denver, a banking director, died September 12 at his home. He was 62. Private funeral services will be held September 15 at Faith Church in Hampden Memorial Gardens.

He was born January 27, 1933, in Ft. Collins. On September 20, 1974, he married Mary Jo Appleton in Colby, Kansas. She preceded him in death.

Holmes was a banking and agricultural director at Commerce State Bank in Littleton, Col., and he was a member of the Farm House Fraternity. He was a lieutenant in the Navy during the Korean War.

He is survived by two sons, Steven Holmes, of Denver, and Fred Holmes, of Chile, and a daughter, Margaret Anne Holmes, of Phoenix.

Formal Professional Announcement

*French & French
is pleased to announce
that*

Susan A. Banes

*has joined the firm
as a partner.
She will be in charge of
Southern Spain Operations.*

New Employee

MEMO
DATE: (Date)
TO: All Employees
FROM: Cleo Barker
SUBJECT: Mr. William A. Carey Joins Glucks as
               System Sales Vice President

We are pleased to announce that Mr. William A. Carey will join Glucks as vice president in charge of system sales, effective June 1. Bill will be in charge of all model lines A, B, and C sales activity, which will be consolidated to our offices from our Seattle and New York offices.

Bill was in charge of automated sales at Z-Rocks for the past seven years and was instrumental in that company's outstanding sales growth of 55 percent during that period.

Please drop by the Sales Department, introduce yourself, and welcome Bill to Glucks.

Focus on the information you want to communicate.

State information in order of importance.

New Policy

MEMO
DATE: (Date)
TO: Department Managers
FROM: Stewart Collins, V. P.
SUBJECT: New Lunch Policy

To alleviate the congestion and long lines in the cafeteria between noon and 1:30 P.M., we will serve lunch in three shifts by department:

Preparation Department   11:30 A.M.

Office Personnel and
    Production Department   Noon

Sales and Shipping   12:30 P.M.

If any employees need another time, please try to assign them equally over the schedule to keep the numbers in each time frame equal.

I appreciate your cooperation in this change. Give me a call if you have any comments or questions.

Be sure to address the *what, who, when, where, why,* and *how.*

Sales Meeting

MEMO
DATE: (Date)
TO: All Sales Representatives
FROM: Ted Garcia, National Sales Manager
SUBJECT: National Sales Meeting, April 10, from
            10:00 A.M. to 3:00 P.M.

A sales meeting will be held on Tuesday, April 10, from 10:00 A.M. until 3:00 P.M., in the Boardroom at Central Headquarters. Lunch will be served.

If you have any items you would like to have addressed, please send them to me by March 18. An agenda will be mailed to you on March 30.

Please let me know immediately if you will be unable to attend. Thanks, I look forward to seeing all of you.

Professional Office Relocation

(Date)

Dear Patients:

I will move my offices to 1400 Clearwater, Suite 540, on July 8. This is what you have been asking for: a new, larger, and more convenient building.

There is free parking under the building and an elevator directly into our lovely new reception area. The new office telephone number is 555-1212.

I look forward to seeing you on your next visit.

Yours truly,

Dr. Charles Rose

New Product

John Henry Ford
1335 North Arapahoe Road
is pleased to announce that

THE NEW MODELS HAVE ARRIVED.

Come take a test drive.
Bring this card and receive
a free Parking Lot Car Locator,
and register for our Mustang Giveaway.
September 15–17,
10:00 A.M.–9:30 P.M.

New Business

Sole Music
is opening in your neighborhood
at 433 West Prince Street
(across from Joe's Deli).
If your feet don't feel like dancing,
bring those shoes on in
and we guarantee
we'll tune them up!
Bring this card for 25% off
your first repair.
10–9 Mon. through Fri.;
noon–9 Sat.
844–1313

ENGAGEMENT ANNOUNCEMENT

Over the past several decades many factors have influenced the traditional practices of announcing an engagement to be married: the changed role of women in our society; the high rate of divorce and remarriage; same-sex relationships; and the dramatic changes in the ages, career status, and financial resources of those becoming engaged. Although we still cling to some of the traditional, time-honored elements of announcing a couple's engagement, many of the old items of protocol are falling away in favor of announcements that more accurately reflect our changed roles.

The most important element in the engagement announcement should be the sharing of the joyous news.

To make the announcement public, it may be printed in newspapers and other publications. Contact the social editor and ask for the desired format. A black-and-white glossy photograph of the engaged couple or just the future bride may appear with the announcement.

Here are some guidelines that are still generally accepted. If a young woman has not been married, her parents usually make the announcement:

▶ "Jack and Julie Bremmer, of Cottonwood Manor, Texas, announce the engagement of their daughter, Katherine Anne Bremmer, to Alex James Smerthington, son of John Z. and Lucy Smerthington, of Minneapolis, Minnesota. A June wedding is planned.

Ms. Bremmer graduated from Texas A&M and is a communications consultant for Beams and Motes Advertising Agency. Mr. Smerthington graduated from Texas A&M. He is associated with Mickey Advertising Agency in New York City."

If one of the future bride's parents is deceased, the announcement is made by the other:

▶ "Mrs. Barbara Gates announces the engagement of her daughter, Ms. Sandra E. Gates, to Dr. David R. Cole…. Ms. Gates is also the daughter of the late Robert Gates."

If a parent of the future groom is deceased:

▶ "… son of Mrs. Abigail R. Wright and the late Mr. George B. Wright."

When the engaged woman is divorced or widowed, her parents may make the announcement, using her current name.

A mature woman, single, divorced, or widowed, may make her own announcement:

▶ "The engagement of Miss [Ms. or Mrs.] Deana Turner to Mr. Jacob Die has been announced…"

When the future bride's parents are divorced, the announcement is usually made by the mother:

▶ "Mrs. Susan Raines announces…Ms. Raines is also the daughter of Mr. Julius B. Raines, of Boston, Massachusetts."

When the divorced parents are cordial, they may announce the engagement together:

▶ "Mr. John Kelly of Ft. Lauderdale, Florida, and Mrs. Margaret B. Waters, of Indianapolis, Indiana, announce…"

If a remarried mother makes the announcement, it may read:

▶ "Mr. Richard R. and Glenda F. Gaines announce the engagement of Mrs. Gaines' daughter, Ellen Sue Bates…. Ms. Bates is also the daughter of Mr. Robert G. Bates, of Riverside, New York."

If the engaged woman was adopted, the family that raised her from infancy has no reason to mention this fact. If she joined the family later and has retained her original surname, the announcement should read:

▶ "Mr. Roy and Mrs. Rose Weinstein announce the engagement of their adopted daughter, Ms. Carla Reid, daughter of the late Mr. Carl and Mrs. Trudy Reid."

If the engaged woman is an orphan, the nearest relative, godparent, or dearest friend may make the announcement, as may the woman, herself, impersonally:

▶ "The engagement of Daisey Marlys Gibson (daughter of the late Mr. Darrel and Mrs. Alta Gibson) is announced…"

The parents of the engaged man may make the announcement when the woman is from another country, has no living relatives, or for some other reason has no contact with her family. The man's parents should not make the announcement in their own names, but in the woman's parents' names:

▶ "The engagement of Miss Sutra Batra, of Bombay, India, daughter of Greg and Seema Batra, of Calcutta, India, to Dr. Walker Dennis Tabor, son of Dr. Walter and Gloria Tabor, of Kentilworth, Illinois, is announced."

The couple may elect to announce their own engagement, either alone, or in concert with their parents:

▶ "Steven Barr and Louise Albright announce their engagement." Or, "Louise Albright and Steven Barr join with their parents, Mark and Helen Albright and Albert and Joan Barr, in announcing the couple's engagement."

If an engagement is canceled, the same persons who received an announcement should also be notified, simply, of this change.

Engagement

*Douglas and Anne Wittenberger
announce
the engagement
of Anne Wittenberger's daughter,*

*Elizabeth Sterling Dunning,
to
Robert Townsend Fielder,*

of New York City.

*Miss Dunning is also the daughter of
Larry Dunning of Phoenix.*

4

CONGRATULATIONS

*Whatever kind word thou speakest,
the like shalt thou hear.*

—ANONYMOUS

Nothing makes our accomplishments sweeter than compliments and praise. We've gotten away from the practice of sending notes and letters of congratulations over the last couple of decades, so if you send one, yours may make a lasting impression. It's reported that former president George Bush made extensive use of personal, handwritten notes of congratulations throughout his career. Some even say this practice was very helpful in getting him into the White House.

DECIDE TO WRITE

Send congratulations for

- Personal achievements such as graduation, award, promotion, successful speech, publication, winning a sports competition, receiving a prize, finishing a marathon, completing a course of study, or receiving a rating for a hobby or avocation
- Family events like marriage, birth or adoption of a child, or an anniversary
- Life events like a birthday, retirement, or a first or new home
- Religious events such as joining a church, a baptism, confirmation, first communion, Bar or Bat Mitzvah, ordination, taking vows, or becoming an elder or a deacon

- Business achievements like an award for top or outstanding sales, promotion, new job, new assignment, new title, starting a new business, getting a new contract, having a book published, joining an association, or other business success
- Elections to office in a club or association, professional society, political post, or a social club

THINK ABOUT CONTENT

- Write immediately. But if you've heard the news long after the fact, or if you have procrastinated, write anyway, and note briefly why your greeting is late: "Congratulations. I may not be swift, but I'm still delighted that you are now a vice president."
- State the occasion for congratulations in the first sentence or two.
- Use the word *congratulations* early.
- Write conversationally, like you'd talk to the person. (A note to a friend will be less formal than one to a business associate.)
- Connect the person to the achievement, occasion, or event.
- If appropriate, relate how you learned the news, include a newspaper clipping, or refer to a shared memory.

- Relate something that bears on the occasion or event, but remember to keep your message focused on the recipient.
- Make sure your message has the ring of sincerity.
- Express your best wishes for the person and your expectation for continued success.
- Make sure your congratulations letter has a single focus.
- Make it short. Three to six sentences is usually sufficient.

ELIMINATE WRONG MESSAGES

- Don't assume a tone improper to the relationship you have with the recipient.
- Avoid being overly flattering. Effusive, unmerited praise is never appropriate.
- Don't mix messages. A congratulations letter should include only congratulations. Use another letter to address other matters.
- Don't include negative phrases like "Who would have believed it?" Especially for occasions like birthdays and anniversaries.
- Don't be insensitive. Know how the recipient regards the event or occasion. For example, if the recipient prefers not to discuss the fact that this is his or her twentieth year with the company and this promotion should have come ten years ago, it is insensitive to refer to the fact that he or she had been passed over so long. If the recipient has very strong feelings about it, don't send the letter at all.
- If you can't be sincere in your congratulations, don't write. If a friend is, in your opinion, marrying the wrong person, don't write a hypocritical letter of congratulations. If a business associate gets a promotion you feel belonged to another, don't write.
- Don't use the congratulations message for "public relations" purposes, as in "Congratulations on opening your new checking account at Fisherman's Bank." A welcome letter is more appropriate.

TAILOR YOUR MESSAGE FOR EXCEPTIONAL SITUATIONS

- Six months after an employee has retired, another congratulations letter that cites some contribution the retiree made to the company, states how the person is missed, and includes continued well wishes will mean a great deal to the recipient. This letter may be signed by all the employees with whom the recipient worked.
- Congratulations on successfully handling a very difficult situation, such as the illness of a family member, divorce, unemployment, or being passed over for promotion, must be handled with great care. Again, such congratulations should reflect a deep personal relationship with the recipient and, if done properly, can be very meaningful.
- Use a public forum to give your greetings when it's appropriate. Many newspapers, for example, have a section for family and friends to print congratulations on an anniversary.
- When using a commercial greeting card to extend congratulations, be sure to make the card personal by writing your own message in addition to the printed one.
- Congratulations on a new family member should be sent immediately. Such greetings have now been extended to include a new pet.
- Tradition no longer dictates that messages to a future bride and groom be different. In this area, at least, we have gained parity. The words *best wishes* or *congratulations* apply to either person.

SELECT A FORMAT

- Personal congratulations usually take the form of a note handwritten on personal stationery. The commercial fold-over notecards are also fine.
- For a birthday or a specific occasion, commercial cards are often used, but be sure you include a handwritten message.
- For associates from business, clubs, politics, professional associations, and other organizations, a more formal, typed letter is better. Base your choice on the relationship you have with the recipient and the importance of the occasion or good news.

WRITE STRONG SENTENCES

Start with an action verb that expresses your feelings. Put it into a phrase, then a sentence:

▶ Congratulations on a job well done.

▶ I am so delighted to learn of your good news.

▶ It's a pleasure to send my congratulations on your promotion.

▶ We are delighted at your news—congratulations!

BUILD EFFECTIVE PARAGRAPHS

Remember, the best notes or letters of congratulations are short. These paragraphs may constitute most or all of your communication.

▶ Congratulations on a terrific job! I was delighted, but not surprised, to read your piece in the *Wall Street Journal.* I've seldom seen a piece so well thought out and so extensively and soundly researched.

▶ Congratulations on receiving the Expert Skier Award. It is well deserved. You sliced through that powder on Saturday like a real pro.

▶ Our warmest congratulations on the birth of William III. He has selected two of the best people we know for parents.

▶ Congratulations on an exceptionally outstanding job in whipping the St. John's Annual Bazaar together. It bore your expert fingerprints, and profits were the best ever.

EDIT, EDIT, EDIT

Keep your congratulations simple, sincere, and in tune with your relationship to the recipient.

Congratulations on a Wedding Anniversary

[Handwritten]
(Date)

Dear Elizabeth,

    Congratulations! Of course we'll attend your fiftieth wedding anniversary celebration, and Jack and I will be proud to relate the story of the weekend on Lake Witless. It remains a favorite in this family.
    You two have achieved a unique level of oneness in your marriage, which we've long admired. Our best wishes for many more years to come.

          Affectionately,

          Katie and Jack

Congratulations on a Career Achievement

[Handwritten]
(Date)

Dear Jennifer,

    Congratulations, Dr. J. E. Jensen. That has a wonderful ring to it. We are so proud of your outstanding achievement. You have demonstrated what determination and hard work can produce, and we know the fruits of your labor will be plentiful.

          All the best,

          Booker and Alice

Congratulations on a Job Well Done

[Handwritten]
(Date)

Dear Bert,

Before you took over Boy Scout Troop IV, the dropout rate was one in two. Over the past year, I have seen George go from dread to anticipation in preparing for the next troop meeting. Congratulations.

          Sincerely,

          Melvin Wellington

Congratulations on Reaching a Personal Goal

[Handwritten]
(Date)

Dear Robert,

    Meeting an imposed deadline is difficult, but reaching a self-set goal (which no one else believes possible) is a feat of extraordinary self-discipline. Congratulations on achieving the AAS designation. I'd like to hear all the details during our Thursday luncheon.

          Your friend,

          Rich

Congratulations on Marriage

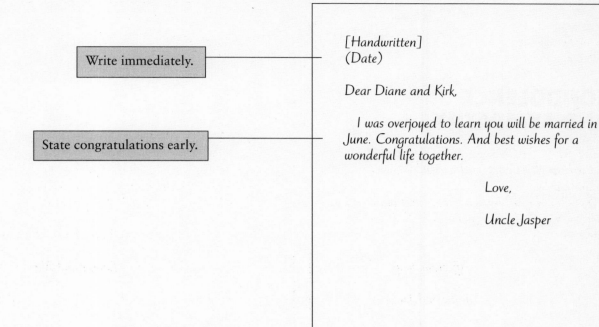

Write immediately.

State congratulations early.

[Handwritten]
(Date)

Dear Diane and Kirk,

I was overjoyed to learn you will be married in June. Congratulations. And best wishes for a wonderful life together.

Love,

Uncle Jasper

Congratulations on a Promotion

[Typed]
(Date)

Dear David:

I was delighted to hear you will be the First Vice President in charge of creativity. Congratulations. A more deserving or talented partner could not have been selected for the post.

I'm looking forward to seeing many more of the unique ideas that brought you the Gold Pick Award at our agency.

Sincerely,

Winnie Backus

Congratulations on the Birth of Children

[Handwritten]
(Date)

Dear Carolyn,

What wonderful news that the twins were born and are doing well.
I'm sure you would much rather have brought them straight home from the hospital, but perhaps this will give you a little time to rest up. I'll call you next week to see what you need. In the meantime, please call me if there's any way I may help.

Lovingly,

Marjorie

5

CONDOLENCE
AND SYMPATHY

... look in thy heart and write.

—SIR PHILIP SYDNEY

It is difficult to express your feelings in writing to someone who is suffering a major loss. Focus on the person you are writing to, and let your knowledge of the recipient and his or her relationship to the loss guide you.

The letter of condolence or sympathy, while one of the most difficult messages to write, is undoubtedly one of the most important. It should be brief, kind, and offer concrete help, if that is appropriate.

DECIDE TO WRITE
Compose a personal note or letter when
- Death touches the life of a relative, friend, neighbor, business associate, or employee.
- Illness or injury strikes a relative, friend, business associate, or neighbor.
- Loss of finances, property, business, or well-being affects a friend, employee, organization you do business with, colleague, or client.
- It's the anniversary of a death, or other significant date, to the person who will experience, again, the loss of the deceased.
- Divorce affects a friend or associate.
- Keen disappointment or misfortune occurs in the life of a friend or associate, such as not winning an election, loss of a job, or not getting a promotion.

THINK ABOUT CONTENT
- The first and most essential step is to empathize with the bereaved recipient.
- Think about what you really feel.
- Use your relationship with the recipient to guide your writing.
- Write immediately, but, if you have just heard of the grief after weeks or months or have put off the task, still write. It's not too late.
- Focus on the recipient and don't misdirect your message toward your own feelings.
- Open with a simple and strong message of sympathy, naming the person, loss, or event for which you are extending condolences: "Lansing and I extend our deepest sympathy to you at the loss of your dear Lindsay."
- It may be difficult, but be sure to write to employees, clients, associates, and colleagues in times of grief or loss.
- Save long messages that reminisce about a loved one for later, when the recipient is better able to reflect upon those memories without such a keen sense of loss.
- Choose your words carefully, using words that relate to the loss, sorrow, or grief of the bereaved. Avoid cold and harsh words like *dead, killed,* or *deceased.*

- Relate a fond memory you have of the deceased, if appropriate.
- Always consider the religious preference, ethnic mores, family wishes, and organizational customs of the bereaved when writing your message.
- Include a message of sympathy to other family members or associates, if appropriate.
- Make a specific offer of help, indicating when and how you will make the next contact to carry through on your offer.
- Close on a warm note.
- Ask the mortuary what the family has requested if you want to send a memento of your feelings in the case of a death, or check the obituary column of the newspaper for this information.
- If you send flowers, write a message to accompany them.
- Inquire verbally of a designated relative or friend, or the mortuary, about any immediate needs the bereaved may have, any service or task you may wish to volunteer for, e.g., pallbearer, a special commemorative service, etc.

ELIMINATE WRONG MESSAGES

- Don't use overcharged language. "The worst tragedy" or "The most dire news I've ever received" does nothing to comfort the bereaved. The same rule applies to overly sentimental, effusive statements.
- Do not moralize or include statements or clichés meant to be sympathetic. These may be misinterpreted. Remember, this is a time of extreme grief and vulnerability for the bereaved, and language like "He's in a better place now" is not appropriate.
- Don't let your message fall into a pitying or maudlin tone. There's a fine line here. Read your message through several times to ensure you haven't failed on this point. Sometimes it helps to place your letter aside for at least a few hours then reread it just to be sure.
- Don't give advice. Your sole purpose is to try to give comfort.
- Avoid empty or vague offers of help. Rather, be specific and offer to take the next step. "I will call Joannie tomorrow to see if there are calls I can return on your behalf, or errands you may need to have run."

CONSIDER SPECIAL SITUATIONS

Take special care in these special circumstances:

- Divorce of a friend, associate, colleague, or employee requires keen sensitivity. You should know the recipient very well. Make sure your message is timely, brief, and focused on the recipient.
- The death of a child, a stillbirth, or a miscarriage should all be treated the same. Don't fall prey to attempts at "consoling" that tend to diminish the recipient's grief. When multiple births result in the loss of a child, offer congratulations on the birth of the surviving children first. Then, in a separate paragraph, express your sympathy at the loss of the other children, taking care not to connect the two emotions.
- For loss of a home in a natural disaster, loss of employment, or a financial reversal, it's best to give your message the legs of real assistance. Inquire to find out what would be helpful and present your gift or offer of help so it does not take on the character of charity. Empty offers of assistance are insulting in the face of crisis.
- The terminally ill person or the person who has suffered a debilitating injury is in a special category. This includes a person who has contracted HIV. Take your lead from what the recipient has expressed about his or her illness. Don't mention death unless he or she has discussed it openly. It's appropriate to include fond memories you share or aspects of your relationship you treasure. Use "Thinking about you," "My thoughts are with you," or other such messages.
- Suicide or a violent crime that results in death or loss is an especially difficult situation. Unless you know the faith and belief system of the bereaved, your message should simply state, "I was so sorry to hear of your loss."
- The death of a pet, especially for an elderly person, can be a great loss. A note to such a person at this time, if sincere, will be greatly appreciated.
- In sending flowers to a funeral home, attach a small card addressed to "David M. Meeks," or to "The funeral of David M. Meeks." The plain, single card (available from the florist, usually two by three inches) should contain a brief message of

sympathy, for example, "Sidney, our thoughts are with you and Ann at this time."

- When contributing to a charity on behalf of the deceased, include your name and address, in addition to a brief statement such as "This contribution is made in the name of Robert C. Walker, 8100 West Chicago, Appelton, WI 55801." This allows the charity to acknowledge that your contribution was received and inform the family of the deceased of your contribution.

- Anniversary dates shared with a person now gone are a good time to send another special, thoughtful note of sympathy to a relative, friend, or associate. It will be extremely meaningful if your relationship is close.

SELECT A FORMAT

- Your message of sympathy must be very personal, and that requires that it be handwritten. Use a commercial card only if it expresses, exactly, your feelings, and then also include a handwritten message. The most popular stationery is a plain, fold-over card, but modest personal stationery (smaller than 8½ by 11 inches) may also be used.

- For business acquaintances you did not know well or work closely with, either a handwritten note or a typed letter of sympathy may be used. The list here may include an employee who has lost a spouse, a customer, client, or colleague. Use white personal business stationery, preferably smaller than the usual 8½ by 11 inches. A five-by-seven-inch size is a good choice.

WRITE STRONG SENTENCES

▶ I was so sorry to hear about your accident.

▶ Our thoughts are with you at this time of loss and sorrow.

▶ Our hopes are set on a full recovery from your accident.

▶ We were so sorry to learn that Martha's courageous battle with AIDS is over; her life was truly an inspiration to all of us.

▶ I'm sorry to hear that you and Jim are divorcing. I know this is an extremely difficult time and my thoughts are with you.

▶ We shall miss David's smiling presence.

▶ Not everyone understands the joy and companionship a pet can bring and how it is missed when it's gone; I was so sorry to hear Smoky died.

BUILD EFFECTIVE PARAGRAPHS

▶ There are never adequate words to express the proper sense of loss at a time like this. I was so saddened to learn Toby is gone from us.

▶ I just wanted to write to express my sympathy at the loss of your home to fire. I know through my own experience it is devastating, and I want you and Jack to know our thoughts are with you. Please accept this gift to help you with the things you'll need immediately. We'd also like to give you the sofa and chair we have in the rec room, several lamps, linens, etc., if you will accept them. There are many other items we'd be happy to loan you. I'll call Saturday to see what you can use and when we might bring things over.

▶ May the joy of life that was George's sustain you in this dark time of losing him. We will all remember his exuberance in the smallest and simplest pleasures. And we'll all miss him a great deal.

▶ Please don't despair. When we were robbed, the lingering sense of having been violated was the most difficult part of the ordeal. I'll call in a couple of days to see if there's anything we have you may want to use until you replace things.

EDIT, EDIT, EDIT

Use the greatest care to ensure your message is clear and sincere.

ALSO SEE "APPRECIATION AND THANK-YOU," PAGE 55, AND "ANNOUNCEMENT," PAGE 23.

The Death of a Neighbor

[Handwritten]
(Date)

Dear David,

Choose your words carefully.

  Anne and I were very saddened to learn of Trudy's death. We respected and admired her contributions to the community and will miss her.

Empathize with the bereaved. Offer help, then follow up.

  Our heartfelt sympathy to you and the children. I will call you Thursday to see how we may help in the weeks ahead.

Sincerely,

Anne and Woody

The Death of a Business Associate

[Handwritten or typed]
(Date)

Dear Martha,

  I was so sorry to learn of Ruth's death. I'm sure this is both a professional and personal loss for you and many others at Banko Corporation.

Use your relationship with the bereaved to guide your writing.

  I and my staff offer our sincerest condolences to you and your department.

Regards,

Dudley

Death in a Friend's Family

[Handwritten]
(Date)

Dear Rodney and Kris,

We were stricken to learn of Jordan's death. He was a wonderful person, your son, and we know how very close you were. May the joy the three of you shared help to sustain you during such a bleak time.

We will bring the Buick over tomorrow for you to use for as long as you need it. We would like to help by running any errands you may need completed, or answering your telephone if you care to forward your calls here. Please let us help by doing anything else you may need.

We will all miss Jordan deeply.

Your friends,

Alice and Art

Financial Loss

[Handwritten]
(Date)

Dear Lea and Alex,

Please accept this gift to help with anything you may need immediately in this difficult time. Not many people have the courage to follow their dreams as you two have. We're sorry for this loss, but we know this great disappointment won't defeat you.

Our hopes and prayers are with you for a very bright future. We'll call next week to see how we can help.

Sincerely,

Mille and Wick

Loss of a Pregnancy

[Handwritten]
(Date)

Dear Jill and Jeff,

We were very saddened to hear of your miscarriage. We know how eager you were to have this new member of your wonderful family. Please accept our warmest sympathies. Our thoughts are with you.

With our love,

Ted and Carol

Illness of a Business Associate

[Handwritten or typed]
(Date)

Dear Margaret,

Your secretary informed me you are in the hospital. I was so sorry to hear you will be out for several weeks recuperating from surgery. I hope you'll enjoy this book by one of my favorite authors. It helped me a great deal during my recovery period.

I'll check with you in a few days to see if you are up to having visitors.

My wishes for a full recovery.

Sincerely,

Joyce Most

6
WELCOME

True friendship's laws are by this rule express'd,
Welcome the coming, speed the parting guest.

—ALEXANDER POPE

A letter of welcome is a great opportunity to start a positive relationship with a new neighbor, a new business, or a new coworker. Whether a business or personal letter, it should be warm and congenial in tone and should convey a friendly "glad you're here" message. It may also extend an offer of help—although it's wise to define the limits of your offer.

In business or social correspondence you may want to tell the reader you are happy in this group (location, etc.) and include a suggestion or two about how the person can fit in, learn the ropes, or get oriented. Your closing should encourage the reader to participate in the group or suggest an initial step the reader can take.

DECIDE TO WRITE

Use the welcome letter in response to the following:
- A new neighbor moves in.
- A new employee starts work.
- A new member joins your club, faculty, school, student association, church, temple, fraternity, or sorority.
- A new business starts.
- A new employee joins a customer's or client's business.
- A new business prospect, customer, client, or associate is added.
- A new person is about to join the family.

THINK ABOUT CONTENT

- Express your enthusiasm and pleasure at making the welcome.
- Keep your message simple and focus on how the other person feels at this time.
- Welcome the person into the organization, family, group, or neighborhood.
- Include, if possible, a complimentary statement about the organization, family, group, or neighborhood.
- Generate some enthusiasm about the future.
- State your best wishes for the person, drawing a relationship between him or her and the organization.
- Be specific and make it as personal as possible.
- Make an offer of help, if appropriate, and suggest a time to meet.
- In the case of an employee, give any details that may be appropriate: work hours, lunch policy and times, parking arrangements, benefits, etc.
- Close with an encouraging comment.

- Timeliness is very important. You lose the opportunity for the greatest impact if you don't send the letter immediately.
- Your offer of help will never be as valued as it is now, but be sure to set limits you can live with and be concrete in your offer.

ELIMINATE WRONG MESSAGES

- Don't mix messages. This is not the place for a sales message, for example.
- Don't include bad news or negative messages.

CONSIDER SPECIAL SITUATIONS

- A welcome to a new family member should ring with warmth and sincerity, expressing your pleasure at having the person join the family.
- Often families in neighborhoods are so insular that it becomes very unusual to welcome a new neighbor with a letter. But we now have so many master-planned communities that the practice of sending a welcome from the homeowners' association should become routine. This can be done very nicely with a welcome basket and a helpful sheet on local shopping, professional services, a directory of families in the neighborhood, etc.
- A personal welcome letter to a new neighbor can be helpful in establishing the type of relationship you desire. "Welcome to the neighborhood. I look forward to having you over for coffee, so please give me a call when you get settled," says you prefer to be called first rather than dropped in on.
- Letters welcoming new employees are often considered the domain of the human resources or personnel department and include a packet of information about insurance coverage, company policy, benefits, etc. Although this may be standard operating procedure, make sure employees are welcomed verbally by other employees and also with welcome letters. This creates better relationships, allows new employees to settle in more quickly, and ensures a greater sense of camaraderie and loyalty.

- Students, attendees, parents, and new faculty members of schools, colleges, or special academic programs will benefit from the information and feel more at ease if they receive a welcome letter. The letter should include a list of the things they will need for the first class or session and an inspiring sentence or two about the session. Naming someone for the new persons to contact before the first session is also helpful.
- With the welcome letter to a potential business customer or client, include a reason for a well-timed follow-up call to help you establish a relationship. "I will call your office next week to arrange a time to stop by briefly and introduce myself, to give you the *Glenwood Directory,* and to answer any questions you may have."
- The welcome wagon or other new-resident service may be a good source of new residents for you to contact if these are potential clients or customers for your business.
- The chamber of commerce, the new business section of the newspaper, and local business publications may be a good source from which to glean the names of new businesses you may wish to contact with a welcome letter.

SELECT A FORMAT

- Business welcome letters, in which you are acting in an official capacity, should be typed on organization letterhead.
- For a welcome letter from you to a new coworker or employee, personal business letterhead may be used, and the letter should be typed.
- New-neighbor welcome messages and those to new members of an informal group, club, etc., are usually handwritten on personal stationery or a commercial card.
- Student and attendee welcomes may best be handled by sending printed or handwritten postcards.

WRITE STRONG SENTENCES

▶ A warm and sincere welcome to you.

▶ I hope you will enjoy your membership as much as I have enjoyed mine over the past fifteen years.

▶ We look forward to a long and mutually rewarding relationship.

▶ Welcome to this warm group, where I have found true fellowship and faithful friends.

BUILD EFFECTIVE PARAGRAPHS

▶ With great pleasure I welcome you to the Press Club of Mobile. Your application has been approved by the Board and ratified by the members.

▶ Welcome to Bentonville! It has been said that anyone who comes never wants to leave, and my family certainly agrees.

▶ Welcome to the Baskerville team. I believe you will find that everyone has the spirit of working together to get the job done. We're very glad to have you, and I invite you to give me a call at any time to discuss questions you may have.

▶ Welcome to West Concord Business Park. I have found this location convenient to all of the metro area and an ideal location from which to get to the ski slopes on Friday afternoons. I'll call next week to see if you would care to get together briefly to discuss park procedures and policies. In the meantime, here's a directory of the businesses in the area.

▶ Welcome to our entrepreneurial family. I believe one of the greatest benefits of becoming a Small Business Chamber of Commerce member is the Members-of-the-Board sessions, where entrepreneurs help solve each others' problems. I know it's the best business decision I've ever made. Happy to have you aboard!

EDIT, EDIT, EDIT

Be sure your message is brief, warm, and personal.

ALSO SEE "EMPLOYEE CORRESPONDENCE," PAGE 101, AND "DIRECT-MAIL," PAGE 233.

To a New Family Member

[Handwritten]
(Date)

Dear Jessie,

David is so special to me. He stayed with his Uncle Jack and I during his mother's lengthy illness when he was four and five, and again when he was ten and his mother had surgery. I've loved him like a son since the moment he was born.

So, when I say I'm very pleased you two have decided to get married, it's the sincerest compliment to you, and the truest belief in the possibility of your extraordinary happiness.

I know you'll have a wonderful life together, and I'm thrilled for you both.

Your aunt,

Bea

To School

[Handwritten]
(Date)

Dear Ms. Alison,

The PTA at Logan wants to welcome you to our group of parents and teachers working together. Our goal is to create a better educational experience for our children.

I feel sure your daughter, Jennifer, will enjoy Ms. Rudy's class. My daughter was one of her students last year, and I found Ms. Rudy to be an extremely skilled and concerned teacher.

Please plan to attend our Thursday social hour, September 18 at 7:30 P.M., in the gym for an informal welcome. I look forward to meeting you.

Sincerely,

June Addison

To a Student

[Handwritten or typed]
(Date)

Susan,

Let me introduce myself and say welcome to the fifth grade at Stanley Academy. My name is Mrs. Moore, and I'll be your homeroom teacher.

I believe you will enjoy our series on "The Birth of Democracy," the four field trips we have planned to the state capitol building and state representatives' offices, and our "Women in U.S. History" project.

It's going to be a wonderful year, and I look forward to meeting you next Thursday in room 43, opposite the administration office. Please bring the items listed in the margin and wear a big smile!

Your teacher,

Mrs. Moore

Reactivated Club Member Welcome

[Handwritten or typed]
(Date)

Dear Sarah,

Welcome, again, to the Toronto Womens' Press Society. We are all delighted you have chosen to reactivate your membership after three years. Yes, we have changed our goals and are much more in tune with the needs of women working in the media today.

This year's programs include several touring luminaries, a special seminar we're calling "The Future of News," and a series of programs on computer research techniques. Of course we'll also continue our member "Shop Talk" evenings, which are a favorite.

We're so pleased to have you back.

With best wishes,

Enid Lubbick

To a New Business

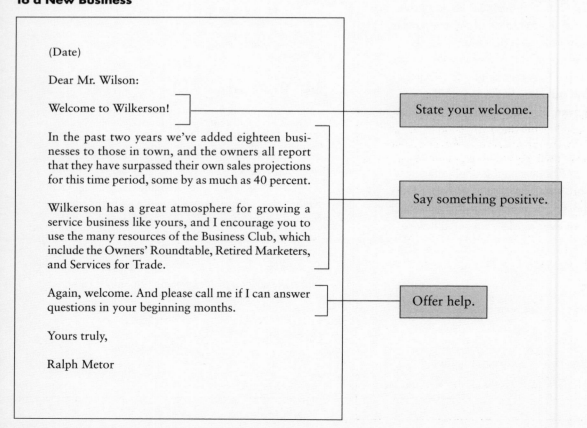

(Date)

Dear Mr. Wilson:

Welcome to Wilkerson! ———— State your welcome.

In the past two years we've added eighteen businesses to those in town, and the owners all report that they have surpassed their own sales projections for this time period, some by as much as 40 percent.

Wilkerson has a great atmosphere for growing a service business like yours, and I encourage you to use the many resources of the Business Club, which include the Owners' Roundtable, Retired Marketers, and Services for Trade. ———— Say something positive.

Again, welcome. And please call me if I can answer questions in your beginning months. ———— Offer help.

Yours truly,

Ralph Metor

As a Volunteer

(Date)

Dear Gary:

Welcome to Big Friends Club. In the next two weeks you will be given three young friend candidates to review before you make your friend choice.

Last year in Cleveland we were able to match 1,250 boys with Big Friends. On the back of this letter we've listed some of the boys' comments about the differences their Big Friends have made in their lives. You'll also see some comments from Big Friends.

Being a Big Friend is inspiring, rewarding, and a lot of work. We're so pleased you have decided to help make a difference in a young boy's life.

Remember, we are always here to help.

Sincerely,

Rodney Baker
President

As a Customer

(Date)

Dear David:

It was a pleasure serving you at the Regiment today, and I welcome you as a customer of the finest men's custom-made clothing store in the city.

As we discussed, your final fitting for the suits will be Friday the 15th, at 4:00 P.M.

I look forward to serving you then. And again, welcome!

Yours truly,

Ted Bunson

To a New Businesswoman

(Date)

Dear Gwen:

Welcome to Marmet, Missouri.

Since this is the "Show Me State," I'd like to suggest a breakfast meeting on the 15th, 8:00 A.M., at Robins Inn, with a group of new residents and a few of us old-timers. It will be a kind of orientation for important things like where to buy the best women's suits for the least, where to go when you need to have dinner for 10 in 40 minutes, and where to take your car for a tune-up.

We'd also like to give you the opportunity to ask us questions. We have all been businesswomen in this town for two to thirty years. (There's a wealth of information here.)

Please call me and tell me you'll attend, 232-7555.

Sincerely,

Joan Slosky

7
INVITATIONS

But all the fun's in how you say a thing.

—ROBERT FROST

Inviting guests to an occasion can be as informal as saying, "Y'all come," or as formal as sending engraved invitations—pieces of art—created and then addressed by a calligrapher. Whether the event's an impromptu pizza party or the 125th Annual Governor's Ball, you'll want the reader to feel you are expressing a special desire to have him or her attend.

More frequently, social occasions cross the lines between the personal and business, making distinction between the two impossible. Certainly all such occasions present an opportunity to solidify relationships, improve morale, create new relationships, or patch up old ones.

DECIDE TO WRITE

You'll use invitations for many get-togethers:
* Informal parties
* Business events, including such things as trade shows, open houses, exhibitions, new product introductions, premieres, etc.
* New business openings
* Fundraisers
* Celebrations of a family, religious, or educational nature, including showers, weddings, anniversaries, christenings, first communions, baptisms, Bar Mitzvahs, Bat Mitzvahs, confirmations, ordinations, graduations, etc.
* Hospitality, such as an invitation to be a weekend houseguest
* Educational programs, such as workshops, seminars, conferences, or speeches
* Cultural events, such as concerts or theater productions
* Social organization events
* Holiday or commemorative events

THINK ABOUT CONTENT
* Make the form and appearance of your invitation consistent with the formality of the occasion. Invitations to business events may take the form of a business communication, and strictly social events should follow the rules for a social invitation.
* Focus on answering the *what, when, why, where, who,* and *how much* in writing an invitation to be sure you include all the essential information.

- Begin with words of personal invitation or state the occasion or event: "The Fifth Annual Goldminers' Ball," "The Grand Opening of Phinney's," "You Are Cordially Invited to the Ninth Annual Preferred Customers' Presale Event."
- List the date and time of the event, including month, day, year, and time, A.M. or P.M. (The day of the week may be listed before the month.)
- The address comes next. A cross street ("at Maple and Main") or brief directions ("turn south off Alameda onto Grant") may be given after the address, or a map may be included with the invitation.
- Supply helpful information for guests, e.g., if food and beverages (and possibly which foods) will be served. Giving the timing sequence is also helpful: "A light luncheon for out-of-town guests will be served at four o'clock, before the six o'clock ceremony."
- Charges and costs, if any, should be listed: "$125 per couple," "Open Bar," "Valet Parking." All this information tells the reader the arrangements and their anticipated expenses involved with attending.
- The R.S.V.P. tradition has become very blurred. Since every host needs to know how many and possibly who will attend, an *R.S.V.P., Please respond, Please R.S.V.P. by* (date), or *Regrets only* should appear in the lower-left corner of the formal invitation with a telephone number and an address. Many such formal invitations enclose a printed or engraved R.S.V.P. card and an envelope addressed and stamped for the reader's reply.
- Optionally, place information about attire in the lower-right corner of the formal invitation. Designations most often used are *informal, semi-formal, formal, black tie, white tie, casual, costume,* and *evening attire.* On informal invitations, the host may say something like "Come in slacks."
- When your invitation includes hospitality, multiple activities, or requires guests to make their own overnight or eating arrangements, provide as much information as possible. Making a statement like "Come prepared to enjoy swimming, tennis, and an evening

hayride" gives guests an idea of the kind of clothing to bring. If your invitation is to a weekend rally for owners of red 1965 Corvettes, it will be helpful if you include hotel suggestions and even information on restaurants in the area and reservation policies.
- The host should not be shy about including the limits of the invitation. For example, "Please plan to arrive Saturday between 3:00 P.M. and 4:00 P.M. and depart Sunday between 2:00 P.M. and 3:00 P.M." "We're a nonsmoking home" will be helpful to the host and guests.
- Inform guests, too, about unusual arrangements:

  "Sleeping arrangements for women at the Gourmet Cowboy Weekend will be in the west camp tents, for men in the east camp tents. Bring your own sleeping bag, towels, and personal items. There is no electricity. Cots are provided."

- Miscellaneous information can be very important. If guests are to arrange their transportation from the airport, make that clear. Parking (and fees), inclement weather information, and notices about alternative plans should all be included: "In the event of rain, we will move inside Grange Hall."
- Most important, make sure the invitation is warm in tone and leaves readers with the sense you look forward to having them attend: "Please R.S.V.P. with an acceptance." "We're so looking forward to seeing you. It has been such a long time. We have some serious catching up to do."
- Corporate informal and general invitations for such things as an in-office party for a retirement, maternity leave, promotion, service celebration, etc., can be made in memo form. List the event, time, date, place, and refreshments. Information on contributions for a gift may be included, and if you need a response, a telephone extension number should be given with a time limit: "Call Susan at ext. 3443 by Thursday at 4:00 P.M. and tell her how many from your department will attend."

- To help ensure a response to your invitation, place the R.S.V.P. in the lower left-hand section of the invitation and enclose a reply card and envelope that is addressed and stamped. Or, list a telephone number or an address for the response:

R.S.V.P.
775-7231

or

R.S.V.P.
110 Forest Lane
Rockport, IL 60641

- If you have not heard from invitees by the time you need to make final preparations, telephone.
- The response card should be a simple fill-in-the-blanks. The printer will have several options to select from, but it can simply say:

M_____

___ regrets ___ accepts
the invitation for
Friday, January fifth
at Willow Creek Country Club

or

M_____
will _____ attend
Friday, January fifth

- When there are inclusions in the invitation, the response card and response envelope, raffle tickets for a benefit, a separate map, or seating tickets for a performance or graduation, these items are placed in front of the invitation with the writing side facing the mailing envelope flap so the reader sees the writing when he or she opens the envelope.
- Dress designations are not as strictly adhered to today, but "white tie" is the most formal, indicating a white tie, wing collar, and tail coat for men. Women wear formal evening gowns. Today this kind of dress is reserved almost exclusively for official and diplomatic occasions. "Black tie" indicates men are to wear a tuxedo and bow tie. Jackets may be patterned and of almost any color. Women wear a gown or cocktail dress.

"Semiformal" has come to mean: "Wear shoes. Don't wear T-shirts or jeans."

- The name game can be confusing. When in doubt, call and ask. Issue the invitation in the names of the hosts, for example, "David Greer and Sally Westmore invite you..." Address invitations to invitees by their preferred names. Many women now use a business name and another social name. Business invitations may list the titles of the hosts. It's also correct to issue an invitation in the name of a club, friends, a fraternity, etc.
- List the times of events in the invitation whenever possible. "Ceremony at six o'clock, reception at half past seven." "Cocktails at six o'clock, dinner at seven thirty."
- The timetable for sending invitations depends upon the occasion, the distance guests must travel, and everyone's social calendar. Wedding invitations should wisely be sent months ahead. For most formal events and dinner parties, invitations should be sent four to six weeks ahead. For informal get-togethers and casual dinners, two to four weeks is adequate (allow an extra ten days to two weeks for getting invitations printed).
- Include a no-gift statement if appropriate: "Your love and friendship are cherished gifts. We respectfully request no other." "No gifts, please." "Please bring the gift of a favorite recipe." "Please bring the gift of a favorite photo or story to share."
- Fundraiser invitations will receive a markedly better response rate if you enclose a postage-paid, addressed reply envelope.
- Invitations to guest speakers, panelists, and prospective conference attendees should contain complete information. Speakers need to know the composition of the audience, the goal of the conference or seminar, other presenters and their topics, time allotments, the room size, accommodations, seating style, audiovisual equipment, and other equipment available for use. Be sure to include a contact person to answer other specific questions. If you are using a hotel for the event, the hotel may offer a complete copy of this information.

THINK ABOUT RESPONDING

- The best rule is to always respond to a personal invitation, whether it's business or social. Both "R.S.V.P." and "Please reply" require a response. "Regrets only" requires a response only if you will not attend. Even if a dinner invitation is in conjunction with an annual sales meeting, board of directors' meeting, or special convention, respond as indicated.
- Use the reply-in-kind rule. If the invitation is formal, reply in a like manner. Use the same language as the invitation. Write, "Mr. and Mrs. Lewis Curtis accept with pleasure the kind invitation of Mr. and Mrs. Peter Graves for dinner on Monday the tenth of November at eight o'clock." Informal written responses may be made on personal stationery.
- Response by either invitee of a married couple is correct. No longer is this considered the domain of women.
- If you must cancel at the last minute after accepting an invitation, telephone or otherwise notify the host by using e-mail, fax, or telegraph and immediately write a personal note of regret.

ELIMINATE WRONG MESSAGES

- Informal invitations may contain informal writing, like abbreviations, but formal invitations should avoid abbreviations except *Mr., Mrs., Ms., Dr., Jr., Sr., Lt., Col.,* and other military designations. In formal invitations, do not abbreviate the states in the address. Numbers in the formal invitation should be spelled out, like "eight fifteen Sherman Street" and "seven o'clock." In conjunction with names, use *second* and *third* without a comma after the name, instead of *II* and *III*. Use a comma before *Jr.* and *Sr.*
- Don't be vague about whom you're inviting. List invited small children by their first names on the envelope under the parents' names. If you are inviting teenagers or older children, each should receive his or her own invitation. If the spouse of an employee is being invited or the invitee may bring a friend, make that clear. Use the individual's name whenever possible.

SELECT A FORMAT

- Formal invitations are usually on high-quality white or cream-colored cards with matching envelopes. Other choices may be embossed or plain cards with a raised border (plate mark). There is a trend toward handcrafted invitations for very special occasions. In either case, select cards with proportions of three units by four units. Good choices are 3 by 4 inches to 4½ by 6 inches. Ask the printer for samples.
- Select a typeface or lettering that is easy to read.
- Printing may be engraved or, more economically, done by thermography, which produces raised letters.
- If you create invitations, use appropriate artwork or even a nice card stock or note paper and formal verbiage, usually in the third person:

"John and Judith Eisner request the pleasure of your company at a dinner party at their home at one hundred Fox Dale Drive on September tenth. Cocktails will be served at seven, dinner at eight. R.S.V.P. 722-1558. Informal."

CREATE STRONG SENTENCES

Start with a key word of invitation and build lean sentences with precise words of invitation. Here are some examples:

▶ We really hope you and Uncle Roy will be able to have Thanksgiving dinner with us this year.

▶ Will you join Joel Walton and me for lunch on Thursday? It would be so good to see you.

▶ During the open house, First Bank's loan officers will be available to answer any questions you may have.

▶ This is your special invitation to our Ninth Annual Pre-Sale Celebration.

BUILD EFFECTIVE PARAGRAPHS

Put precise, complete information in its logical order.

▶ Please stop by our booth, #566, at the Chicago Convention Center, Expo 104, September 10–12, and see the new Model 415. There'll be a registration for a free two-week vacation giveaway, and a 25 percent discount on the new models.

▶ This is your invitation to a one-month free membership to Valley Racquet Club, 4300 Miners Road, Englewood. This entitles you to full use of the entire health club facilities, with the exception of the indoor tennis courts.

▶ Please bring the enclosed 25 percent off certificate in during our "Madman Special," Thursday, November 5, between 10:00 A.M. and 6:00 P.M. Free hot dogs and sodas for the kids.

▶ The Marketing Department is hosting an after-hours reception to show-and-tell the fall campaign on Friday, August 30, 5:00 P.M. to 6:30 P.M. Please respond with a list of those from your department who will attend.

▶ Monday Night Football happens at my house one hour before kickoff. Won't you and Sally join the rest of the softball team?

EDIT, EDIT, EDIT

The best invitations contain complete, concise information.

Invitation to a Formal Dinner

*Roosevelt and
Suzanne Connors
request the pleasure of your company
at dinner
on Friday, the tenth of September,
at half after seven o'clock
at the Town Club
Heathertown, New York*

*R.S.V.P.
20 Applewood Lane
Heathertown, New York 10045*

Invitation to a Formal Ball

*The Governors
of Gateside Country Club
invite you to subscribe to
the Annual Springtime Ball
to be held at
The Gateside Country Club
on Saturday, the twenty-fifth of April
Nineteen hundred and ninety-nine
at eight o'clock
Applewood, Connecticut*

*R.S.V.P.
Georgia Geiger
722-4212*

Invitation to an Informal Business Open House

[Typed or handwritten]
(Date)

Dear Allyson,

I hope you will come by the hospitality suite, room 430, at the Westmoreland Hotel on Thursday, April 27, between 7:00 and 9:30 P.M., and introduce yourself to our marketing team attending the Booksellers' Convention. I'd like you to meet Bill Ashton. I believe he will be a great contact for the Grizzly project.

This promises to be our best convention yet. There are already well over 125,000 registered attendees.

Best wishes,

Titus Teeter

Invitation to an Informal Social Open House

Willow Creek Country Club
will hold its thirty-fifth annual
open house for new members

One o'clock to five o'clock
Saturday the fifth of May
4500 South Willow Creek Drive

Refreshments   *Informal Dress*
Drawing

Invitation to an Informal Get-Together

[Handwritten]
(Date)

Dear Rachel,

I would be so pleased if you would join us after baby Jennifer's christening on Sunday, the 12th, from 1:30 P.M. to 3:30 P.M. It will just be a small celebration with a few special relatives and friends.

We certainly hope you can make it. Please let us know: 755-4330.

Yours truly,

Celeste Castle

Informal Invitation to a Working Business Dinner

[Typed]
(Date)

Dear Jim:

I'm hosting an informal get-together on Thursday, May 12, at 7:00 p.m. for the key players in the Adams restructuring. We will have dinner and plan on reviewing the proposed elements of the agreement, which I've enclosed. A map is enclosed with complete instructions.

Please call my secretary at 445-6700 by Wednesday, and let her know if you can make it. I'll also need your comments on the enclosed draft by Friday so I can have everyone's feedback distributed to all those coming on the 12th.

Sincerely,

Agatha Jeevers

Invitation to a Graduation Reception

Jerald and Olivia Soderholm
request the honor of your company
at a reception to celebrate the college
graduation of their son
Christopher David Soderholm
Sunday afternoon, June twenty-fourth
at three o'clock
in the Crown Room of the Highmoor
420 Eastman Drive
Cleveland Springs, Ohio

Please reply to
744 Tamarac Drive
Cleveland Springs, OH 44704

Acceptance of a Dinner Invitation

[Handwritten]

Ted and Jane Turnett accept with pleasure the kind invitation of Reginald and Jennifer Trumpet to dinner on Friday, the tenth of September, at half after seven o'clock.

Regrets to an Informal Invitation

[Handwritten]
(Date)

Dear Electra and Warren,

Dede and I are so disappointed. We will be unable to accept your kind invitation to dinner at the Metro Club on May 12 for your retirement celebration. We are scheduled to be in France for the entire month.

Have a wonderful time. We'll look forward to getting together when we return and hearing all about the event. I'll call when we return to arrange a time.

Best,

Bill

8

APPRECIATION AND THANK-YOU

*Life is not so short but that there is always
time enough for courtesy.*

—RALPH WALDO EMERSON

You will distinguish yourself if you express appreciation in personal and business relationships. The letter of appreciation is appropriate in situations where the recipient has performed in a manner that is notable or extraordinary; or when there is a mutuality in your exchange with the recipient, but you want to extend the goodwill effort of expressing appreciation.

A thank-you letter was once common courtesy and is a tradition that merits revival. Send a thank-you for gifts or acts of kindness. These notes should be brief, pleasant, and informal.

DECIDE TO WRITE
Send a note of appreciation or thanks in response to
- Outstanding addresses, speeches, and instruction sessions
- Employees' extraordinary performance
- Early, prompt, or prepayment by a customer
- Expressions of sympathy
- Letters or acts of congratulations
- Offers of assistance
- Complimentary remarks or acknowledgments in speeches, books, etc.
- Invitations to speak, chair a committee, sing, sit on a panel, etc.

- Salary increases or bonuses
- Outstanding or beneficial conduct or acts of a teacher, family member, friend, associate, or supervisor
- Financial contributions
- Volunteers' efforts
- Job interviews
- Business orders
- Referrals of clients, customers, or patients
- Reference for a business position
- Hospitality
- Contributions to fund-raising events or drives
- Membership in a club, association, or professional organization

THINK ABOUT CONTENT
- Begin with the point of appreciation or thanks, and the rest will flow more easily.
- Make it brief and sincere.
- Use a tone that is pleasant, even enthusiastic, and one that reflects the way you would talk to the recipient.
- Mention the appropriateness of the gift or act.
- Add some detail about how the gift or act benefits you.

55

- If appropriate, offer to reciprocate.
- End with a reference to the future. If appropriate, encourage the recipient to contribute again or express your desire for a future meeting.

ELIMINATE WRONG MESSAGES

- Don't mix messages. Keep news items, meeting announcements, etc., for another communication. Don't tack a thank-you onto a letter with another purpose. (See "Sales," page 231.)
- Stay away from general statements; make it specific.
- Don't let your prose go beyond your true feelings. Flowery insincerity will defeat your purpose, and your letter will be pronounced a fraud. Use, instead, a simple "thank you very much."
- For letters concerning a gift of money, the mention of the amount received is sometimes considered tactless. If you know the recipient well, you may conclude that to say, "Thank you, Uncle Joe, for the check for $50," will not offend him. For others you don't know well, say, "Thank you for the check" instead.
- In the short thank-you, the use of "Thanks again" in concluding the note does not work well. Instead, conclude with a sincere compliment to the recipient.
- Examine your motives if you are having difficulty. It may be that another type of letter is more suitable, or that a letter of appreciation or thanks isn't merited.

CONSIDER SPECIAL SITUATIONS

- The best advice is *don't procrastinate*. A late thank-you or letter of appreciation carries with it a ring of insincerity and must also be explained. Still, write it, and don't belabor its tardiness. ("I'm so sorry this note is late. The tornado hit just as we were arriving home." Or, "I'm sorry for not having written sooner to tell you how much I love the red sweater. It's a perfect match with my tartan plaid skirt.")
- Verbal thank-yous for gifts don't substitute for written ones. If you've verbally thanked the giver, still send a personal, written note.

- A written thank-you is required when a thank-you gift has been given.
- Thank-yous for condolences, flowers, contributions, and acts of kindness in the case of a death in the family must always be sent. Even written letters of sympathy should be acknowledged with a return note of thanks. These thank-yous may be written by the person closest to the deceased or by a close family member or friend. At such times, it is wise to have someone make a record to ease the task and make sure no one's kindness is overlooked. There is obviously much leeway in timing here, but generally thank-yous should be sent within six weeks of the funeral.
- A letter in response to an offer of assistance should express appreciation, accept or reject the offer, and suggest the next step if the offer is being accepted.
- A letter to a team, committee, department, or group of people may address them as a whole. If appropriate, a copy may be sent to each member. Be sure to include everyone.
- Business thank-yous should be sent by regular modes of transmission. To fax or use e-mail to transmit a personal thank-you would detract, considerably, from its personal quality. A routine thank-you for a regular business luncheon may be combined with a letter with another main message. It may be faxed.
- Sometimes appreciation must be combined with refusal. If there is an offer to serve on a committee or a gift is sent that you must refuse, emphasize your appreciation first (see "Refusal," page 186).

SELECT A FORMAT

- Handwritten personal notes of appreciation and thank-you notes should be the first choice. Use personal stationery or fold-over notes.
- Formal printed cards or stationery are sometimes used to express thanks, especially for very large events, like large weddings, or political campaigns. Still, a personal, handwritten note is in order for gifts.
- Business letters of appreciation and thank-yous should be typed on letterhead, personal business stationery, or quality paper if the recipient is associated with another organization.
- For internal business appreciation, it is usually best to use the interoffice memo.
- When hospitality was extended in a business associate's home, the thank-you is addressed to the home address.
- For routine, quick messages of appreciation for such things as product orders, a postcard may be used.
- When there are exceptionally large numbers of people to thank or there is the possibility of oversight, as in the death of a community leader, or when many people have contributed to a political campaign, it is important to include a public thank-you in local and appropriate publications.
- A formal announcement of thanks does not, of course, substitute for personal ones to people whose efforts or gifts were exceptional.

WRITE STRONG SENTENCES

▶ Your contribution to the new plant scheduling policy is one of the best I've seen in twenty years with the company.

▶ I felt your insight helped the committee do a much better job than any of us expected.

▶ Please call on me if I can return the favor.

▶ All of the family was touched by your act of kindness in serving as head pallbearer at Dad's funeral.

▶ I can't tell you how wonderful it was to see you come through that door in such a dark hour.

▶ I can't remember attending a more relaxing and enjoyable dinner party.

▶ It was extremely kind of you to call me about the opening at Formed Container.

▶ Thank you for referring Alice Bannock to Adams, and more precisely, to me.

▶ Thanks to all of you at White & White for contributing the time and energy to the Women's Corner project, answering the phones during the viewers' fundraiser.

▶ Tickets to "Sherman's Forces" were unavailable, and we would have missed the event if it hadn't been for your generosity.

BUILD EFFECTIVE PARAGRAPHS

▶ It was extremely thoughtful of you to volunteer to be on hand for the courtroom drama. I really appreciate your vote of confidence.

▶ Taking over for Karen Gross when she became ill was way beyond the call of duty. Your extra efforts and dedication to making the organization look good are greatly appreciated.

▶ I really appreciated your demonstrated leadership in last night's meeting. You kept the whole issue from exploding.

EDIT, EDIT, EDIT

Thank-you letters are generally no longer than a paragraph or two. Make every word count.

In Response to Prompt Payment

[Typed]
(Date)

Dear Mr. Jepson:

We just received your letter and check for the landscaping of Green Acres. We appreciate your prompt payment.

It was a pleasure working on this lovely project, and we do hope you'll call us for further planning or maintaining the grounds.

We look forward to hearing from you.

Yours truly,

Annie Schmidt

> Name what you appreciate.

> Refer to the future.

In Response to a Letter of Recommendation

[Handwritten]
(Date)

Bob,

I have just received the copy of your letter of recommendation to Begones on my behalf. (Is this me you're talking about?)

I greatly appreciate your kind efforts and I will certainly keep you informed of the progress and outcome as the selection process goes on.

Kind regards,

Dave

In Response to Extra Effort

[Typed]
(Date)

Dear Mr. Richardson:

I have just received the reworked architectural plans for the addition to the children's wing of St. Joseph's. I know a lot of overtime went into responding in this tight timeframe to enable us to present the plans at the board meeting, and we appreciate it. You did a great job.

The board meets in the morning, and I will be back in touch with you tomorrow afternoon to let you know how it went. I truly appreciate your fine work.

Sincerely,

Bill Babson

In Response to Volunteering

State what you appreciate early.

State *why* you are appreciative.

Offer to reciprocate.

[Typed]
(Date)

Dear Janice:

It is very thoughtful of you to volunteer to take over three of my class sessions next semester while I attend the workshops. I thought I would have to reschedule the class sessions, and that presented some insurmountable problems. Your offer is a wonderful solution.

I will telephone you next week to set a time to go over the lesson plans. Please allow me to stand in for you next semester, Janice.

Best regards,

Nancy Letterer

For the Party

[Handwritten]
(Date)

Caroline,

I've never been so totally surprised! How did you ever plan a fifty-person party of office staff, organize it, and pull it off right under my nose, complete with those fantastic Caribbean decorations? I never suspected. You are truly a wonder and a very dear friend.

Now when, exactly, is your birthday?

Affectionately,

Karen

For the Gift

[Handwritten]
(Date)

Dear Aunt Jennifer,

I've deposited your very generous check in my college fund. I'll use the money to purchase an alarm clock, so I expect I may experience mixed emotions when I hear it go off. But I'll always think fondly of you for your gift.

Thank you.

Your niece,

Lois

III. JOB-SEARCH

9
NETWORKING

Good writing is a kind of skating which carries off the performer where he would not go.

—RALPH WALDO EMERSON

The networking (sometimes called "broadcast") letter is a personal sales letter, hopefully some of your best persuasive writing. It is used to locate job openings or even to be the stimulus for creating them, and it must include enough crisp, powerful statements about your abilities to entice the reader to want to learn more. In our present job culture, where the dynamics of employee and employer are changing rapidly, this letter is becoming an increasingly important tool.

A networking letter should be sent out as an essential part of a job-search campaign to specifically identified individuals within carefully targeted organizations. It is the most positive, effective, and time-saving way to take up the job search.

Do not enclose your resume, but, rather, end the letter by requesting an exploratory interview. Enclose a self-addressed, stamped envelope for the reply to increase your response rate.

If you have gotten no response after four weeks, send a slightly different networking letter to the same executive or another carefully selected executive within the organization. The response rate for second mailings is consistently as good as that for first mailings.

Networking letters are, incidentally, most success-fully used by mature, established professionals.

DECIDE TO WRITE
Send this letter to
- Request a personal interview in your present career field
- Investigate career-change possibilities
- Gather job or career information
- Get noticed by a number of people within a company
- Follow up after your cover letter and resume haven't gotten a response
- Get the interest of headhunters

RESEARCH
Corporate directories, newspaper ads and articles, and other sources will help identify organizations and key people. Start with standard resources.
1. *Dun and Bradstreet's Reference Book of Corporate Management*
2. *Million Dollar Directory,* Dun and Bradstreet
3. *Standard and Poor's Register of Corporations, Directors, and Executives*
4. State industrial directories

5. Industry associations
6. Yellow Pages
7. *Thomas Register of American Manufacturers*
8. *Fortune Magazine*'s annual supplement listing of the largest corporations
9. *Forbes Magazine*'s annual listing of corporations
10. *The Standard Directory of Advertisers*
11. American Management Association publications
12. *MacRae's Blue Book* (an industry guide located in the reference section of your library)
13. Trade magazines
14. Association publications
15. The *Wall Street Journal*
16. State manufacturers' guides
17. Chamber of commerce publications
18. City directories

If you still need help, check the latest *Guide to American Directories* (B. Kline & Company, 11 Third Street, Rye, NY 10050). For trade and professional associations, check the *National Trade and Professional Associations of the United States and Canada* (Columbia Books, Inc., Washington, DC).

THINK ABOUT CONTENT

Write so the reader will want to learn more about you. The reader has to see something in your letter that identifies closely with a problem he or she is having at the moment that needs to be solved. All businesses, no matter how smoothly they run, experience one problem after another. Your letter must include actual, factual deeds you have accomplished, problems you have solved. Here are some general rules to think about as you begin writing:

- Use action words, verbs instead of nouns, whenever possible.
- Be sure your statements convey a sense of power.
- Be specific, not general. Remember you are asking about a specific kind of position, your specialty.
- Address your letter to the company president, chief operating officer, or chief executive officer, whenever possible, the person with the power to hire. Remember, in organizations things move much better from top to bottom than bottom to top.

More specifically, there are two types of openings to use in a networking letter: topical and accomplishment.

Topical Openings

Topical openings capitalize on current trends, current events, and identified industry needs. Timing and circumstances play a very important role here, making this opening difficult. A topical opening still is, however, the most electrifying opening if used properly.

If Sweetie Company is buying lots of TV ad time for their wild animal ads and you are an integral part of that, you might start your letter:

> I was filming charging rhinos in Nairobi last week as the ad director for the Sweetie account. I am responsible for all phases of the $36.2 million in annual billings.

Here is another example:

> I believe there are still many practices of Japanese manufacturing we need to use in this country. I have just returned from Japan after five years of living and working there. I am now home to stay in Dallas.

Accomplishment Openings

This opening is much more useful than a topical opening because it is simply more adaptable. Where the topical opening depends on the right timing and particular circumstances, the accomplishment opening can almost be lifted right out of your resume. Use one that fits the business situation or cycle at the moment. Here are examples:

> I created new-home ads that produced more than 455 visitors a day every Saturday and Sunday.

> I increased sales by 32 percent by implementing a new marketing policy.

> I reversed an operating loss and turned a net profit of 21 percent of sales before taxes.

Paragraph Two

Your second paragraph should tell the reader why you are writing:

> Your marketing department may need a person with my skills and experience. If so, you may be interested in some of my other accomplishments.

Or, try some of these transitional second paragraphs:

> Your company may need a marketing manager. My experience, therefore, may interest you.

> If your company needs a marketing manager with my training, experience, and expertise, you may be interested in some of my other accomplishments.

> You may have need of a marketing manager with my experience.

> You may be expanding your marketing program and therefore need someone with my experience and background.

Show Me

Then come the "for instances." Lift three, four, or even five of the right items from your resume and transplant them into the networking or broadcast letter.

Don't overload your letter. Less is more. Let your examples stand out as if you'd thrown shocking red paint on a canvas.

Try to use no more than ten to twelve words per sentence, keeping paragraphs between three and six lines each. This will take some work and some rework.

You may want to throw in the name of your school but not necessarily your specific degree. Name the school and degree if they say in an understated fashion: quality product. For example, if you earned an MBA from one of the country's top MBA programs, list it. Also, if you know the addressee graduated from your alma mater, list it. Many such items have been real door openers.

The Ending

In closing ask or suggest action within the power of the reader. Don't be shy. Ask for the exploratory interview. With as much zing as possible, say something like, "I'd like to discuss the details of my experience with you in a personal interview." Or, "I'll call you to arrange a time for a personal interview." You want to make sure that the ending will be the beginning.

Again, do not include a resume, and don't mention it in your closing paragraph.

ELIMINATE WRONG MESSAGES

* Don't write, "... discuss any possible positions that you might have to offer." This statement weakens your letter.
* Don't mention your resume. If you do, the reader will ask you to mail it, and you may have lost the interview opportunity.
* Never write, "I would like to show you how I can help increase your profits." The reader may consider this presumptuous from an outsider.
* Don't mention any specific kind of training that could adversely affect the intended direction of your letter. Do mention your educational background. This usually adds to the reader's receptivity.

GET THE WORD OUT

* Develop your own mailing list, select the proper recipient, and check to be sure of the name spelling and current title.
* Send out 100 to 200 letters per week.
* Continue the campaign until you have accepted a position and have started work.

SELECT A FORMAT

* Letters should be typed on personal letterhead or stationery.
* Use a computer or word processor so you can individualize letters easily.
* The visual appearance of the completed letter should be open and inviting. Indent points and create wide margins to produce a lot of white space.

WRITE STRONG SENTENCES

Use action words. Replace nouns with power verbs whenever possible.

▶ Eliminated employee pilfering that had cost the company $500,000 per year.

▶ Doubled sales in eighteen months.

▶ Expanded the market for the Model X-123 by 31 percent by designing four attachments.

BUILD EFFECTIVE PARAGRAPHS

▶ I'd like to discuss further details of my experience in a personal interview. I shall call you next Wednesday to arrange a time and place.

▶ As Marketing Manager for Reholdt, Inc., I increased sales 18 percent in twelve months by instituting a new marketing policy. I believe you would find the details of this policy very interesting.

▶ The ads we developed launched the new product in great style. In the first year, it obtained a 23-percent market share.

▶ As a department manager in the largest department store in the state, I doubled the sales volume of the ready-to-wear merchandise in three years. Profits were 13 percent above the store's previous average.

EDIT, EDIT, EDIT

After finishing your letter, put it on the shelf for a day or two so you can reread it with a fresh perspective. You may also want to ask people whose opinions you respect to read it and comment on it before you write the final draft.

ALSO SEE "RESUME," PAGE 74, AND "RESUME COVER LETTER," PAGE 69.

Seeking Engineer Position

(Date)
Mr. Ivan Prather, Vice President, Engineering

Dear Mr. Prather:

As Chief Engineer I expanded the market for the Ryan Model 880 by improving the tolerances by 34 percent. This improved product has secured new sales in high-temperature and high-load applications not previously possible.

I believe Ramsburg's Model 4000 has similar product application potential, and I would like the opportunity to discuss my engineering approach with you.

I shall call your office next week to arrange a time and place.

Sincerely,

Lydia S. Squares

Seeking Sales Manager Opportunity

(Date)
Mr. Ruben Sternberg, President

Dear Mr. Sternberg:

As National Sales Manager of RemKo, I increased sales volume 32 percent in an industry that was growing at the rate of 4 percent a year. If your company faces growth challenges, you may be interested in how I accomplished this. My multi-faceted plan achieved the following improvements:

• combined five sales regions into two,
• reduced manpower costs by 17 percent, and
• increased profits by 22 percent.

Achieving this level of performance required recruiting and developing a top team of sales professionals, instituting a sales incentive program, and dramatically increasing—by 19 percent—the sales in two product lines. We were awarded the National Sales Association's "Top Performers" award four out of the past five years.

I'd like to talk to you about how several ideas I have might benefit your company. I'll call your office next Thursday to see about arranging a time.

Cordially,

Calvin R. Clements

Seeking Entry-Level Marketing Opening

(Date)

Ms. Jeannine Trump
President

Dear Ms. Trump:

I just graduated from Duke University, where I majored in marketing and graduated *cum laude*. I was the first African-American student to receive the coveted Student-of-the-Year award. Perhaps your marketing department would be interested in someone with my enthusiasm and capabilities. During the four years I worked before returning to college for my final year, I completed the following projects:

- Organized direct-mail campaigns of over 20,000,000 letters and brochures that received an 11 percent response rate
- Completed market research and sales forecasting that sold our services to four accounts for over $500,000
- Created a promotional package that established sales distribution in a twenty-three-state area and gained a 67 percent label recognition for a start-up mineral water

Trump / (Date) / page 2

I would like to discuss my education and experience with you. I will call you next week to arrange a time and place.

Very truly yours,

Juliet S. Guest

Seeking Marketing Manager Position

(Date)
Mr. Clive Abbott
Chief Operating Officer

Dear Mr. Abbott:

As marketing manager for Critters Manufacturing, I increased sales by 42 percent. You may be interested in a woman with my marketing and sales experience. Here are a few of my other accomplishments:

Get the reader's attention.

- Launched a new product. Triggered first-year sales of $4.2 million in new markets.
- Recruited and trained twenty-five salesmen who—within one year—were the top producers for the company.
- Forecasted sales with 94 percent accuracy.

List some accomplishments.

I graduated from the Wharton Business School, where I specialized in sales management and marketing.

I would be happy to discuss details of my experience with you in a personal interview. I will call your office on Thursday morning to arrange a time.

State that you will make the next contact and when.

Sincerely,

Daisy L. Sluggs

Seeking Public Relations Opening

(Date)
William J. Barker, President

Dear Mr. Barker:

I just read the Hot Rox piece in *Creative* magazine, and I'm impressed by your dynamic organization's commitment to finding new creative talent. I believe some of my accomplishments fit your desired employee profile:

* Created and established a department that drew strong support from the community and 85 percent of the employees
* Recruited, trained, and motivated a highly diverse group of personnel from six departments into an effective team
* Developed and executed a community relations program that has won national recognition

Perhaps my search for a growth opportunity will fit with your search for an innovative, creative, and productive public relations leader. I will call later this week to arrange an appointment time.

Sincerely yours,

Dumar Q. Tyler

Seeking Sales Manager Opening

(Date)
Mr. John Rogers
President

Dear Mr. Rogers:

I just read about your plans to expand into manufacturing an upper-end line of home furniture, and I'd like the opportunity to discuss with you my experience in this area.

* As sales manager for a small Midwest manufacturer of fine furniture, I increased sales over 225 percent in two years.
* While managing a sales force of twenty-two, I added two dealers and a manufacturer's representative to expand sales to forty-two states.
* When I instituted inventory procedures that reduced inventory by 16 percent, I maintained 96 percent customer satisfaction.

I will be in Columbus on April 10 for the National Furniture Convention, and I would like the opportunity to discuss details of my experience with you. I will contact you next week to arrange a time and place.

Sincerely,

Frederika R. Fink

Seeking Accounting Opening

(Date)
Mr. Todd Ryder, President

Dear Mr. Ryder:

I have been in Dawes Prison thirty-seven times. Each time I performed a professional audit as a public accountant examining accounts, costs, and management records of the prison.

Evergreen may need a diversified, well-seasoned professional to assume accounting responsibilities. If so, you may be interested in my background and achievements.

I have completed general audit work for twenty-four government entities, seventy-six different business enterprises, fifty-three industrial manufacturers, and over 135 public and private institutions.

I designed the accounting system used for the townships of Marek County, which became a model statewide.

I would welcome the opportunity to discuss with you how my skills can benefit Evergreen, and I will call you next week to arrange a time.

Yours truly,

Jamie S. Small

10
RESUME COVER LETTER

*If you would not be forgotten, as soon as you
are dead and rotten, either write things worth
reading, or do things worth the writing.*

—BENJAMIN FRANKLIN

 The resume cover letter is a sales letter, and one of the most important sales letters you will ever write.

While the cover letter or transmittal letter (see "Cover Letter," page 167) for reports and proposals may be primarily a laundry list of the "covered" document contents, the resume cover letter must sell and call the reader to action.

The goal of the resume cover letter is to get the reader to delve into your enclosed resume and get him or her to call you to arrange an interview. Focus on one or two precise skills the employer needs. Highlight your achievements in those areas—with numbers whenever possible. Make your letter brief.

DECIDE TO WRITE

- Find out who's responsible for hiring for the position you want. Address your letter to that person. Personalize your letter, if possible, to demonstrate that you have done your homework. Beginning with "Dear Sir," "Gentlemen," or "Madam" does not convey the kind of message you need. There are many ways you may obtain the name of a particular person. Certainly calling the organization and asking for the person's name is one of the most direct.

- Identify yourself in terms of a specific job.
- Write something unique. It's important to convey something of your personality, eliminating the flavor of a form letter.
- Take a few risks. You must tell the reader why he or she should interview you. Describe the value you can bring to the organization. Be sure to communicate your achievements and capabilities in a way that suggests assistance and support.
- Speak the language. Every specialty has its own particular terms. Use them. But be sure you don't overdo it.
- Keep your language conversational and friendly.
- Keep your sentences short.
- Demonstrate energy and enthusiasm.
- Cut to the chase.
- Use a brief paragraph to define your achievements, skills, and value.
- Give full information on how you can be contacted. Give the where, when, and how, and any precautions on confidentiality.
- Be innovative to get extra attention. A colored dot or a star adhered to one corner of your letter and resume, a unique design approach, or even an audiovisual presentation (if acceptable within

69

your field) can work to bring extra attention to your qualifications.

- Close with a friendly but proactive statement that promises or requests further contact. Ask for the next step: a meeting or conversation with the reader. Be as specific as you can. For example, "I am going to be in Boston the week of the fifteenth. I would like to meet with you at that time. I will call your office Thursday morning to set a date and time."
- Rewrite and edit to give your letter punch.

ELIMINATE WRONG MESSAGES

- Avoid formal, dry, and vague words and terms.
- Don't get lengthy.
- Do not use general statements. Be specific.
- Don't lift sections from your resume verbatim.
- Don't address your letter to the personnel department unless absolutely necessary.

CONSIDER SPECIAL SITUATIONS

- When you determine it's better *not* to send a resume, use a networking letter. (See "Networking," page 63.)
- If you know all the specifications of a job opening, you may want to use a comparative listing of your qualifications, sometimes called an "executive summary," "briefing," or "skill summary."
- When sending your resume cover letter to a head-hunter, you may be more informal; in that case, you may certainly concentrate on the job you are seeking and your qualifications.

SELECT A FORMAT

- White or open space gives the pleasing impression that your letter can be quickly and easily read.
- Quality matching paper and envelopes are a must. Select something neutral but slightly distinctive, like an off-white or cream-colored stationery.
- Select a typeface that is consistent with both your resume and your field.
- Hand-addressing the envelope to the specific person may increase the chances that the person will read it.
- Be creative. In the very competitive job market, make your letter distinctive but still within the realm of what is acceptable in your field. People in the arts, advertising, and public relations professions usually have more latitude than those in banking and publishing, for example.

WRITE STRONG SENTENCES

Start with a power verb to properly focus your sentences. *Created, restructured, initiated, launched, conducted, controlled, administered, constructed, managed, interceded, established, enacted,* and *marketed* are some examples.

▶ I thrive on challenges such as the one you advertised in Sunday's *Job Weekly.*

▶ Having proven myself as an associate director, I am ready to step up to a position of director, such as the one you now have open at Health Programs.

▶ Theodore Sturgeon recommended I contact you concerning the office manager position.

▶ I offer a solid electrical engineering background and education, as well as award-winning design experience.

BUILD EFFECTIVE PARAGRAPHS

▶ I am very interested in the position of administrator of Korda's legal department. I believe my enclosed resume suggests some ways I can add value.

▶ I have been the legal administrator for two firms with thirteen and twenty-five attorneys, respectively. Both went through some serious downsizing due to market conditions. Still, during these extremely challenging times, I maintained healthy profit margins and kept employee satisfaction high.

▶ Other details of my experience are covered in the enclosed resume. I look forward to an interview. I'll call your office on Wednesday at 10:00 A.M. to arrange a place and time.

EDIT, EDIT, EDIT

Polishing your final letter is vital. Before sending it you may want to have several persons whose opinions you respect read it.

Follow-up After a Chance Meeting

(Date)

Mr. Frank Brown, Chief Executive Officer, Atulac

Dear Mr. Brown:

It was a pleasure meeting you at the National Home Builders' Association convention in Dallas last week. I enjoyed the opportunity to see the operation of your electronic skylights. I'm following up our discussion, as you suggested, with this letter.

Over the last ten months with Wilson Windows, I have successfully introduced a new product line, trained forty-five sales representatives, and have already realized substantial market penetration, with profits for the year estimated to be in excess of $3.4 million (compared with $2.2 million last year). You can see in my enclosed resume other skills that could benefit Atulac.

I'd like to discuss my experience with you in detail. Wednesday morning I'll contact your office about arranging a meeting for the week of January 21.

Sincerely,

Germaine Q. Ruddick

Referral for Summer Job

(Date)

Jennifer Beales

Head Librarian

Dear Ms. Beales:

My friend on your staff, Mr. Rob Anderson, suggested I send you my resume and request an interview for the position of summer clerk. I am pursuing a library science degree at the University of Michigan and am a lifelong lover of books.

I have held several volunteer positions working with children and young adults through the Girl Scouts, the Literacy League, and Children at Risk. I have also volunteered at Vulcan Library as a Children's Hour storyteller.

I will call you next week to request an interview time convenient to your schedule.

Sincerely,

Joan Diddly

Sending Resume After Telephone Contact

(Date)
Philip Tinsdale
Vice President

Dear Mr. Tinsdale:

Thank you for the invitation to submit a resume for your international sales manager position. As I mentioned over the telephone, Jack Belzer was enthusiastic about my contacting you. He did, in fact, cover many of the requirements of the position.

For the past five years, I have headed the international sales efforts at Manchester, a position that included the following:

- creating sales offices in Belgium, France, Germany, and Great Britain;
- recruiting and managing a group of thirty-four independent sales representatives;
- providing full training of all European representatives;
- securing 43 percent, 34 percent, 28 percent, and 37 percent of the Belgian, French, German, and British markets, respectively; and
- surpassing $45 million in annual sales with excellent margins.

Contact the right person, preferably the person who will hire the successful candidate.

Introduce yourself by making a connection with the reader.

Define your accomplishments.

Tinsdale / (Date) / page 2

I look forward to discussing details of my experience with you, including how I feel I can benefit Smith. I shall call your office Monday morning about 10:00 A.M. to arrange a time and place.

Sincerely,

Jacob Seles

Make a strong close, stating when you will make the next contact.

Comparison Letter—Responding to Ad

(Date)
Celeste Vickers, Vice President

Dear Ms. Vickers:

I noted with interest your advertisement for an Accounting Manager in Sunday's *Tribune*. I am looking for just such a growth opportunity.

I believe my skills and experience closely align with the qualifications you are seeking:

Applegate Requirements	My Skills and Experience
Accounting degree and several years accounting experience.	C.A. degree, 1989, from DePaul, and over five years experience.
Demonstrated ability to manage and motivate staff.	Effectively managed staff of fourteen, including two senior accountants.
Strong analytical and administrative skills.	Developed a base reference library with Lotus 1-2-3 for 350 clients.
Outstanding oral and written communication skills.	Initiated department staff meetings. Created skill-training classes for four personnel levels with 95 percent participant "excellent" rating.

Vickers / (Date) / page 2

Some of my other achievements are outlined on the enclosed resume. I would welcome the opportunity for an interview and will call your office next week to arrange a convenient time.

Yours truly,

Jamie Baxter

Response to Blind Ad

(Date)
Chairman of the Board

Dear Chairman of the Board:

The North Chicago Chapter of the A.M.A. dubbed me the "turn-around king" in the *C.M.A. Journal,* issue IV, June 15. Over the past ten years, I've taken three companies from the bankruptcy court to profits of $500,000, $2.l million, and $1.8 million. One of these companies is Plastic Forms in Hollywood, Florida.

I would like the opportunity to discuss with you the details of what I've done and how my skills might work for your organization. I'm enclosing a resume for your review.

I will call your office next week to arrange a time convenient for a brief meeting.

Sincerely,

Cordelius M. Conover

11
RESUME

The perfect resume is, "commander in chief, United States of America."

—ANONYMOUS

Your resume is a synopsis of what you have to offer. It should include what you have done, what you know, and who you are. It must have the meat and muscle of facts and figures, and it should have a certain flair, technique, and pizzazz. The proper balance of these elements provides the impact you'll need to sell yourself as a worthy candidate.

The secret to writing a great resume is first knowing the audience—the person doing the hiring—and the organization. The key, then, is writing your resume to show that you are the best person for the specific job.

DECIDE TO WRITE

Send your resume

- In response to newspaper and other media ads
- In response to an invitation from an organization
- As part of your job-search campaign
- To accompany a proposal, report, or other document that is based on your qualifications and experience
- In connection with running for political, club, or association office
- To document your qualifications as a speaker, author, expert witness, or other type of authority

DECIDE ON RESUME TYPE

There are three basic styles of resumes: the chronological, the functional, and the creative. Select the style that showcases you the best and is best matched to your target audience, based on your own experience and capabilities and the position you are targeting. There is no "correct" or "incorrect" form. You may even want to use one style for one audience and another style for a different audience. And sometimes you may want to combine styles to best illustrate why you are the best person for the position.

Chronological Resume

The chronological resume is the most traditional. It uses a time sequence to list work experience and education, usually appearing in a reverse order beginning with the present.

Use a chronological resume when

- You are pursuing traditional fields (government, education).
- Your work history shows a strong growth pattern or direction.
- Your title progression is impressive.
- You're continuing on the same career path.
- Your present or last employer is important.

The chronological resume is not the best form for everyone. If any of the following applies to you, it is probably better to use one of the other styles.

Don't use a chronological resume when
- You are just entering the job market (a recent graduate).
- You're changing career direction or goal.
- You have holes in your work experience (periods of unemployment).
- Your career has plateaued and remained there for some time.
- You are returning to the job market after a long absence.
- You do not wish to divulge your age.
- You've changed employers frequently.

Functional Resume

The functional resume focuses on capability and skills. Usually these are listed by areas and may or may not include dates.

Use a functional resume when
- You are changing careers.
- You are entering the job market.
- You are reentering the job market.
- Your experience lacks a demonstrated career path.
- You are a consultant, freelancer, or have completed temporary work.
- Your latest job appears to be a demotion over previous ones.
- Your work experience seems somewhat unconnected to the position you are applying for.

Don't use a functional resume when
- You have not targeted your resume toward a certain position.
- You do not have well-defined accomplishments and capabilities.
- You do not have enough experience to demonstrate functions performed.

Creative Resume

The creative resume is a free-form style and can be extremely effective in showcasing your skills and capabilities—particularly for artists, writers, actors, public relations personnel, and people in the media. An account executive looking for a new position in an advertising agency effectively used a resume with cartoons to land a high-powered position. A C.E.O. of a public relations agency was elected to an important association president post by preparing audiotapes of voice impersonations touting the various attributes that made him the best person for the job. He played it for association members at a campaign luncheon.

Executives of various disciplines and actors have used audiovisual resumes in cassette-tape form to land sales jobs, manager jobs, acting roles, and public service jobs.

And computer experts, graphic designers, actors, and photographers have created interactive resumes that they put on Internet systems or mailed on diskettes, wrapped in a cover letter, to employers.

Use a creative resume when
- The target of your resume is a creative or specialized audience who will appreciate it.
- You decide it is the only medium that can adequately express who you are.
- You especially want to showcase your creative talents.

Don't use a creative resume when
- You are seeking a position in a traditional field, such as banking or government.
- You are not well-grounded in your own creativity.
- It won't be otherwise "acceptable" to your audience.

THINK ABOUT CONTENT

Learn as much as possible about the employer and target audience. Assess the position you are seeking—preferably a specific position within a specific organization—and the key ingredients needed to fill it.

Then work through the following steps of writing, rewriting, and editing your information, keeping in mind the resume style you have selected. Create separate categories of information, or use index cards for ease in completing your final draft:

1. Make an inventory of your personal information, focusing on your skills, abilities, and strong points. There are really two types of skills: general and specific.

    General skills, like analyzing, communicating, and writing, are often taken for granted because they seem like things everyone can do. List the general skills you use in your work, because every job requires them. The inventory on the opposite page can help you identify your general skills and their job applications.

2. Select your twelve strongest general skills from the list, and translate them into specific technical skills that produce measurable results. These are job-related skills like inputting on a keyboard, which produces a piece of correspondence. Here are a couple of examples:

General skill:	*Organizing*
Related activities:	*Making order out of chaos, establishing physical order, categorizing facts*
Applications:	*Setting up a filing system, creating a systematic way to categorize inventory in a warehouse, and rewriting and editing reports*
General skill:	*Negotiating*
Related activities:	*Bartering, holding a position, convincing others, arranging terms, establishing standards*

Applications:	*Setting up conferences with hotels, establishing sales prices for products, developing contract terms, arranging details of sales, establishing salaries*

3. Factor into your skill statements those things that express your personal characteristics, and select those that best describe you. These words may not appear in your completed resume, but they will help you in forming your final statements.

___ Able	___ Intense
___ Ambitious	___ Intuitive
___ Assertive	___ Loyal
___ Careful	___ Masterful
___ Caring	___ Open-minded
___ Communicative	___ Organized
___ Creative	___ Persistent
___ Decisive	___ Persuasive
___ Dedicated	___ Political
___ Determined	___ Precise
___ Diligent	___ Quick
___ Easygoing	___ Responsible
___ Energetic	___ Results-oriented
___ Flexible	___ Rigid
___ Forthright	___ Sensitive
___ Friendly	___ Strong
___ Hardworking	___ Supportive
___ Helpful	___ Tactful
___ Honest	___ Thorough
___ Humorous	___ Trustworthy
___ Imaginative	___ Warm
___ Intellectual	___ Willing
___ Intelligent	

4. List your accomplishments in the most powerful way.

5. Include any pertinent special-interest areas, school results, training results, sports and hobby results, military and service results, community activities results, home results, and, of course, work experience results.

GENERAL SKILL INVENTORY

Skill	Direct Job Application	Indirect Job Application
Acknowledging Others		
Acting		
Analyzing		
Building		
Classifying		
Communicating		
Conceptualizing		
Convincing Others		
Cooking		
Counseling		
Dancing		
Drawing		
Driving		
Entertaining		
Following Instructions		
Growing Things		
Innovating		
Interior Decorating		
Keeping Records		
Learning New Material		
Managing People		
Manual Dexterity		
Meeting Deadlines		
Meeting New People		
Negotiating		
Nurturing		
Organizing		
Painting		
Planning		
Reading		
Remembering		
Repairing Things		
Researching		
Running		
Supervising Others		
Supporting Others		
Teaching		
Traveling		
Understanding New Material		
Using Mechanical Tools		
Visualizing		
Working with Numbers		
Writing		

Education results examples:

▶ Achieved a 3.8 G.P.A. while working twenty hours a week and participating in two extracurricular sports.

▶ Established the Women's Republican Club and solicited membership from 1,320 undergraduates.

▶ Served as editor of the class yearbook.

▶ Initiated an Easter Seal spring frolic, which raised $5,240 for the Kids' Summer Camp program.

Special-interest examples:

▶ Organized a tennis tournament for 520 participants.

▶ Read the complete Great Books of the Western World.

▶ Designed and created three new, complicated quilt patterns.

▶ Improved my U.S.T.A. tennis ability level from a 2.0 to a 4.5 in three months.

Training results examples:

▶ Taught myself how to speed write and accurately take dictation up to 110 words per minute.

▶ Graduated number two from the effective-sales program.

▶ Completed the AMA marketing-for-profit workshop.

▶ Completed the Xerox sales training program.

▶ Graduated from a women-in-business managing-your-time seminar.

Sport/hobby examples:

▶ Organized and initiated a fiction-writing group of ten members.

▶ Organized a tennis league and tournament for fifty-four participants.

▶ Redesigned and remodeled a seven-room house in my spare time in fourteen months.

Military examples:

▶ Completed airborne training second in my group of seventy-six.

▶ Learned conversational German in five months.

▶ Mastered an AS-11 guidance system in five months.

Community activity examples:

▶ Organized a group gubernatorial campaign for leading candidates in four months.

▶ Implemented a meals-on-wheels program for the aged for 1,500 participants.

▶ Initiated, organized, and conducted seven health-care programs for 5,000 participants.

▶ Successfully petitioned—obtaining 5,500 signatures—against irresponsible mining operations.

Family and household examples:

▶ Established a family trust fund for seven siblings.

▶ Managed an annual family budget of $56,000 for nine.

▶ Repaired five small home appliances.

6. List your last four jobs, starting with the most recent, and work backwards. Carefully sort through your experience results, enumerating five distinct results for each position you held. Think in terms of results you can express in concrete terms of facts and figures. Make your results as action oriented and as power based as possible. Here are a few examples:

▶ Organized a company library of 5,000 volumes.

▶ Prepared a career-advancement plan for five entry-level careers.

▶ Increased production by 20 percent by eliminating four procedural steps in clerical activities.

▶ Planned and administrated the orientation program for thirty-five employees.

Position: _____

Dates: _____

Employer: _____

Five results: _____

_____

_____

_____

_____

7. Focus on how the results you have listed relate to your career future. Go back over the items you have selected and use a three-number rating system to indicate their relevance to your future career: a *1* to represent very career-oriented results, a *2* to represent somewhat career-oriented results, and a *3* to represent results that are not relevant to your career.

- Think in terms of your career objective. You will want to divide your information into skills, work history, education, training, and licenses.
- Arrange the elements of your resume to showcase what you bring to a particular position.
- List experience in a straightforward manner, with the employer's name, but not address, recorded.
- Education, for anyone who has more than three years' work experience, should appear at the bottom of the resume.
- Use power phrases and use indented "bulleted" statements. Resumes do not have to have subjects and predicates.
- Make your most powerful statements first. Those with less power should appear in diminishing order.
- Keep it simple. If the position you are applying for is very specialized, use the simplest terms possible.
- State what you did, not what the reader should think about you. For example, "I am an excellent writer" is an evaluation. "I wrote four marketing analyses rated excellent by six department heads" exemplifies your expertise.
- Include personal awards or achievements if they are pertinent or if they will be important to the reader. Examples might be "wrote a best-selling novel," "ran the New York marathon in 1988," or "have read the Great Books of the Western World."

- Part-time jobs may be used by recent graduates looking for their first job. If the information is especially pertinent, it should be distilled and used.
- Professional associations can be very important to your career, especially if you held a prominent office. List all of them that might apply to the position you are targeting.
- Pertinent licenses, certificates, and other qualifications should be listed.
- Personal references should not appear, but have them recorded and prepared in the event they are requested.

ELIMINATE WRONG MESSAGES

- Do not exaggerate, distort the facts, embellish, or lie. Include only information that is true and verifiable.
- Check to be sure all errors have been removed.
- Do not include an "objective" that states your individual goals. Focus, instead, on what you can do for the organization.
- Never state the salary you are seeking.
- Don't overload your resume. It should not include everything you have ever done.
- Don't use long sentences or paragraphs. Use sentences with ten to twelve words and paragraphs of three to six lines.
- Don't be shy. This is the place to state—clearly and succinctly—your best attributes. At the same time, be sure your resume does not contain a braggart or flippant tone.
- Get rid of statements that do not stress results. Review what you've written down: Does it focus on description or does it stress results?
- Eliminate wimpy words that make your resume weak. Any adverbs, those anemic "ly" words, should be deleted. Take this sentence: "I actively pursued…" Adverbs weaken the verb or act as a crutch; "I pursued" is stronger.
- Eliminate articles—*the, a, an*—whenever possible and select strong verbs to convey the meaning you want.

- Eliminate unnecessary descriptive words and modifiers: "creative, innovative, hard-working, futuristic, dedicated, bottom-line oriented." Dull resumes contain lots of descriptive statements that look like they were copied right out of corporate personnel manuals.
- Unless it is relevant to the position, don't include personal information like age, weight, height, marital status, religion, or political affiliation; salary information; references; statements like "references will be furnished upon request"; or a picture of yourself.
- Never include information about past or part-time jobs that have no relevance to the job you are applying for. Your job description for these experiences should be distilled into a simple statement that covers a broad range of time or activities unless this is your strongest work experience.
- Don't clutter your resume with too-precise dates.
- Eliminate vagueness and jargon.
- In reviewing, check that your statements contain power verbs and precise, hard facts and figures.

CHECK YOUR FINAL DRAFT

- The employment section of your resume should include a maximum of four or five positions held. In the chronological listing, do not leave periods of time unaccounted for.
- Document your pertinent education, association memberships, pertinent personal information, if any, and skills or training.
- Enlist the help of friends and professional associates whose judgment you trust. Ask them to critique your resume, using the following checklist:

	Yes	No
1. Are statements clear and concise?	___	___
2. Are there any superfluous or unnecessary words?	___	___
3. Have I included what should be eliminated?	___	___
4. Is it easy to follow?	___	___
5. Are my accomplishments well showcased?	___	___
6. Have I accounted for all the time covered?	___	___
7. Have I included my address, phone number, and a place where I can be easily reached?	___	___

SELECT A FORMAT

- Computers and word processors make it possible for you to target each resume. And high-quality printers allow you to produce professional-looking typefaces (fonts). Don't use a dot-matrix-printed resume.
- Try to put all your information on a single sheet.
- Position your name, address, and contact numbers centered, flush left, or in a manner so your resume looks balanced.
- For typeface, usually Helvetica, Times Roman, Schoolbook, or New Century are good choices. Don't combine styles unless you're an expert. Use boldface type, strong italics (many are too weak), large type, and attention-getting spacing to make your point. Your name and telephone number, your job titles, your objectives, and capabilities statements—these are items you may want to stand out.
- Balance your material vertically and horizontally on the page so that it looks open and clean on the paper. Use the white space to get the reader's attention.
- Select a quality bond. If you're answering an ad, your resume may be one of hundreds. Isn't it worth the risk of color (buff or cream) to get extra attention? Using pastels and "shocking" colors is taking considerably more risk, however, so use these only if you know the target reader well and are sure your choice of paper won't be labeled unprofessional. Test your paper selection to be sure it copies well. Select envelopes that match your resume paper.
- Check to ensure you have no typos. These are embarrassing and unacceptable. Use the computer spell checker, but go over the resume to catch correctly spelled words used incorrectly, like *to* for *too*.
- Give the resume a little aging time before your final proofing. It's amazing how much difference just a little time can make in your ability to have a completely fresh, objective look.

Pilot Resume

Daniel R. Flowers
6800 East Yale, #55
Omaha, Nebraska 68108

(402) 780-6550

Experience

1964–1993   **CAPTAIN**
United Airlines

In 29 years, I logged 14,437 accident- and injury-free hours in the air.

1990–1993	DC-10 Captain
1988–1990	DC-8-71 Captain
1983–1988	B-727 Captain
1968–1983	B-727, DC-8, DC-10 First Officer (Co-Pilot)
	DC-6B, DC-8 Second Officer (Flight Engineer)
1964–1965	Flight Engineer Trainee

Military

1957–1964   **CAPTAIN**
United States Air Force

- In the 44th Air Transport Squadron (MATS), Travis AFB, CA, I was assigned to fly the C-135B (B-707) in worldwide rapid deployment of troops to Tan Son Nhut (Saigon).

- During a tour of duty at Wheeler AB, Tripoli, Libya, I flew the T-33 jet trainer throughout Europe and the Mediterranean.

- During my assignment to the 56th Air Rescue Squadron, Sidi Slimane AB, Morocco, I flew helicopter rescue missions in limited visibility and gale force wind conditions to find and rescue victims of floods, fires, downed aircraft, and sinking ships.

Education

1952–1956   Bachelor of Science in Business Administration
University of Idaho
Moscow, Idaho

Current   ATP
FAA Medical Certificate First Class

1

Pilot Resume Attachment

Daniel R. Flowers

Attachment I
Flight Time History

Total Flight Time   17,723
Total Pilot in Command Time   7,500

Civilian Flight Time

Aircraft Type	PIC Time	Total Flight Hours
DC-6B	0	346
DC-8	1,000	5,061
DC-10	2,000	4,186
B-727	3,000	484
	6,000	14,437

Military Flight Time

Fixed Wing Aircraft	PIC Time	Total Flight Hours
T-34	20	40
T-28	45	100
T-33	360	460
C-47/DC-3	0	118
C-135/B-707	1,000	2,200
	1,425	2,918

Rotary Wing Aircraft	PIC Time	Total Flight Hours
H-13	15	30
H-19/H-21	100	338
	1,540	3,286

2

Conrad Cunningham Manchester
25 Outrigger Street
Marina Del Rey, CA 90292
(310) 553-7443

PROFESSIONAL EXPERIENCE

SENIOR FINANCIAL ANALYST Los Angeles, CA
Houlihan Lokey Howard & Zukin 1992–Present
- Managed all facets of securities analyses. Completed over 30 midsized corporation due diligence pro formas in 12 months, including quantitative financial analyses, debt restructuring, and offering memoranda for principal investment groups.

- Conducted over 20 separate real estate investment services, including in-depth debt restructuring, quantitative financial analyses, and due diligence on 30 deals.

- Completed merger and acquisition services on up to seven deals at a time, including 24 private placement and 23 exclusive sales of middle-market companies. Purchased and placed $125 million in corporate business debt. Executed 24 business valuations including fairness and solvency opinions.

- Developed 35 new business opportunities with middle-market companies for purchase and corporate bond reissues.

MEMBER, BOARD OF GOVERNORS San Francisco, CA
University of San Francisco 1992–Present
- Propose alternative fiscal plans to the Board of Directors. Establish student scholarship criteria. Represent Southern California alumni in fundraising activities and public relations.

ANALYST, RESTRUCTURING/LITIGATION GROUP Los Angeles, CA
Price Waterhouse 1990–1992
- Provided restructuring and bankruptcy advice to 45 creditor corporations. Included due diligence and debt restructuring analyses.

- Prepared internal financials for 45 client corporations and evaluated alternative strategic plans for 37 restructured companies.

- Designed financial models for 36 distressed companies.

EDUCATION

HONOR STUDENT San Francisco, CA
University of San Francisco 1990
Bachelors of Arts, Economics/Philosophy

COMPUTER SKILLS

Proficient in Lotus 1-2-3, WordPerfect, Paradox, and Harvard Graphics.

Chronological Resumes

Middle Manager Resume

Jennifer Maynard Boyles
1765 West Island Way
St. Charles, VA 29741
(803) 554-9875

PROFILE

Middle manager in health-care setting with excellent communication skills and a keen eye for detail and accuracy. Self-starter with strong customer service skills and the ability to work effectively in high-pressure environment. Possess fine ability in accounting, bookkeeping, and math.

EXPERIENCE

Resource Coordinator, MERCY HOSPITAL, Charleston, SC   1993–Present
Work closely with physicians to identify and evaluate patients who need extended care. Attend all Med/Surg rounds to conduct patient psychosocial assessments. Consult with families to advise on extended care placement. Consult with physicians and social workers to implement patient care programs. Organize and implement two health-care teams. Coordinate all patient discharge, transfer, and referral records. Create statistical reports for extended care placement using spreadsheet software. Design and create database file system to update extended care and rehabilitation facilities.

Patient Care Coordinator, ST. FRANCIS HOSPITAL, Charleston, SC   1991–1993
Coordinated and supervised all patient floor records and services. Received admissions and arranged discharges. Kept medical records current. Ordered and compiled lab work records. Inventoried, maintained, and ordered supplies as needed with 98 percent accuracy.

Program Coordinator, ST. FRANCIS HOSPICE, Charleston, SC   1987–1991
Created and implemented new budget utilizing Lotus 1-2-3. Prepared payroll for 65 employees and performed and oversaw accounting functions.

EDUCATION

Clemson University, Clemson, SC
B.S. in Human Services Management

COMPUTER

Lotus 1-2-3, WordPerfect, Microsoft Word

Emma Cornell Worthington
1145 Evert Street
Cleveland, Ohio 44101
(440) 755-7883

OBJECTIVE: Restaurant Assistant Manager Trainee

RESTAURANT EXPERIENCE

Management
- Prepared payroll for staff of 25
- Completed light bookkeeping, made bank deposits, and maintained records for taxes
- Opened, balanced, and closed cash registers
- Ordered supplies and arranged for equipment maintenance
- Decorated restaurant
- Arranged special events for reservations of 15 or more

Personnel Supervision and Training
- Trained and supervised 20 waitresses and 12 hostesses
- Hired and terminated staff
- Successfully mediated dozens of employee disputes
- Completed work schedules for 25 employees

Menus, Food Preparation, and Presentation
- Ordered over $50,000 per month in food and liquor supplies
- Maintained inventory and organized stockroom, which resulted in savings of 15 percent
- Oversaw sanitation and preparation of food
- Planned menus and oversaw quality and accuracy of deliveries, which resulted in savings of 7 percent each month
- Supervised food presentation, which resulted in 22 percent higher customer satisfaction

Education
Associate of Culinary Arts, New York College of Culinary Arts, 1994

Jennifer M. Bateman, R.N.
3212 East Burlington Street
Wilmette, IL 60651
(312) 554-8210

QUALIFICATION HIGHLIGHTS

- Skilled in working with people in crisis.
- Work well independently or as a team member.
- 10 years successful research and collection of data as clinical nurse.

PROFESSIONAL EXPERIENCE

Counseling
- Crisis intervention and long-term counseling with individuals of diverse backgrounds and problems, including confinement, terminal illness, and institutional group living.
- Advised study-group volunteers of positive test results including venereal disease, TB, high blood pressure, and other abnormal blood values.
- Directed and coordinated the medical follow-up for 300 individuals with problems.

Research
- Completed 40 human nutrition research studies.
- Established critical test procedures.
- Prepared samples for analysis and transport.

Management/Supervision
- Head nurse in charge of supervising support staff, research volunteers, and graduate students for a Northwestern University nutritional study.
- Authored two procedural manuals and delivered in-service training talks to staff.
- Taught data-collection and handling techniques to research participants.
- Assembled data and wrote 42 reports of studies. (See bibliography.)

EMPLOYMENT

1989–Present   Research/Clinical Nurse II   Northwestern University/U.S.D.A.
1994–Present   Health Consultant   Chicago School District

EDUCATION

B.A., Journalism, DePaul, 1986
R.N., Northwestern, 1989

Creative/Combination Resumes

Health Education Administrator Resume

Denise Leah Golightly
2345 West Highline Drive
Leadville, CO 98540
715/344-6440

OBJECTIVE
Community Health Education Administrator

QUALIFICATIONS

- Award-winning assessment and communication skills.
- Proficiency in program development, presentation, and group facilitation.
- Over 10 years experience in varied and complex human relations responsibilities.
- M.S.W. degree with fieldwork experience in medical and psychiatric settings.
- Proven ability to work independently and with multidisciplinary team.

PROFESSIONAL EXPERIENCE

Community Relations and Education

- Agency liaison to 24 secondary, high school, and college classes; lectured on health and education issues.
- Recruited 45 adoptive couples for hard-to-place children. Developed, organized, and coordinated 12 training sessions and 10 support groups.
- Developed and presented 32 special community education programs.
- Organized 18 community parents participation in schoolwork workshop programs.

Administration

- Established 10 in-house and interagency programs on extended medical care and adoptions.
- Prepared 15 comprehensive, expert reports and recommendations for agency and court use.
- Contributed to establishing $2.5 million in budgets, and worked with financial officer to authorize monthly disbursements of $9,000 to $25,000 monthly budgets.
- Supervised 17 case workers and technicians.

Counseling

- Achieved 87 percent improvement rate with individuals and families through use of crisis intervention techniques and long-term counseling. Those counseled came from diverse backgrounds and status, and problems included life stress, illness, disability, and life transitions.
- Performed in-depth investigative interviewing and personal assessments.

EMPLOYMENT

1992–Present	Kaiser Hospitals, San Francisco, CA
	Medical Social Worker
1990–1992	Marin Human Resources Agency, Marin, CA
	Counselor for Adoption—Child Abuse
1986–1990	San Francisco Social Services
	Case Worker—Low-Income Families

EDUCATION

B.A. *cum laude* Sociology—University of San Francisco
M.S.W. University of San Francisco

Creative/Combination Resumes

Computer Service Manager Resume

Franklin Q. O'Day
13245 Osprey Drive
Wadsworth, Florida 33597
(352) 655-7897

OBJECTIVE

Computer Service Manager

QUALIFICATIONS

- Diagnose and repair at 97% accuracy rate.
- Skilled in all major computer equipment types.
- Experienced both in working independently and supervising others.

EXPERIENCE

- Used Commodore's diagnostic programs to locate defective components on PET computers.
- Found and solved problems beyond the scope of diagnostic programs, such as thermal integrated circuit failure and unstripped wire in keyboard connector.
- Kept electronic equipment operating at 96 percent efficiency, including microcomputers.

EMPLOYMENT

1992-Present   Senior Electronics Technician

University of California, Berkeley, CA

Radio Astronomy Laboratory

Test and install sensitive receivers and computer control equipment for radio and optical telescopes working from engineer sketches and diagrams.

1988-1992   Electronics Technician

Beckman Instruments, Richmond, CA

Developed, tested, and repaired prototypes for high-speed electronics counters.

EDUCATION

- Santa Monica City College, Santa Monica, CA. Engineering major, three years.
- University of California, Berkeley, CA. Electrical Engineering major, two years.

12

RECOMMENDATION

He who says there is no such thing as an honest man, you may be sure is himself a knave.

—GEORGE BERKELEY

The terms *reference letter, letter of evaluation,* and *letter of recommendation* are often used interchangeably. In strictest definition, the *reference* letter is the most general of the three and is used to document personal history: dates, position, credit, and place of schooling and employment. This letter often includes a general recommendation about character and was once used very routinely, addressed "To Whom It May Concern," when an employee left an organization's employment.

Though reference letters are not usually required in today's business world, employers, prospective employers, or other organizations often want verification of scholarship, character, credit, and employment and may request a letter of reference.

In response, send the letter specifically to the person requesting it, and supply only the information requested.

The letter of *evaluation* is used to give a more thorough accounting of both the negative and positive aspects of a person's history. This letter is routinely completed as part of an employee's review process and is placed in the personnel file.

The letter of *recommendation* is generally written by a former superior in the workplace or school in response to a request by the employee or student.

The organization and content of these three types of letters is very similar, but this chapter will concentrate on the letter of recommendation. Most everything here applies to the other letters as well. (See the letter samples at the end of the chapter.)

The letter of recommendation promotes one person to another. To write an effective letter you must be familiar enough with the person's abilities, skills, and performance to offer specific information. Before you start, review your organization's policies. They may prohibit you from answering a request for information on a former employee or associate. If you do respond, stay away from information about the person's age, race, religion, sex, marital status, pregnancy, criminal record, citizenship, organization memberships, and mental and physical handicaps, unless—in an unusual case—the information is clearly related to the position. Many organizations have a policy that limits reporting to only certain broad, verifiable facts.

If you are not very familiar with the person, or you cannot recommend him or her, decline (remember, in most instances the person will be able to read your letter under the provisions of the Privacy Act).

DECIDE TO WRITE

You will need to compose this letter to

- Respond to a request about a former employee or company you have been associated with
- Promote a candidate for club, sorority, fraternity, association, or honor society membership
- Recommend a candidate for a job, grant, scholarship, or special award

THINK ABOUT CONTENT

- Address your letter to a specific person.
- Identify the request.
- Be sure you know the position for which the person is applying, and write the recommendation in light of that knowledge.
- Explain your relationship with the person, stating your position, title, and any other pertinent information.
- State the person or company's full name, position, or status. Include dates of employment or association, position titles, primary responsibilities, and professional or honorary associations.
- Give a general recommendation that sets up the organization of the letter. Use a tone that is businesslike but friendly, warm, and informal. A cold or overly formal letter will not help the person being recommended.
- Be explicit and substantive. Vague and general statements distance you from the person you are recommending and are not persuasive.
- Be honest and truthful, and give every fact the emphasis it deserves. If you are reporting a negative point, for instance, give only enough emphasis to convey an accurate picture. Because negative facts are usually given more weight in the reader's mind, it will be best to subordinate any negative facts given.
- Detail two or three characteristics in their order of importance. Instead of "John is a good negotiator," write, "John purchased and placed $500 million of corporate debt." Rather than "Julie has excellent skills," write, "Julie consistently inputs 110 words a minute using WordPerfect, Paradox, or Harvard Graphics software." Listing more than three examples diffuses the impact of your letter.

- Verify the reason for the resignation or termination of an employee or relationship, as appropriate.
- Reaffirm and summarize your recommendation. Invite the reader to write or call for more information.
- End on a note of goodwill or best wishes.

ELIMINATE WRONG MESSAGES

- Don't go overboard or make statements you cannot prove.
- Don't advise the reader with statements like "You should hire her fast," etc. This could work against the person being recommended.
- If in doubt, check out the request, refuse to supply a recommendation, or give the information verbally.

CONSIDER SPECIAL SITUATIONS

- Because we live in a litigious society, caution must be used in deciding the contents of your letter of recommendation, reference, or evaluation. Some organizations are not giving this information either over the telephone or in writing, only confirming the person was employed, the dates of employment, and the person's title. Litigation charging negligence has ensued where the former employer did not disclose that the former employee had been charged with theft or other problems.
- Assume that anything you write may end up in a court of law, and if you do not want to defend it, don't write it.
- If there is any question about your statements being actionable, consult legal counsel before sending the letter.
- Using a subject line that identifies the request and the person being recommended helps get your letter off to a direct start.

SELECT A FORMAT

- Type on letterhead, personal stationery, or quality bond. The appearance should be professional.
- Interoffice recommendations, references, and evaluations may be done in memo form.

WRITE STRONG SENTENCES

Start with a powerful verb, and then construct strong, concise sentences:

▶ She earned the respect of her coworkers.

▶ Jennifer sorted out and deposited $11 million in unpaid royalties in the correct accounts in four months.

▶ Carla increased production by 17 percent in seven months.

▶ Employee satisfaction increased over 30 percent during Myron's first year as director of personnel.

BUILD EFFECTIVE PARAGRAPHS

▶ It was a sad day in this office when Elsie Walkio resigned to move to Phoenix with her husband. For over ten years she kept me prepared and on time. I don't expect I'll ever find another secretary as fine or as efficient as Elsie.

▶ Here are just a couple of examples. Elsie worked an entire weekend preparing separate project packets for a national sales meeting because our copy equipment had failed the week before and no one else knew how to assemble the packets. She saved our company hundreds of thousands of dollars by revising the manual review procedures, and she never missed an administrative employee's birthday.

▶ Let me know if you need any additional information.

EDIT, EDIT, EDIT

Make your recommendation clear, concise, and detailed enough to be credible.

ALSO SEE "RESUME," PAGE 74; "INTRODUCTION," PAGE 108; AND "APPRECIATION AND THANK-YOU," PAGE 55.

Personal Reference for Friend

(Date)

Dear Mr. Archibald:

I'm writing in response to your May 18 letter requesting a personal reference for Saul Bellweather. I have known him for eleven years. His father and I are partners in the same law firm, and his mother has been my wife's CPA for fifteen years. Our families have gotten together socially over the years of our affiliation, and Saul and my son, Teddy, are best friends.

Saul possesses fine character traits. He has always pursued his own path, excelled in what he set out to do, and carried through on assigned tasks.

If you need further information, please call me. Obviously, I give Saul the highest recommendation.

Sincerely,

Barclay Withers

Recommendation for Promotion Within Company

MEMO

DATE: September 5, 2003
TO: Derek Woodward
FROM: Maria Whitmore, V.P. of Sales
SUBJECT: Leah Harvey Promotion

Leah Harvey has completed her tour here in the fast-track program. Although the youngest in the Sales Department, Leah has performed well in decision-making, problem-solving, and negotiating skills. In fact, she is our number-one performer. She closes at the highest rate (76 percent) and in the shortest time (31.5 minutes) of anyone in the department.

Leah desires to be a district sales manager, and I believe she possesses the skills to be one of the best. I recommend we place her in the opening for Region Thirteen.

Recommendation for New Law School Graduate by Professor

(Date)

Reference: Your Letter of May 12 Requesting a Recommendation for a First-Year Lawyer

Dear George:

Yes, I have an exceptional recommendation for the position at Krause & Krause. I was fortunate enough to have Neil R. Reynoldo in three of my classes at Stanford Law School. He is a breath of fresh air. Not only did he finish in the top of his class, he demonstrated rare leadership skills on special team projects. Neil has an intuitive sense of justice—real justice—and came up with completely innovative ways to carry out solutions to the advantage of all involved. I've never seen another student with this ability. I could go on and on.

I tried to get Neil in at Stanton & Gregg, but we took three new graduates last year, and our practice is presently undergoing some changes in scope and direction.

Neil comes with my highest recommendation. If I can offer any additional information, please call.

Sincerely,

Benardo Blackburn

> Restate the request.

> Name the person.
> State your relationship with the person.

> Make your recommendations as precise as possible.

> Reaffirm your recommendation; offer further help, if appropriate.

Recommendation for a Long-Time Customer

(Date)

Reference: Your Request of April 15 to Supply a Reference for Sidney Wales

Mr. Ray Karnes:

We have done business with Mr. Sidney Wales for twelve years. We are pleased to refer him as an outstanding customer who conducts his business in a conscientious manner. There has never been an unresolved dispute or an overdue notice in all these years. Oh, that all our customers were so prompt and honest.

If you have any further questions, please call.

Cordially,

Samuel Wise

Recommendation for a Former Employee

(Date)

Dear Mr. Bellows:

I highly recommend Robert Levine. He worked as my secretary in the office of the president and as statistical clerk for five years. He had a confident, take-charge manner that was, at the same time, cordial, and his statistical work was accurate.

In five years, Robert missed three work days. He was always eager to see a project through to completion, even if it meant staying after hours. I don't believe Robert ever angered a telephone caller, and his skills in dealing with clients and callers in this office were outstanding.

Sincerely,

Nathan Neustetter

Recommendation of Former Graduate Student

(Date)

Dear Dean Callan:

Dr. Edward A. Meyers is an outstanding scholar, a capable teacher, and a diligent and tireless worker.

Dr. Meyers's scholarship is demonstrated by his 3.8 GPA (out of 4.0) here at Marquette, as well as his performance in undergraduate work at MOO U. He was in two of my human resources classes, and he did excellent work, making As in both. He demonstrated a keen, scholarly inquisitiveness and worked diligently to excel. I expect that trait will help him make a great contribution in the field.

I believe he has already begun on that course with the publication of portions of his dissertation in *HR Magazine* and *Administrators' Digest*.

I have heard three of his speeches, and he did an excellent job. And I have observed many of his classroom sessions while he served as my graduate assistant for two years. He entered the classroom well-prepared, maintained a thoughtful learning atmosphere, and challenged the students to stretch a bit.

Callan/(Date)/page 2

In summary, I recommend Dr. Meyers as a teacher of behavioral management. I'll be pleased to discuss any of this information in greater detail if you care to call me.

Sincerely,

Dr. Herbert K. Kline

Declining to Give Recommendation

(Date)

Dear Jackson:

My secretary relayed the message that you called and asked for a recommendation to Breakers for the position you have applied for.

Reflecting on the years we worked together, I do not feel I worked closely enough with you to offer a meaningful evaluation and recommendation on those factors that Breakers will want. I certainly will confirm your employment and salary history if you would like to have someone contact me for that information.

Best wishes in your job future.

Sincerely,

Stanley Blacker

Offering a Neutral Recommendation

(Date)

Dear Oswaldo:

Star Reising held the position of customer service representative with Stiches from May 10, 1992, to March 15, 1998. During this period of time she was promoted twice within the department with appropriate salary increases.

Star left Stiches to return to college.

Sincerely,

Melvin Whales

13
REFUSING AN APPLICANT

A powerful agent is the right word.

—MARK TWAIN

 Since this letter is bad news given to a recipient who may be in a stressful situation, the utmost tact must be used in phrasing it.

THINK ABOUT CONTENT
- Thank the reader for applying, using a positive statement about his or her skills or qualifications.
- Set up the explanation for refusal, stating only the organization requirements.
- Make a clear, positive statement of refusal.
- Tell the applicant what will happen to his or her application and future prospects with the organization.
- Close with a goodwill statement, offer suggestions, or alternatives, or compliment the reader. Any well-thought-out suggestion, referral, or compliment will enhance your goodwill efforts.

ELIMINATE WRONG MESSAGES
- Do not make negative statements.
- Make no comparisons with the winning candidate.
- Offer no excuses, and leave no question about the finality of your decision.
- Never blame others for the refusal.

SELECT A FORMAT
- Business refusals should be typed on letterhead.

WRITE STRONG SENTENCES
▶ Thank you for applying for the office manager position.

▶ The committee has selected a candidate with extensive experience in this exact research.

▶ It was a pleasure meeting you.

BUILD EFFECTIVE PARAGRAPHS
▶ It was apparent to the Reems selection committee that you have a very bright future in genetic engineering. They were especially impressed with your ideas on cell division.

▶ Thank you for your resume in response to our opening for a Marketing Director (April *Marketing News*). We have reviewed your qualifications carefully and have determined they do not match the requirements for this senior position.

▶ I would like to suggest you contact Mr. Ray Miller of IN-PLANT Placement. He has done an extraordinary service in connecting positions and candidates in this field.

▶ With your permission we will keep your resume on file so we may consider you for a future opening. Our procedure is to review existing resumes first when a position opens up or is created. Perhaps we will have the privilege of considering you for a position with Carlisle in the future. We will be pleased to do so.

EDIT, EDIT, EDIT

Deliver your negative message in the most positive terms possible.

ALSO SEE "DECLINING A POSITION," PAGE 97, AND "REFUSAL," PAGE 186.

Refusing a Production Management Applicant

(Date)

Dear Jack:

Thank you for applying for the production manager job. Both Mr. Reynolds and I were very impressed with your accomplishments over the past five years. You should be very proud. We have, however, selected a candidate with ten years experience in our very specialized area.

Your inquiry will, of course, be kept confidential, and we will keep your resume in the engineering file should something else open up in the next six months. I wish you continued success in your career.

Yours truly,

Jack Buboinis

Refusing an Underqualified Candidate

(Date)

Dear Ms. Curtis:

Thank you for considering Mason & Mason Engineering as a place of employment. You made a very positive impression here with your outstanding work history and interview skills. As we discussed, however, the present status of our design department and the projects we have in-house demand we hire a candidate with skills and experience in these specialized areas.

We would like to keep your resume and copies of your work samples on file. We anticipate that six to eight months down the road we may be expanding the design department. We would like the opportunity to consider you as a candidate again at that time.

Best wishes for what we know will be a brilliant career.

Sincerely,

Kim Sanders

Refusing a Candidate Due to Internal Delay

(Date)

Dear Ms. Schneider:

I was pleased to meet you and discuss the position at General Television for an administrative assistant to the executive director. I was very favorably impressed with your skill levels.

Since the interview, however, we have had other changes in the organization, which have required that we delay hiring an administrative assistant for at least five months.

I would like to keep your resume on file to reconsider at that time, and I invite you to contact us in four months about the position. Again, thank you for coming in. Perhaps we will have the opportunity to discuss this position or another one at a future time.

Sincerely,

Sally Weinstein

DECLINING A POSITION

*Tact consists in knowing how far
we may go too far.*

—JEAN COCTEAU

 The letter used to decline a job offer is a refusal letter with the central theme of goodwill (see "Refusal," page 186).

DECIDE TO WRITE

- Open with a friendly statement.
- Thank the employer for the job offer.
- Review the facts and give an explanation, if applicable.
- State in definite, clear, and positive terms that you must decline the offer based on the information you presented.
- End the letter on a cordial note.

THINK ABOUT CONTENT

- Make sure you understand the time frame and respond within it.
- Always leave a situation with goodwill and open for future contact.
- Keep the lines of communication open even after the decision process.

ELIMINATE WRONG MESSAGES

- Do not leave your decision open to debate.
- Don't belabor the bad news.

SELECT A FORMAT

The letter should be typed on personal stationery.

WRITE STRONG SENTENCES

▶ It was a pleasure meeting your fine staff of engineers yesterday.

▶ I was very impressed with the efficiency of the quality control operation.

▶ Thank you for orchestrating the interview process and for the offer of the marketing manager position.

BUILD EFFECTIVE PARAGRAPHS

▶ I have enjoyed the past month of interviews and screening for the position of plant manager at Wickliff. I believe that you, Brad Williams, and Dennis Bradley make an outstanding team.

▶ I am flattered by the offer of vice president of client affairs at Metcalf & Metcalf. It's an exceptional opportunity, but after careful consideration, I shall have to decline.

▶ Your generous offer of a partnership at Lockhart & Wendell is everything I've worked for these past twelve years, and I'm honored you, David, Lance, and Jacob feel confident in my abilities to fill the position. Ironically, after two days of soul searching and lengthy discussions with Carol and the boys, I must decline.

▶ Meeting you and the other people at Cruthers was a pleasure. I was very impressed with the attention to detail the entire department exhibited in doing their work. And I was, of course, pleased to receive the generous job offer that followed the interviews.

EDIT, EDIT, EDIT

Your ultimate task when declining a position is saying no with a written smile.

Declining Position Due to Accepting a More Suitable One

(Date)

Dear Mr. Broward:

Yes, I did receive your second offer. It was very generous of you to increase the benefit package.

I appreciated the courtesies extended to me during the interview process, and certainly the after-hours interview arrangements.

I enjoyed meeting the therapy team, too, and feel your program is a very important one. I'm sure it will do well over the next several years with the goals you have set.

All this made it extremely difficult for me to come to the decision to accept another position in Los Angeles, which fits not only my career goals but allows complete coordination with my wife's career as well.

Thank you for all your efforts on my behalf. I greatly appreciate your thoughtfulness and hope we will be able to serve together on one of the various professional committees in the future.

Sincerely,

Dr. Reginald McDonald

Declining Position Due to Accepting a More Suitable One

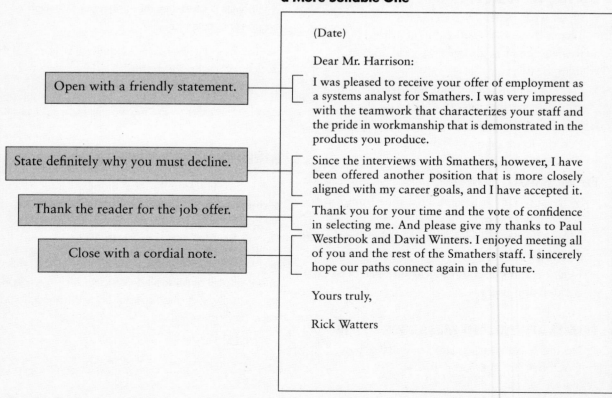

Open with a friendly statement.

State definitely why you must decline.

Thank the reader for the job offer.

Close with a cordial note.

(Date)

Dear Mr. Harrison:

I was pleased to receive your offer of employment as a systems analyst for Smathers. I was very impressed with the teamwork that characterizes your staff and the pride in workmanship that is demonstrated in the products you produce.

Since the interviews with Smathers, however, I have been offered another position that is more closely aligned with my career goals, and I have accepted it.

Thank you for your time and the vote of confidence in selecting me. And please give my thanks to Paul Westbrook and David Winters. I enjoyed meeting all of you and the rest of the Smathers staff. I sincerely hope our paths connect again in the future.

Yours truly,

Rick Watters

IV. BUSINESS AND EMPLOYMENT

15
EMPLOYEE CORRESPONDENCE

The only agreements that ever caused me trouble were the ones I wrote with a handshake.

—ANONYMOUS

Employment correspondence is a category rather than a specific type of letter. It's important to think of these as a group of communications that details the history of the relationship between the employer and the employee.

Both the employee's and the employer's perspectives are reflected in this chapter because all this correspondence is important to the history of that relationship.

Starting when an applicant tries to secure a position, he or she may write a number of letters to the organization. Obviously, it's in the applicant's best interest to make as many appropriate, positive contacts with a potential employer as possible. During each telephone conversation and each face-to-face meeting, for example, the applicant may create the opportunity to follow up with a letter. These letters can be pivotal in demonstrating his or her writing skills.

During the course of employment, written communications between the employer and the employee become even more important in documenting the history of the relationship.

Some of the most important communications to document, because of our litigious society, are difficult or negative messages, such as a reprimand, termination, or resignation. Because they are so important, they need special consideration.

The letter of *reprimand* is used when an employee or associate has committed an error or a willful breach of policy, procedure, or practice. The effective reprimand separates the act from the person and deals only with the act that needs to be corrected.

You must first know the facts. Conduct any investigation necessary and record precise facts. This should be done in an objective way, without implicating anyone. Keep this information confidential.

To be effective, your anger must first be dealt with so your letter is objective, yet the reprimand should be written as soon after the offensive behavior as possible. The letter should not, however, substitute for a face-to-face meeting. It should be a follow-up record and a notice of corrective action.

An indirect or direct approach may be used (see "Refusal," page 186). You must decide, based on your knowledge of the person involved. In the case of a direct subordinate in the workplace, a direct approach is usually best.

Make the letter short. Introduce the problem; state it; give any succinct, constructive criticism and action to be taken; and end on a note of encouragement and goodwill, if appropriate.

Remember, your objective is to effect a positive change in behavior. Focus on the act, not the person, and set realistic, attainable, and measurable goals for improvement or correction, within a set time frame. List any ramifications or any corrective action and give the person an opportunity to respond.

When the offense is against another employee, such as sexual harassment, consult specialized legal counsel. Both punishment and education may be indicated. A record should be kept in the organization's central headquarters. The organization must have stepped procedures for corrective action, and if the behavior isn't corrected, the employee should be terminated. These procedures should be reviewed by an attorney specializing in gender, sexual harassment, and diversity issues.

A letter of *termination* should never come as a bolt out of the blue. This news should first be given verbally in a face-to-face meeting, if at all possible.

If an employee is being terminated because of his or her actions or failures, opportunities to correct the situation should first have been given.

Before writing this letter, be sure the criteria of pertinent laws, regulations, and organization policies and procedures have been met.

The letter must be direct, stating the reason for the termination, and you should set the stage by stating your regrets. Avoid being negative or hostile, but do not leave any doubt that the employee is being fired—and don't lay the blame on someone else. Finally, assure the recipient that you will not be giving a negative reference and end on a cordial or encouraging note, if you can without sounding false.

The letter of *resignation* is a refusal letter and should be written using those guidelines. The bad news may be given indirectly or directly—depending upon the situation (see "Refusal," page 186). In either case, make your letter as positive as possible, using tactful, supportive statements. Assume full responsibility for your resignation and include an acceptable reason for resigning, if possible. Be specific or vague as the situation dictates, but do not write a negative or angry letter. If you must air any grievances or complaints, do so orally.

Start with an expression of goodwill and follow with the logical resignation statement, making it clear and positive. State that you are resigning your position (use your title) and give the effective date. Don't forget to state the good points of having worked for the organization. End with a goodwill statement of appreciation for experience, training, and relationships.

Usually resignations are made orally, but it is sometimes more practical or comfortable to resign in writing. Often a verbal resignation is followed by a letter of resignation to create a written record.

DECIDE TO WRITE

This group of letters, memos, and other documents may be used to
- Respond to a job applicant or candidate
- Apply for a job
- Communicate with an employee
- Communicate with an employer

THINK ABOUT CONTENT

- It is important to have a written record of agreements, changes of status, and decisions made between employer and employee. Make sure you commit these to writing and keep copies in the appropriate personnel records.
- In addition to following the instructions for the type of letter being written, make sure your letter is crystal clear and to the point.
- Keep job applicants informed. This is an important time to create a positive impression of the organization.
- Make it a practice to tell people when they are doing a good job. It does wonders for goodwill and usually improves work quality.
- In our litigious society it's important to document all corrective actions that are taken and make these a part of the employee record.
- Keep current on legal requirements in relationships between employers and employees, and keep all related records.
- State the subject of the letter clearly and concisely.
- Offer the explanation, backing it up with facts.
- Close with a statement of goodwill or on an upbeat note, if possible.

ELIMINATE WRONG MESSAGES

- Avoid any statements that could result in a legal battle; review pertinent laws, regulations, and policies before writing.
- Don't write negative messages if you can avoid it. Almost anything you have to say can be said positively. If you are angry, process your anger privately, not in a letter that can be made public.
- When writing a difficult communication—for example, a letter of reprimand or termination—be sure to have another person well-versed in company policy and the appropriate regulations read your letter before you send it to ensure your objectivity and compliance with regulations and policies. Don't violate any confidentiality issues, however.
- Don't use a written message to avoid a verbal exchange. The written employee message, for example, should usually be used to document what has been said in a face-to-face meeting.

SELECT A FORMAT

- The interoffice memo is the most commonly used vehicle for employer and employee communications. The exceptions are the letters of employment, termination, and resignation. In these instances a formal, typed letter on letterhead is appropriate. Be sure to place a copy in the employee's file.

WRITE STRONG SENTENCES

▶ Two invoices marked "original" were sent for October, November, and December to the Baker Grand Rapids and Sioux City offices.

▶ I am sorry to deliver this message, but we must terminate your employment, effective immediately.

▶ There was no safety officer on duty from midnight to 8:00 A.M. on February 17 through 25.

▶ Your scheduled date for the complete physical examination is July 5.

▶ Thank you for your request to go on a flextime work schedule.

▶ I look forward to a new attitude in your work performance.

▶ This letter is to notify you that I am resigning my position as purchasing agent with Harold and Harold on July 15, three weeks from today.

BUILD EFFECTIVE PARAGRAPHS

▶ As I discussed with you, the vacation schedule you designed for your department for July and August impaired business operations and resulted in extra expenditures, and possibly the loss of two accounts. We had twenty-three customer complaints of double billing, for example, because payments had not been entered in the computer, and there were about two dozen complaints from our personnel that there was no one in your department to answer questions.

▶ I've reviewed your request for a leave of absence from March 1 through July 31. Please be in my office at 10:00 A.M. Monday to discuss this, and bring a copy of your physician's recommendation for this leave.

▶ I'm sorry to learn of the interpersonal conflict within the marketing department. I have, as you requested, reviewed possible transfers for you. There are three options open. Please be in my office at 10:00 A.M. on Friday to discuss them.

▶ Copies of all facts and violations of company policy are attached for your review. These are the same documents that were reviewed during your employee hearing on June 6.

▶ With this letter I offer my resignation from my position as general manager at Maxims, effective May 1. My decision was a difficult one, and I have deliberated for many months; but I feel this is the right decision for me.

EDIT, EDIT, EDIT

Cut out unnecessary words and arrange paragraphs so the reader may easily understand the message. And even with reprimands, terminations, and other difficult communications, end on as positive a note as possible.

SEE ALSO "COVER LETTER," PAGE 167;
"APPRECIATION AND THANK-YOU," PAGE 55;
"RESUME," PAGE 74; "WELCOME," PAGE 43;
"REFUSING AN APPLICANT," PAGE 95;
"REQUESTS AND INQUIRIES," PAGE 155; AND
"CONGRATULATIONS," PAGE 33.

State your business.
Offer an explanation.

Close with a goodwill statement.

Changing the Employee Reporting Relationship

(Date)

Dear Dean:

Starting Monday you will report to Jim Harris, sales manager, as we discussed, because we are changing the shipping department reporting relationship. We believe this will produce a better flow in the marketing process, result in fewer errors, and improve customer relations. (See the new organizational chart attached.)

I will expect your new operations report on August 1. Thanks for your cooperation.

Sincerely,

Margo Lancet

Retiring for a Negative Reason

(Date)

Dear Mr. Walrus:

This is to notify you that I shall take an early retirement, effective May 31, from my position of scheduling director.

I have six weeks of accrued vacation time, and request to take it starting April 15, my last working day.

Yours truly,

Leland Miles

Position Terminated Due to Downsizing

(Date)

Dear Rachel:

As we discussed, the economic slowdown in the Cleveland market for HighFlyers demands we close the regional office. Sadly, this eliminates your position.

We will terminate your employment with us on July 1, as agreed, and you will receive severance pay equal to three months' salary. The company will pay your medical insurance for the remainder of the year. In lieu of our bonus program, you have agreed to accept a one-time payment of $6,000. Your retirement benefits will be retained by the company until we receive instructions from you. The personnel department will send you a letter containing all the actual figures.

Rachel, we will all miss you here, but we are confident that your skills will land you an excellent opportunity very soon. Please use my name for a reference.

Sincerely,

Marika Lovelace

Sexual Harassment Claim

(Date)

Dear Lisa:

I have reviewed your complaint of sexual harassment by your supervisor, Allan Reek. Again, Dimensions wants to provide a positive work environment for all our employees, and that means we will not tolerate sexual harassment.

I have initiated a full investigation by Mort Jansen, plant manager, and Jennifer Swan, vice president for Human Relations. One or both of them will contact you in the manner you requested in the next couple of days.

We will make every effort to resolve this situation swiftly and justly. Please contact Jennifer Swan or me if you have any other questions or comments.

Sincerely,

Marla Drapples

Warning About Intoxication

(Date)

Dear Lars:

Following up on our discussion of this morning, this is your second and final warning that McGraw does not tolerate intoxication on the job. Your first warning was issued on May 15 for the incident on May 12 when you were found to be intoxicated (report copies are attached).

Please be in my office at 9:30 A.M. tomorrow to tell the employee committee why you should not be terminated effective June 15. The committee will give you their response on Thursday. As you know, there is a required treatment plan to follow to remain employed here.

Lars, we all want to see you turn this around. We don't want to lose you.

Sincerely,

Joseph Dutton

Maternity Leave

(Date)

Dear Julie:

Congratulations on the anticipated birth of your baby. We are extremely happy for you. I have arranged for you to take a leave of absence, as you requested, from July 1 through December 1. Jayne Dorsett of personnel will contact you to determine all the related information.

What an extremely exciting time for you and Bill. We all wish you the best.

Sincerely,

Alexandria LaSasso

Promotion Denied

(Date)

Dear Alex:

Thank you for your bid for the job opening number 9-9821. It was an extremely difficult decision, and you were well in the running. But after final evaluation of all of the twenty-one applicants, Mel Berger was awarded the position.

I was sorry to deliver this disappointing news in our meeting this morning, but I'm sure that your skills and outstanding record will allow you to obtain an equal position in one of the openings coming up in the next few months.

Sincerely,

Martina McPhee

Resolving Favoritism Complaint

Memo
To: Nicole Lazar, Manager
From: Sandra Lewis, Director of Personnel
Date: September 10, 2001
Subject: Employee Complaints

As I discussed with you this morning, we have had four complaints alleging favoritism in your treatment of subordinates. I believe you can resolve this problem by holding a department meeting and explaining the criteria and the selection process that resulted in JoAnn Beales being promoted to assistant manager.

Please let me know by October 12 whether you feel this is satisfactorily resolved without intervention from personnel. We will have someone from this department attend the meeting and give the job description and qualifications, if you like.

The subordinates involved have also been asked to indicate their response to personnel if they wish.

I will get back to you on October 17 to discuss the resolution of this complaint.

Recommendation for Employee Promotion

Memo
To: Jackson Davis
From: Vivian Long
Date: January 10, 2004
Subject: Daniel Viders' Promotion

I recommend Daniel Viders for the Region Four Sales Manager position effective July 1. His performance over the past eighteen months meets the criteria, even surpasses it in some areas.

His sales are the highest in Region Four. Dan sold 11 percent over his own projected goals, 17 percent over mine.

His management skills as demonstrated in his customer correspondence and during customer interviews rank at a 98 percent "very satisfied." He is also held in high esteem by all the other sales people.

Dan's planning and other activity levels I must rate very high also. He set a goal of forty-five new customers this year and he has fifty-seven. He planned the mailout of four new direct mail pieces and met that goal with a 12 percent response rate.

Termination for Poor Performance

(Date)

Cassidy Lindsay
433 Birch Lane
Rockville, MD 20852

Dear Cassidy:

Regrettably, it is necessary to terminate your employment at Bikers. After several discussions with you, and three reviews of your work, you have not improved your performance to match the duties of the job description.

Although separation from a company is never easy, it is often the best solution for everyone involved. After a careful review of all the facts, I believe this is true here.

I assure you we will strictly observe Bikers' policy in giving any future references concerning your employment here: We will release only the dates of your employment and your job title, and we will verify your salary with us only if the caller has obtained that salary information from you.

We do wish you every success in your future work.

Sincerely,

Donna Laurent

Davis/January 10, 2004/page 2

His follow-up converted all these respondents to customers, and he brought in another 10 percent from his original mailing list. He has also demonstrated the ability to change directions and adjust his planning to company changes.

As far as product knowledge and new product applications are concerned, Dan has performed far above average and demonstrates a willingness to work on this area.

I conclude that Dan rates very high in our criteria for both can-do and will-do, and even though he is junior in seniority, we should reward him with this promotion.

Report of Unsatisfactory Performance

Memo
To: Richard Parks
From: Jim Fuchs
Date: October 5, 2003
Subject: Rick Hanson's Unsatisfactory
          Performance

I have just received the fourth customer call this month that Rick Hanson has made a substantial error in analyzing a customer account. Dick, these errors occurred on four of our top accounts (see attached reports).

All of these customers have requested a change of analysts. Would you please handle this and let me know by Friday who the new analysts will be.

Resigning to Take Another Job—Positive Departure

(Date)

Dear Mauricio:

Working for you as assistant program director for the past five years has been a great learning experience. I have been able to grow as an administrator under your watchful eye.

As we have often discussed, I shall receive my M.B.A. in May. To stretch myself and take another important step toward my career goals, I must tender my resignation at JCHH effective June 31. I have accepted a position with Systema Corporation as program director.

I shall always remember my experience here with fondness. I greatly appreciate all your help over the years, and that of all the other program directors and staff. I plan not to lose contact. Let's continue our friendship.

Thank you.

Sincerely,

Abdul Kouri

Reprimand for Tardiness

(Date)

Dear Marie:

On five occasions in the past three weeks you have been from thirty minutes to one hour late in arriving at the office. Marie, the work of your department depends on your being on time, and company policy clearly states that administrative personnel will start work at 8:00 A.M.

> State the specific reprimand.

If there is something I should know about the facts that created this tardiness, please make an appointment with Alice to discuss it with me before Friday. Otherwise I will expect to see you in your office by 8:00 A.M. each morning.

> Give an opportunity to respond.

I appreciate your cooperation in getting this problem resolved.

> End on a positive note.

Sincerely,

Julie Adams

16
INTRODUCTION

*In this world, you must be a little too kind
in order to be kind enough.*

—PIERRE MARIVAUX

The letter of introduction was created for a much different society, to introduce one person to another. It was not created as an announcement, a recommendation, a letter of reference, or a sales letter.

Because we live in a very mobile society, equipped with many forms of instant communication, and a business and social climate of assertiveness, the letter of introduction is seldom used. When it is used for business introduction, it carries little obligation; the social introduction carries more.

DECIDE TO WRITE
Use this letter when you want to introduce
- One person to another
- A new employee
- One service or organization to another

THINK ABOUT CONTENT
- Since the letter of introduction implies the approval of the person being introduced, agree to write it only if you can do so wholeheartedly.

- Give the full name of the person you're introducing and some of his or her background. For a new employee, state the person's position, effective date of employment, and, if appropriate, the person to whom he or she has reporting responsibility. List the pertinent information: new employee's experience, education, expertise, past employers, major clients, special projects, and awards. Ask other employees to welcome the new employee.
- State why you want to introduce the two people. Give any characteristics, points of interest the person and the reader may have in common, and any other helpful information.
- Make your letter cordial and brief.
- Offer more than one or two points of commonality, if possible.
- Suggest a meeting time, place, and an arrangement that does not obligate the recipient to entertain the person you are introducing.
- Tell the reader the possible benefits of meeting the person, service, or organization.
- Give the reader an opportunity to decline the meeting.
- Thank the reader.

ELIMINATE WRONG MESSAGES

- Do not presume the reader will be anxious to meet the person, and don't make statements like "I know you'll be glad to meet him."
- Don't just plunge in. Give full consideration to the reader, even though you may be making the introduction as a favor to the person you are introducing.
- The letter of introduction should not obligate the reader to socially entertain the person you are introducing. Be sure not to imply or suggest this.

CONSIDER SPECIAL SITUATIONS

When you use a letter of introduction to introduce a new sales employee to customers or clients, all the same rules apply. In addition, it's important to affirm your support to both parties.

SELECT A FORMAT

- Unless the recipient is a personal friend to whom you send handwritten letters, the letter of introduction should be typed on letterhead, business or personal, or on plain stationery.
- A form letter may be used when the message is being conveyed to a number of recipients, such as the introduction of a new sales representative or a salesperson to customers or clients.
- Introductions to clubs, groups, or associations are best typed on personal stationery or the appropriate letterhead but certainly may be handwritten.

WRITE STRONG SENTENCES

▶ Maybe you can spare thirty minutes to meet her.

▶ I've heard you mention you would like to meet Dr. Allan Beard.

▶ One of my dearest friends, Alex Rivers, will be in Los Angeles next week.

▶ You have heard me mention Joan Brookstone in reference to the new theory on disease control.

BUILD EFFECTIVE PARAGRAPHS

▶ My good friend Jenny Creighton will be in Los Angeles the week of the twenty-first for the National Advertising Convention. I believe her graphic designs are just what you are looking for to use in the Cooler campaign.

▶ As I said on the telephone, Alice Bradford will be staying at the downtown Empire Hotel, and a message may be left for her any time after the evening of the twentieth. She said she has no plans for lunch on the twenty-second or twenty-third, and as we discussed, I told her you may call her.

▶ In addition to her great campaign work, Tink is a fine person with interests in several areas similar to your own: quarter horses and hang gliding. I believe you could use her skills on future projects. I hope this works out.

EDIT, EDIT, EDIT

Your job is only to create an opportunity. Make sure your information is direct, clear, and concise.

ALSO SEE "RECOMMENDATION," PAGE 90.

Introducing a Friend

(Date)

Dear Claire,

As I mentioned to you on the telephone, Adeline McDougell is a designer for Limon's. She will be in Baltimore next week for the Women's Forum and will be staying at the downtown Fairmount Hotel. I believe the two of you would enjoy each other's company, and since you will both be attending the Forum, what better time to meet?

Well, I'll leave the rest up to you. Adeline and I will understand if your prior commitments to the production of the Forum make it impossible for you to schedule a time to get together.

All the best wishes for the success of this important event.

Sincerely,

Stella Dire

Introducing a Sales Rep to a Customer

(Date)

Dear Bernie:

This will introduce Ned Remick, Smith & French's new regional representative for your area. He will be calling on Rx Inc. next week.

Ned spent seven years with Johns & Johns sterile products' division in New Jersey, where he distinguished himself for five years as sales representative of the year for their medical instrumentation division after graduating from Victoria College. (He's a stock car driver and huge Buff's fan.)

I think you will find him extremely knowledgeable about our entire product line. He has a well-earned reputation as one of the finest and most conscientious salespersons around. Do take a few extra minutes to talk to Ned. I believe you will think as highly of him as I do.

Cordially,

George Cordiss

Introducing Friends to a Club

(Date)

Dear Rex,

It is a pleasure for Sandra and I to introduce Winn and Gloria Stickler to the Greenwood Country Club. The Sticklers have been distinguished members of the Shaker Heights Country Club in Omaha for over fifteen years and have just moved to Denver in the past three months.

It has been our privilege to have been both business associates and personal friends of the Sticklers for over seventeen years. They are truly two of the finest people we know, and people who have contributed greatly to the community in terms of fundraising for lung disease.

If the Sticklers desire to join Greenwood, Sandra and I would be honored to sponsor them. (They could help us win that illusive mixed doubles tennis championship.)

Sincerely,

Dexter Dowd

Introducing Friends

(Date)

Dear Ruth,

A good friend and business associate, Jubilee Hoskins, will be in Atlanta next week on a buying trip. She is just finishing the interior decorating of three restored mansions in the Country Club area of Dallas.

She has completed some extraordinary research and restoration of nineteenth-century furniture pieces as part of these assignments. I thought this might be very helpful for you to hear about in light of that chapter for your new book. She would love to hear about your book project and show you some restorations you may want to include.

Both she and I understand you may be committed next week, and she will also be extremely busy, but she should have an hour either midday or late afternoon when she could meet with you at her hotel, the Brown. She'll check in about noon on Tuesday.

If you can work it in, call her after that time at 994-3322, room 221.

Best regards,

Gloria Needles

Introducing a Business Associate

(Date)

Dear Conchita:

It's my pleasure to introduce Margaret Merritt, who served as vice president in charge of book buying for Bookworms for over fifteen years. Since a family move takes her from us to Bakersville, our considerable loss may be your gain.

Margaret is fully capable of stepping directly into the management of your store, so you may start that carefree retirement you heartily deserve.

Margaret and her husband, Jim, are in Bakersville until the 25th, and I'm sure she would be happy to arrange an appointment. You can reach her at 544-7887.

So nice to hear from you. Give my best to Ralph, and I look forward to receiving those postcards from remote and exotic places. You've earned it!

Best,

Jo Roberts

Introducing a Business Associate

(Date)

Dear Ben:

I'd like to introduce Roger Eggbert from the *Chicago Herald*. As I mentioned on the telephone, Roger is doing a special series on small business practices that work, including marketing techniques that make a real difference in sales volumes. Yes, I can tell you with confidence that Roger has never misquoted me, nor presented a one-sided or biased report.

As part of Roger's research, he is putting similar companies from different geographical locations together in a long-distance teleconferencing program. I sat in on several of these groupings, which meet through the miracle of telecommunications, and it's amazing what they are accomplishing. I think you would find it very helpful.

Roger will call you next week and set a time to meet with you if you are interested.

Sincerely,

Bea Ross

Introducing a Business Associate

(Date)

Dear Jake:

My legal assistant, Laurie McCall, is relocating to Atlanta after five years in our offices. She is the best. She orchestrates my cases without a hitch, and I am, as you can imagine, very sorry to lose her.

I understand from Ted Young that you will be in Detroit next week. If you would like to talk with Laurie at that time, please call her at our offices.

Give me a call, too, and let's get together for lunch.

Regards,

Kermit Devers

17

MEMO

… the King went on, "I shall never, never forget!" "You will, though," the Queen said, "if you don't make a memorandum of it."

—LEWIS CARROLL

The memorandum, or memo, is the lifeblood of an organization. It is the written communication used within the organization between its members. A memo may be a short note, a report, or a much longer proposal.

Although memos vary in formality and length, the quality of writing in the memo should be as high as that for corresponding with people outside the organization. The language used should be tailored to the reader, but it should still be conversational. A few organizations still call these communications *internal letters, interoffice letters,* or *intraorganizational reports.*

Effective memos are essential to the success of any organization because they provide a clear record of decisions made and actions taken. They also inform, delegate, instruct, announce, request, or transmit documents. And it's important to know that careers are made and broken on memo-writing power or the lack of it. Remember, each good memo you write will help your reputation and promotability.

DECIDE TO WRITE

Use the memo wisely to

- Distribute information across organizational lines
- Communicate policy and procedures up and down organizational ranks
- Create a permanent, organizational record of plans, decisions, and actions
- With many organizations using a participatory management style, the memo is often a written confirmation of verbal discussions and decisions

THINK ABOUT CONTENT

- Understand your organization's memo policies and protocol.
- Determine the need for your memo. (Creating a paper blizzard or electronic fodder is not your objective.)
- Consult the people affected to get their input.
- Make sure you have all the background facts and information.
- Apply the principles in "Getting Started," page 1, to ensure your best writing.
- Remember, one message equals one memo. Two messages equal two memos.

- Distill the subject matter into a concise core statement.
- Have your reader firmly in mind and select language best suited to your reader.
- Outline the memo points, dividing your information into introduction, body, conclusion, summary, and recommendation parts. You may select a time-sequence pattern if the information lends itself to this format or the cause-and-effect pattern if this is the more logical choice. Use subheadings and numbers whenever they will increase clarity and invite readership.
- Write concisely.
- Use positive statements whenever possible.
- Use action words whenever possible.

ELIMINATE WRONG MESSAGES

- Don't be ambiguous or vague.
- Don't use an autocratic tone (e.g., "I demand," "You must," etc.). It is unacceptable in most organizations today.
- Don't assign blame.
- Don't whine.
- Don't pad. There is a tendency in memo writing to say more than is necessary. Keep your memo to the essential point.
- Don't hedge. If you find yourself unable to take a clear position, reexamine the need to write the memo.
- Don't use officious, stuffy, or formal words when simpler words will work better, or you may be regarded as rigid and lacking in the kind of leadership flexibility needed in your organization. Do use the correct technical word when it's the most precise and acceptable.
- Don't use unnecessary words; edit your memo until it's clean.
- Avoid negative or harsh words and phrases. Negative emotions of irritation, disdain, anger,

revenge, or condemnation should not be expressed in your memo. Allow yourself time to cool off. Then, if these emotions are still present, have someone else write the memo. Here are some examples of words and phrases not to use:

"I cannot understand why you"
"you have failed to"
"I insist"
"I require"
"compelled"
"ignore"
"remit promptly"
"unsatisfactory"
"failure on your part"
"you made an inexcusable error"
"delinquent"
"I must demand"
"no excuse will be accepted"
"a wrong action has been taken"
"cancel the order"
"tardy for work"
"unsatisfactory performance"

- Avoid superlatives. Facts, numbers, and statistics are much better.
- Follow the management protocol of your organization's memo policy when you decide who to address and who to "copy." Here's an example: In many organizations, if a middle manager addresses his supervisor and a vice president, this indicates the manager has a direct reporting relationship to both. Copying the vice president, in this example, may indicate a direct reporting responsibility to the supervisor and reporting access to the vice president.
- Always think in terms of your reader and then the information to be conveyed. This will help focus your thoughts.

- Use the subject line to tell the reader what your memo is about. Be specific. For example: "Subject: New Newton Model 150 Copier Will Be Installed Friday." Remember the subject line will also be used to file the memo. Here are several examples:

Change this	To this
Subject: Performance Evaluation	Subject: Robert Kurtz Performance Evaluation
Reference: Vacation Schedule for July and August	Reference: Shipping Department Vacation Schedule for July and August
Subject: Sales Training Seminars	Subject: Sales Assistant Training Seminar May 10-25

- Organize the information you're conveying so it gets to the reader in logical order.
- Start by making an outline, but don't try to get your first draft perfect. Just get your ideas down, realizing you will edit later.
- With your draft in hand, shape it.
- Reread, delete, rearrange more logically, and edit out the nonessential. Ask yourself:

  –Have I included all the facts the reader will need to know?

  –Have I answered who, what, why, where, when, and how?

  –Do the points in my memo progress logically?

  –Have I used section headings and numbers where they could add clarity?

  –Does it flow?

  –Have I used transitions to carry the reader from one paragraph to the next?

  –Does my memo have a conclusion or a call to action?

- When the organization and structure are right, do your final editing. Then set the memo aside for a period of time, even an hour, if possible. This gives you a new objectivity about your writing.
- Make your language conversational and businesslike but easy for the reader to understand.
- Be sure you have summarized or concluded your memo properly and have made a recommendation or outlined the next step of action.
- Finally, read your memo aloud to yourself. It's amazing what hearing it can do. Overused words will show up. If the tone isn't natural, you'll hear it. Stilted words or phrases will jump out at you. Refer to the lists at the end of this chapter and those in "Getting Started," page 1, for examples of words to substitute or cut.

CONSIDER SPECIAL SITUATIONS

- It is important to avoid memo content that could be actionable. One way to avoid problems is to keep your memo free of gender reference. If you have any questions about the content of your memo, consult an attorney.
- Know that anything you write can come back to haunt you in a very public way, even if you've labeled it "confidential." Your memo could one day be published right after your name.
- Always give yourself "think time." Tomorrow you may not want to send that negative memo. In fact, try to put every memo in a positive form.
- The visual layout of your memo helps your message.
- Measure the words you've used, don't go to extremes. *Never* and *always* aren't good choices, nor are accusing names or characterizations. (Incidentally, make sure you destroy what you've thought better of. Wastebaskets can give up their contents in embarrassing places.)
- Don't generalize, and be sure to document what you've written.
- Use the proper organizational channels. Don't circumvent the lines of authority. Skipping over your boss isn't wise.

- Memos not only cover tails, but they also document sources. Put your ideas down. Good ideas should be put into memo form and copies kept in your files. If your organization allows it, copy up the organizational line to superiors.
- If you state a problem, offer a solution, or at least a plan for further action.
- For memos about upcoming meetings, state your objective and outline the plan of action. Assign tasks to people to ensure they are involved and come prepared to participate. Then ask *who, what, when,* and *where* to check for complete content. Give reasons and credit for the meeting; for example, if the meeting is in response to staff requests, point that out.
- For meeting agendas, give your agenda an action bias and list the *who, what, when,* and *where.* (The *how* and *why* may be the goals of the meeting.)
- For progress reports, use significant action headings and action words, and make the report succinct but complete. Finish by summarizing the action.
- For announcements, make organization members feel involved. Major changes should be discussed, comments and feedback considered, and alternatives weighed before decisions are made. This eliminates the possibility of people feeling insulted or uninvolved.
- Promotions, resignations, and transfers should be given verbally and followed up with a written announcement.
- For personnel appointments, it is helpful to include a statement or two about the person's interests and hobbies.
- For bad-news memos, make sure members of your organization hear it from you first, not from outside sources. State specifically what the problem or bad news is and what the organization is doing about it. Take responsibility for any errors or misjudgments you've made: State them clearly but don't grovel. Then, relate the impact on the organization and its members and ask for specific cooperation. Promise to keep members informed and keep that promise.

- For policies and procedures memos, be specific about *why* changes are being implemented and be sure to give the *who, what, where, when,* and *how.* Always explain the nature of the changes in terms of what exists now. Make a response as easy as possible and make the information clear. Use bullets, numbers, and headings to help readers absorb points more easily.
- For recommendations, put them up front. Give the reasons for the recommendations and state, briefly, the benefits. End by restating your recommendation and telling the reader the next action step to be taken.

NOTE SOME EXCEPTIONS

- A few organizations use memos to communicate with other organizations. One example is public relations or advertising agencies, which often use memos to communicate with client organizations. A "Client Memo" or "Contact Report" from the agency to the client organization records decisions and supplies information for accounting purposes. (Also see "Technical and Special Reports," page 142).
- A few organizations use form memos, so handwritten messages to customers are quick and easy. The forms have several sheets, and a copy of the original message stays with copies of responses.
- Subsidiary organizations under one corporate umbrella may use interorganizational memos.

SELECT A FORMAT

- Follow your organization's policies, procedures, and formatting requirements for memos sent by e-mail.
- Some organizations print forms or special internal stationery for memos, including special second pages. First sheets may be printed as follows:

Memo
To:
From:
Date:
Subject:

- Sometimes "confidential" forms are available for restricted-distribution memos. Some organizations print

    __ *for your information*
    __ *for your action*
    __ *for your reply*

    on message-and-reply "speedy messages." (Replies may be handwritten.) Forms may be printed in half sheets (8½-inch-by-5 ½-inch) or regular (8½-inch-by-11-inch) letter size. These memos may be color-coded, triplicate perforated forms with well-established distribution lines.
- The subject line functions like a report title and aids in filing and later retrieval. Make sure it is topical and complete. Capitalize all major words in the subject line except articles, conjunctions, and prepositions of fewer than four letters, unless the word is first or last.
- Signing or initialing a memo is a matter of choice. Your initials or signature usually go beside your typed name.

WRITE STRONG SENTENCES

Use simple, strong words and eliminate unnecessary ones.

▶ Thank you for your recommendations for the assistant director position.

▶ Unfortunately I cannot approve your July 1 to 15 vacation request.

▶ April production figures slipped 4 percent below projections.

▶ For the first time, production figures surpassed estimates.

▶ A special sexual harassment seminar will be held for all manufacturing supervisors, level II or above, May 16-17, 9:30 A.M. to 4:00 P.M. (lunch will be served) at the Regency Hotel.

BUILD EFFECTIVE PARAGRAPHS

▶ Subject: Flextime Increases Production and Reduces Absenteeism at Drexel

Drexel Systems reports a 16 percent increase in production and a reduction of 15 percent in absenteeism over six months after converting level II personnel to flextime. I believe we can adapt Drexel's flextime changeover plan to work well at Lexington. Here is the background information, a discussion of the advantages and disadvantages (including impact on other divisions), a fiscal impact statement, and recommendations for implementation.

▶ Subject: Final Fisher Contract

Attached is the final Fisher contract as amended during our conference call today. Please review it. If you find any items not in compliance with the necessary safety requirements, contact me by 4:00 P.M. today. Here is a list of the changes:

    <u>Page 7</u>
    Line 4 changed from *"to all those involved"* to *"assembly line personnel"*
    <u>Page 9</u>
    Line 12 changed from *"The contract shall be in effect for 7 months"* to *"The contract shall be in effect for 9 months."*

▶ Subject: Graystone Hotel Collateral Pieces Status Report

I met with Joe Adams to complete the review of the insert sheets for the new sales brochure. Everything was approved. I am waiting for his final figures so we can finish the typesetting and complete the printing. The folders are now being printed.

EDIT, EDIT, EDIT

Use simple, clear, powerful words. Take a look at "Getting Started," page 1, for a list of simple, strong words.

Assignments for Board of Directors Meeting

MEMO

DATE: February 9, 1998

TO: Kent Casewitt, Ed Endres, Alicia Mohr, Sally Brill

FROM: Marilyn Q. Moorespeed

SUBJECT: Assignments for the Board of Directors Meeting,
             October 10, 2:00 P.M., Main Boardroom

Presenter	Agenda Item	Purpose	Time Allotted	Background Reading
K.C.	Production	Information	10 mins.	Mfg. Report
E.E.	Cost Analysis	Information	10 mins.	Financial Reports
A.M	Market Report	Discussion	45 mins.	Market Research Report
S.B.	Facilities	Information	15 mins.	Operations Report
M.M.	Long-term Plan	Decision	45 mins.	Annual & Planning Reports

Appointment Announcement

MEMO

To: All Marco Employees
From: Al Perkins
Date: March 10, 1998
Subject: Aimee Spicer Named Vice President
         of Marketing

I'm pleased to announce that Aimee Spicer will become our Vice President of Marketing on April 1. Aimee has been with Adams Electronic Systems as Assistant Marketing Director for the past five years and has helped Adams grow from $21 million in gross annual sales to over $35 million. She knows our business extremely well and has already begun to formulate plans for the expansion of the Circuit Board Division.

A graduate of MIT, Aimee spent the first three years of her career on the West Coast with Pacific Systems. There she served as regional chairperson for the United Way.

Memo/All Marco Employees/March 10, 1998/ page 2

In both Walnut Creek and Boston, Aimee coached little league teams. Several won the city championship under her coaching. She has also played co-ed softball for six years; in three of those years her teams won the state championship.

Let the recruiting for our softball teams officially begin! And please make Aimee feel welcome.

Request for Recommendations

MEMO
To: Department Heads
From: Calvin Cook
Date: January 10, 1999
Subject: Personnel Manual Recommendations
           Due February 10 for Departmental
           Revision Meeting May 10

February 10 is the deadline for recommended changes to our Personnel Manual. Here's how we will handle the revision process:

1. Please review the present manual, discuss recommended changes with your department personnel, and make notations on policies your people feel need to be changed.

2. Submit these recommendations to me, in writing, by February 10.

3. I will prepare and return to you a complete set of all recommendations, "Employee Manual Recommendations," by April 25.

Memo/Department Heads/January 10, 1999/ page 2

4. Please discuss these recommendations in your department and return any further comments to me by May 1.

5. Department heads will meet May 10 at 9:30 A.M. in the boardroom to make final revision decisions.

Client Memo

MEMO
To: Anne King, Fischer Co.
From: Leah Freer
Date: May 24, 1998
Subject: Chateaux Advertising/Sponsorship in the
           Steve Watson Golf Classic

I talked with the producers of the Steve Watson Golf Classic Program this morning and reserved the ¼-page black-and-white ad in the *Classic Program* magazine. This makes us a "Hole Sponsor," which includes two tickets to play in the golf tournament and two tickets each to the banquet, breakfast, and luncheon. We may now elect one (or none) of three options:

1. Upgrade the Hole Sponsorship to a full-page, four-color ad (instead of the ¼-page black-and-white ad) for $1,600.

2. Add one golf player to the Hole Sponsorship for an additional $250.

Memo/Anne King/May 24, 1998/ page 2

3. Select a "Corporate Sponsorship"—we could enter three golf players—for $2,250. For this price, we would not get the bells and whistles— the banquet, the breakfast, and the luncheon—but we could host a table in the hospitality tent.

I recommend we select item number one. This is the best value because it allows us to narrowcast our advertising in this publication (10,000 are being printed), which will be kept as a memento.

Please let me know your decision by May 26.

Establishing a New Program

MEMO
To: Jack Levine
From: Alice Squire
Date: April 15, 1999
Subject: Establishing a Residential and
         Commercial Real Estate Internship
         Program at Woods

I would like to discuss with you the possibility of establishing a residential and commercial real estate education/internship program here at Woods, using NACREE members as guest lecturers. Can you meet Friday, April 23, at 2:00 P.M. in the boardroom for a sixty-minute discussion of program topics, specific people, and dates?

Meeting Announcement

MEMO
To: All Department Heads
From: Joan Alexander
Date: May 10, 1998
Subject: Weekly Department Head Meeting,
         May 17, 9:30 A.M., Boardroom

Agenda:

1. Vote on the Vacation Policy.
2. Elect a media spokesperson.
3. Introduce the new vice president of Marketing, Mark Halpern.

Loss of Account

MEMO
To: Kevin Hatterfield
From: Sally Speer
Date: September 4, 1998
Subject: Loss of U.S. Army Telephone
         Services Account

I am sorry to announce that the new U.S. Army Telephone Services contract, which represented 35 percent of our business this year, was awarded to Action Systems, beginning November 1. This will slice our gross income at TTI by approximately 42 percent.

This, of course, will affect all departments. I will have complete information on the details of that impact after Jim Harrison, C.F.O., finishes his computations on November 4.

It is important to say that TTI personnel performed well on the U.S. Army account and the change in services contractor is routine. It does not reflect any customer dissatisfaction.

Memo/Kevin Hatterfield/September 4, 1998/page 2

It is also important to tell you that our Sales and Marketing Department is in final negotiations on $24 M in bids to three potential customers for contracts that will begin January 1. The department has another $45 M in bids in process with contract dates to begin between February and May. (The Sales and Marketing Department has secured nearly 65 percent of its bids over the past two years.)

Immediately, the loss of the Army account has made it necessary to furlough eight service technicians, four home-office accounting personnel, and eight part-time clerks. These people have all been notified. Also, the position of Assistant Marketing Director held by Henry Madison has been eliminated; Henry will leave TTI on Friday. I do not believe any additional staff reductions will be necessary.

I will keep you informed of new developments, and I request your best efforts to help all TTI departments pull together in these transitional weeks ahead.

18

MEETING NOTICES, AGENDAS, AND MINUTES

To drift is to be in hell, to be in heaven is to steer.

—GEORGE BERNARD SHAW

Organizations are powered by meetings, and meetings operate best if there's a stated purpose and a plan known to those who will participate.

It's also important to create a permanent record and to let those who don't attend know what happened at a meeting. For these reasons, meeting notices, agendas, and minutes were created.

The meeting notice gives the place, date, time, and purpose of the meeting. It usually asks for a response concerning attendance, and sometimes a vote.

The agenda includes the place, date, and time of the meeting, too, but its primary function is to list topics that will be covered.

Meeting minutes provide a chronological, written, and accurate record of what happened at the meeting. Minutes may be a brief outline or a very detailed and prescribed form, depending on the audience. Besides providing a record, the process of taking minutes helps direct the group to take action. Minutes also inform absent members and a larger audience (if circulated) about what went on.

The meeting report, unlike the minutes, is not comprehensive. The report (see "Informal Report," page 138) presents conclusions, recommendations, and sometimes a summary of the points and discussion.

THINK ABOUT CONTENT
Notice of Meeting

- Meeting notices are sometimes given long in advance and sometimes on the spur of the moment. In either case, inform enough participants to make sure there will be the attendance needed to conduct business (the number of qualified participants needed to vote on issues and whether absentee or proxy voting can be used must be checked with the organization bylaws).
- The written notice must include the date, place, time, and the business to be conducted. Remember to cover the *who, where, when, what,* and *why.*
- Ask for confirmation of attendance. Include the meeting agenda and make any premeeting assignments or requests.
- Include all materials necessary so that participants will understand the issues to be discussed.
- Enclose an absentee ballot or a proxy voting form, if provided for in the organization bylaws.

Attendance Response

* To confirm attendance, state you will attend; confirm the place, date, time, and any travel arrangements; confirm that you will complete any premeeting assignment; and give input on any agenda items.
* To decline attendance, identify the meeting; state why you can't attend; mention how you plan to follow up (reading minutes, sending someone in your place, telephoning an attendee, etc.); and give any input, approvals, voting power, comments, suggestions, etc., that will be helpful or necessary to the success of the meeting.

Agenda

* Identify the date, place, and time of the meeting. When a speaker, meal, or other item is included, the agenda may be called a *program* (*Robert's Rules of Order* covers procedures for the agenda).
* Arrange items of business in a logical order. Times may be listed for each of the items. The order is usually the call to order, reading of minutes from the last meeting, reports from the officers and committees, old business, new business, announcements, and adjournment.

Minutes

* Minutes are difficult to write. The recorder must thoroughly understand the dynamics of the group and the history of the subject. The recorder, usually the secretary, must summarize the reasoning of the group without being subjective. Select this person carefully.
* List the date, time, place, and kind of meeting; the name of the group; and those in attendance and absent.
* Produce minutes in abbreviated or full form, depending upon the organization bylaws, but certain information should always be included. List any substitutes or guests present. Record whether the minutes of the last meeting were approved, and any corrections made, and include a mention or summaries of any reports. Copies may be attached.

All main motions in their final form with the names of the sponsor and seconds must be listed. Give the decision made concerning each motion. Record all the action as it happens. Finally, list the date the minutes are written and the name and signature of the writer.

* Complete the writing of the minutes effectively. Tape meetings, on audio or video tape, if formal minutes are required, and write the minutes as soon as possible after the meeting. Have others review minutes to make sure dates, days, names, and actions are accurate, and make any corrections before they are finally edited.
* Keep a copy of the minutes in a permanent file and distribute copies at following meetings.

ELIMINATE WRONG MESSAGES

* Omit summarizing discussions and routine announcements from minutes.
* Never include personal comments or opinions. Make sure the minutes are completely objective.

SELECT A FORMAT

* Format is dictated by the organization. Minutes should be on organization letterhead, typed, single spaced, and arranged with a minimum of one inch of white space on all sides.
* Use headings, subheads, numbers, and indentation to make minutes easier to understand and visually appealing.

Announcing a Meeting

(Date)
Dylan Readers

Dear Dylan:

I have scheduled a producers' meeting for 2:00 to 4:00 P.M., July 7, in conference room 4B on the lot. Can you make it?

We need to decide on final details, cost factors, and the cast for the *Last Knight* production. We also need to fill the remaining staff openings. (See my list of issues and candidates enclosed.)

Come with your choices and recommendations. We need your input to get this wrapped up.

Sincerely,

Jeff Spellbinder

New Organization Meeting Announcement

(Date)
Audrey Chambers

Dear Audrey:

I finally have some news about the meeting of the ARRF alumni in the Savannah area. We will meet on August 6 from 6 to 8 P.M. in the Brown Palace Regency Room.

The purpose of the meeting is to get acquainted with other alumni and to decide if we will form a local chapter. Mr. Edward Keivers, executive director of the alumni organization in Los Angeles, will give a thirty-minute presentation on what their chapter is doing. He'll also answer any questions about local activities.

There are over thirty local ARRF alumni organizations across the country, and Ralph Weiner will take about fifteen minutes to give us an overview of what those organizations have accomplished for members and their communities.

Chambers/(Date)/page 2

Please return the enclosed card, indicating if you will attend and your interest in forming a local chapter. If you have any questions, call Myron Meeker at (213) 445-7800.

I look forward to seeing you on the sixth. Please come early and get acquainted.

Sincerely,

Byron Bennett

Meeting Notice and Agenda Letter

(Date)
Ellen Grover
Sales Representative

Dear Ellen:

The Regional Sales Representative Quarterly Meeting is set for March 12 at the Executive Inn (I-25 and Belleview) in the Orchids Room from 9 A.M. to 5 P.M. Please arrange your schedule so you may attend.

We will have full details on the new product lines with complete training sessions. Here is the agenda:

9:00 A.M. – 10:30 A.M.	Customer Profile *Darlene Darling*
10:45 A.M. – 12:30 P.M.	You, the Salesperson *Logan Greene*
12:30 – 2:30 P.M.	Luncheon Big Sales Country *Cleo Pengass*

Grover/(Date)/page 2

2:30 – 6:30 P.M.	Seminar Breakout Sessions *Frank Dickens, Alex Saunders, Jennifer Fenders, Marilyn Dougherty*

See you there.

Sincerely,

Robertson Givens

Meeting Minutes

AARD Meeting Minutes

Meeting was September 14, 1998
Commission Members Present: Jerry Holder, Janice Johnson, Bill Wesson, David Wrestler
Staff Members Present: David Weaver, Daphne Justice, Warner Stiles
Staff Members Absent: June Cummings

A regular meeting of the AARD Commission was called to order at 7:05 p.m. on Wednesday, September 14, 1998, at the headquarters conference room, 3400 Riverfront Drive, Phoenix, AZ. The president was in the chair, and the secretary was present.

The minutes of the August meeting were read and approved upon motion by Jerry Holder.

The treasurer's report was a financial statement with a balance on hand, as of September 1, of $455,655.76.

AARD Meeting Minutes/September 14, 1998/page 2

New business included a motion by David Weaver "that we appoint a subcommittee to review the possibility of investing Commission funds for greater financial return."

A motion was made by Daphne Justice "to hold the annual picnic as we did last year."

After a review of the new approval procedure, the meeting adjourned at 9:35 P.M.

[Signature]
Janice Johnson
Secretary

Meeting Agenda

GREEN ACRES HOMEOWNERS' ASSOCIATION
BOARD OF DIRECTORS MEETING

January 11, 1998
7–9 P.M., Club House
Residents Welcome

Agenda

Call to Order

Minutes of the Last Meeting

Management Report, Harry Stropp and David Piper

Financial Report, Jeff Sandler

Old Business
    Surveys, Bill Waverly
    Recycling, Bill Waverly

New Business
    Landscaping/Gardening Recommendation,
    Kathy Klein

GAHA Board of Directors Meeting/January 11, 1998/page 2

Financial Committee Proposal, Jeff Drummer
    Audit
    Cash Management Policies
    Reserves/Dues Increase

Management Contract Bids Review
Misc.

Adjournment

Letter Confirming Meeting Attendance

(Date)

Dear Dexter:

Of course I'll be at the September 15 meeting at the Broadmoar in Colorado Springs. I agree the four mornings will be very heavy.

Yes, I'd be pleased to make my "Marketing Blunders" presentation. Given the schedule, I'll make it interactive. I'll need a blackboard, an overhead projector, and a portable microphone. Will you have your department arrange these items?

Please confirm my hotel late arrival on the 14th. I can't get in until 10:45 P.M.

I look forward to the meeting. It sounds like an outstanding lineup.

Sincerely,

Sidney Bartles

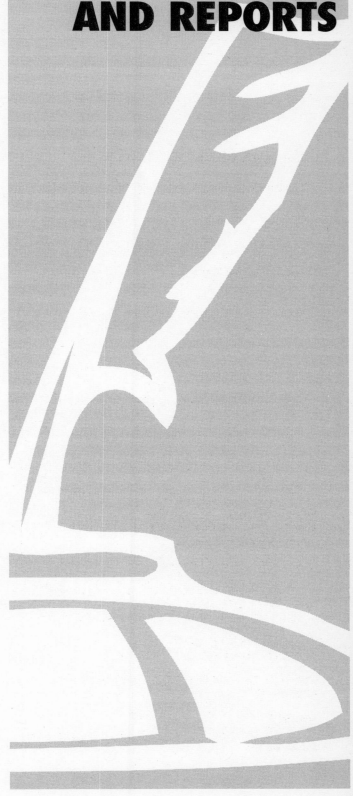

V. PROPOSALS AND REPORTS

19
PROPOSAL

The difficulty is not to write, but to write what you mean, not to affect your reader, but to affect him precisely as you wish.

—ROBERT LOUIS STEVENSON

A proposal is basically a plan to do something. Its purpose is, of course, to persuade. It is usually written in response to an invitation to supply a solution to a need or desire, but not always. Sometimes a proposal is submitted unsolicited or on speculation.

It may be as short as a sentence or as long as a number of volumes. It may be as informal as an interoffice memo or a verbal presentation, or as formal and complex as a lengthy government document.

A proposal is direct. It must be well organized and complete, whether it is unsolicited or requested, informal or formal, short or long. It should start with the reader's needs converted into the writer's purpose. A proposal must not skimp on background elements, a full description of the proposed plan, details (time requirements, schedule, costs, alternative factors, performance standards, etc.), ability to deliver, qualifications, benefits, and a summary or conclusion. All this information should point to the writer's recommendations—the focus of the proposal.

UNDERSTAND THE TERMS

- An internal proposal usually recommends change within your organization.
- An external proposal is made to an outside organization.
- A sales proposal, technical proposal, or budget proposal recommends products or services to a customer.
- An unsolicited or speculative proposal is one you submit without an invitation. Inquire to see if it will be considered.
- A solicited or requested proposal is one you submit after receiving a request for proposal (RFP) or a request for a bid.
- Bid specifications (specs) or guidelines are the rules and requirements that proposal writers or bidders receive from the customer and must follow.
- Nonresponsive means the bidder didn't comply with the specifications.

THINK ABOUT CONTENT

- Qualify for the proposal process. Many government and private, for-profit proposal processes are conducted on an invitation-to-bid basis or a request for proposal (RFP). You must go through a preliminary qualifying process in order to get the opportunity to submit a proposal.

- Research. Complete knowledge of the problem, need, or desire of the recipient is the essential first step. Certainly, knowledge of the reader is vital, too. If past or similar proposals are available, review them as part of the research process.

- Study and know your reader. This must govern your proposal writing from beginning to end. To persuade the reader you must be able to talk to him or her. That means knowing his or her level of knowledge of the subject, bias, examples he or she will respect, and how he or she will best be persuaded.

- Open with a clear and concise preview of your message. This will grab the attention of the reader and set the stage.

- If the reader is not interested, put your strongest points first. If the reader's interest is high, put your strongest points last.

- Choose your "testimonials" from people and examples the reader knows, if possible.

- Tailor your proposal to the reader's attitudes and beliefs, if you can.

- Use well-organized headings, subheadings, and divisions to make your proposal easy to follow.

- Develop an effective solution that will appeal to the reader.

- Start with an introduction. Begin with a statement of purpose and a statement of the reader's need or problem. When the proposal is being submitted in response to an invitation, this should be stated here. When the proposal is unsolicited, you must get the reader's attention and overcome any resistance in this section.

- Insert a statement of background information, a detailed description of the need or problem. In the case of a proposal to reorganize a corporation, for example, this section would give a historical description of the corporation and its development, which explains the need to reorganize.

- Include a need or problem statement. The background will naturally flow into a statement of the need or problem. In a very brief proposal, this section may appear without a background statement.

- Develop a plan. This is the core of the proposal: What the writer proposes to do. It must be well organized, clear, and complete.

- Include enough details to make your plan clear and appealing. In a long proposal, this section will contain the timetables, materials, costs, requirements, performance standards, quality controls, etc. The writer must anticipate the reader's questions and objections and answer them in this section.

- List your qualifications. The writer must give sound reasons here why he or she (or the organization) is uniquely qualified to perform the proposed plan. This may include giving personal qualifications like resumes, job references, operating procedures, and financial statements. Overall, this section must include evidence that the writer can perform.

- List the benefits. Cover the positive results if your proposal is completed. If, for example, a corporation is reorganized, it will be more efficient, be able to expand into new areas, reduce waste, etc.

- Include a summary and conclusion. In a long proposal, briefly summarize the proposal points. Any additional information needed will also appear here, and the conclusion must call for action.

- Give a recommendation. If it hasn't already been stated, this is where your most persuasive statement belongs. It's best to close the circle by referring back to the beginning: "This plan will meet your needs of realizing a 15 percent return by..."

ELIMINATE WRONG MESSAGES

- Do not use sensational claims or facts. Stick to examples within the reader's scope of experience.
- Do not propose elements you cannot back up, but remember that you will not change the reader's attitude by presenting information alone.
- Eliminate everything that isn't carefully focused.
- Eliminate stilted prose and jargon.
- Never mention people or examples without considering the effect on your reader.

CONSIDER SPECIAL SITUATIONS

- Getting on the qualified list of bidders for government work or some for-profit accounts can be a long and difficult process. Start early.
- Study every related, successful proposal you can get your hands on.

SELECT A FORMAT

- Internal proposals often use the memo form.
- Use enumerations and subheads for impact, understanding, visual interest, and clarity.
- A formal proposal format:

I. Table of Contents
II. Introduction
III. Need/Problem
  A. Scope
    1. *Objectives.* The overall objective and specific accomplishments. Give the rationale.
    2. *Approach.* Clearly outline the work plan and the phases.
    3. *Materials, Labor, and Methods.* Details and methodology you will use. Cover your expertise and any difficulties.
    4. *Timetable, Schedule, or Level of Accomplishment.* Break this into relative parts.

  B. Qualifications
    1. *Experience.* General background, specific, and similar experience.
    2. *Personnel.* Qualifications/resumes. Name the responsible person and subcontract sources.

- A proposal may include some or all of these features:

Cover Materials

  – *Cover Letter or Letter of Transmittal*
  – *Title Page*
  – *Table of Contents*
  – *Table of Illustrations*
  – *Abstract or Summary*
  – *Introductory Materials*
  – *Introduction (Grabber)*
  – *Statement of Purpose (Reference to any association with the organization or any association with the problem)*
  – *Problem or Need*
  – *Background (of Problem)*
  – *Needs Analysis*
  – *Solution Statement*
  – *Benefits to be Gained from Solution*
  – *Methodology*
  – *Feasibility of Solution*
  – *Personnel or Staffing Plan*
  – *Design and Organization of Personnel Team*
  – *Personnel Qualifications*
  – *Task Breakdown or Specific Responsibilities*
  – *Time and Work Schedule*
  – *Testing*
  – *Evaluation Procedures*
  – *Progress Reports or Checks*

Management

- *Project Organization and Management*
- *Administrative Structure*
- *Management Policies*
- *Cost-Accounting Methods*
- *Payroll and Timekeeping Methods and Procedures*
- *Credit References and Ratings*
- *Facilities*
- *Quality Control and Assurance Guidelines*
- *Personnel Qualifications and Subcontractors*
- *Experience*
- *Financial Qualifications and Resources*
- *Organizational Support*

Budget

- *Direct Costs*
- *Indirect Costs*
- *Subcontracts*
- *Contract Definition and Terms*
- *Method and Timetable of Payments*
- *Late Penalties*

Close

- *Summary*
- *Conclusion*
- *Call to Action*

Appendices

- *Letters of Reference*
- *Recommendation, Letters of Support, and "Testimonials"*
- *Resumes of Key Personnel*
- *Applicable Policy Statements, etc.*

EDIT, EDIT, EDIT

Before your proposal is finished, it will undoubtedly go through several rewriting and editing processes. Use all your writing skills to make it as clear and persuasive as possible.

SEE ALSO "COVER LETTER," PAGE 167; "RESUME," PAGE 74, AND "REQUESTS AND INQUIRIES," PAGE 155.

Work Proposal

Rose Design Group
200 West Petunia
Oakland, Missouri 64101

(660) 890-7600

Proposal

(Date)

Crystal Lake Homeowners' Association
5200 East Walker Drive
Oakland, Missouri 64101

Attention: Sawyer Applewood, President

Reference: <u>Landscaping Renovation</u>

   This proposal includes completing the following work by (date).
To accept, sign the attached sheet, General Conditions.

	Cost
1. Prepare the site thoroughly, including, but not limited to the following:	$ 935
a) remove and dispose of existing junipers	
b) grind out pear tree stumps	
c) remove lowest branches on existing rock mulches	
2. Furnish and install 5 yards of compost.	440
3. Furnish and install 110 feet of edging.	145
4. Furnish and install flagstone step stones.	290
5. Rebuild existing rock wall at west side of garage.	430
6. Remove and dispose of existing exposed aggregate.	460
7. Prepare the site, including, but not limited to the following:	1,100
a) remove and dispose of plants.	
b) grind out stumps.	
c) remove and dispose of existing rock mulches.	
	————
	$3,800

In its simplest form, the proposal communicates to the reader all the information he or she needs to know to make an informed decision. The proposal, when agreed to, can become the contract between the writer and the reader. This requires that the proposal be crystal clear, down to the last detail.

Proposal/Crystal Lake Homeowner's Association/(Date)/page 2 of 2

GENERAL CONDITIONS

UNFORESEEN SITE CONDITIONS

The contractor has made a reasonable effort to accurately estimate the costs for Material and Labor required to complete the project as specified. However, the Contractor may be required to revise this Contract based on "unforeseen" and/or "undetectable" circumstances, which may arise during the completion of the project. Should any "unforeseen" and/or "undetectable" circumstances arise, the Contractor shall notify the Owner of estimated additional costs required to rectify the situation and obtain written authorization to proceed through the use of a Change Order.

MATERIAL QUANTITIES

The Material quantities specified in the Contract are considered to be appropriate quantities, plus or minus 10%. If any additional Materials are necessary to complete the job, the Contractor shall notify the Owner of the additional costs required to rectify the situation and obtain written authorization to proceed through the use of a Change Order. If less Material is needed to complete the job, the cost shall be credited back to the Owner.

CHANGE ORDERS

All additional Work to the conditions of the Contract shall be subject to additional charges and the Contract price adjusted accordingly. No additional Work shall be performed by the Contractor unless written authorization (Change Order) to proceed with such Work, including the price of such Work, shall be issued by the Owner.

UNDERGROUND UTILITIES

The Contractor shall be responsible to have all underground utilities located.

PERMITS, TAXES, REGULATIONS, CODES

The Contractor is obligated to obtain and pay the cost of all permits, licenses, certificates, inspection and other legal fees that are necessary to do the Work, as applicable.

INSURANCES

The Contractor shall be required to carry and keep in force throughout the duration of the Work General Liability and Workers' Compensation Insurances.

CLEAN UP

The contractor shall leave the site free of debris and surplus material at all times and, at the completion of Work, remove all waste, rubbish, excess materials and equipment generated by the Contractor and leave the site in a clean, completed condition ready for Owner's full use and enjoyment.

DISPUTES/ARBITRATION

Any controversy or claim arising out of or relating to this Contract, or the breach thereof, shall be settled by arbitration in accordance with the Construction Industry Arbitration Rules of the American Arbitration Association or the procedures of the Arbitration Committee of the Associated Landscape Contractors of Colorado. Arbitration shall be binding and the decision to enter into such Arbitration shall be initiated by either party of this agreement.

PLANT WARRANTY

All plant material (excluding annuals, bulbs and transplanted materials) shall be guaranteed to be alive and in satisfactory growth one year following the date of installation. Any material that is considered dead shall be replaced, one time only, by the Contractor at no charge to the Owner. The Owner shall notify the Contractor immediately as soon as any plant material begins to show signs of stress (e.g. yellowing, wilting). The Contractor shall not be responsible for plants that have been adversely affected by factors or circumstances beyond the Contractor's control, including, but not limited to, severe winter or unusual temperature fluctuations during any given time of the year, tornado, vandalism, animal damage, improper application of fertilizers or pesticides and lack or excess of moisture.

IRRIGATION SYSTEM WARRANTY

All components of the irrigation system shall be guaranteed to be free of defects and in good working order for one year following the date on installation. This warranty does not cover the system if it has been damaged due to freezing conditions. It is the Owner's responsibility to insure that the system is protected from temperatures below 32 degrees F.

OWNER————————————————   DATE————————————————

CONTRACTOR————————————   DATE————————————————

This second page of the proposal, when signed, becomes the legal contract between the writer and the reader.

20
FORMAL REPORT

Whatever we conceive well we express clearly.

—NICOLAS BOILEAU-DESPRÉAUX

The formal report collects and interprets data and reports information. It may, in the course of doing these tasks, include an analysis and make recommendations for a course of action.

Reports are used to inform, analyze, recommend, and persuade. They are usually written in indirect order—presenting information, analyzing it, making conclusions, and making recommendations.

The formal report is often very complex and may even be produced in bound book volumes. In the business setting, the informal report is usually used for internal distribution, and the formal report is prepared for external distribution to stockholders, customers, and the general public. The formal report is often a written account of a major project. Examples of subject matter include new technologies, the advisability of launching a new product line, results of a study or experiment, analysis of locations for corporate relocation, an annual report, or a year-end review of developments in the field.

Careful planning and meticulous organization are necessary to guide readers through the material.

Three main sections—front material, body, and back material—help give the report form. These sections may contain the following:

Preliminary (Front) Material
– *Title Page*
– *Letter of Authorization*
– *Letter of Transmittal*
– *Table of Contents*
– *List of Figures*
– *List of Tables*
– *List of Symbols and/or Abbreviations*
– *Statement of Problem, Abstract, Synopsis, or Summary*
– *Foreword*
– *Preface*

Body
– *Executive Summary*
– *Introduction*
– *Text (with appropriate headings, subheadings)*
– *Conclusions or Summary*
– *Recommendations*

Supplemental (Back) Material
– *References*
– *Bibliography*
– *Appendices*
– *Glossary*
– *Index*

THINK ABOUT CONTENT

- Remember that most *formal* reports use an *indirect* approach. This approach introduces the problem, then gives the facts, with analyses (when needed), and summarizes the information given. If your goal is to make a conclusion, you do that next. If your goal is to recommend action, you offer the analyses, draw conclusions, and then, based on this, make your recommendations.

  The *informal* report often uses the *direct* approach, offering the conclusion or recommendation, followed by the facts, often given much more briefly. (See "Informal Report," page 138.)

- Begin by answering why this report is needed, and make your need statement specific. It may be to convey information, to analyze, or to recommend a course of action, or all three.

  The need statement should include the reader. For example, "Our sales representatives need to know why competitive products X, Y, and Z are outselling our product A." Focus your need statement on a specific goal or purpose. It can be expressed as a question or a declarative statement, or you can begin with an infinitive phrase:

  > Question: "What do our sales representatives need to know about competitive products X, Y, and Z in order to effectively sell product A?"

  > Declarative Statement: "Our sales representatives need to know the features of competitive products X, Y, and Z in order to effectively sell product A."

  > Infinitive Phrase: "To sell product A effectively, our sales representatives need to know the features of competitive products X, Y, and Z."

- Divide the task into its component parts. You will want to look at subtopics within the purpose statement.

- If you are reporting information, such as the results of an experiment or a list of books on a topic, the structure will be a straightforward, logical narrative. To make sure your report is objective, base it on facts. This helps free it of opinion and bias.

- If you are making analyses, drawing conclusions, or making recommendations, you probably need to carefully organize some additional elements. Take the case of our product, for example. After defining the broad subtopics—product X, product Y, product Z—you may want to complete some initial observations or surveys of competitive products. You are given these responses to the question "Why are products X, Y, and Z outselling product A?":

1. Products X and Z are cheaper than product A.
2. Products Y and Z are available in designer colors; product A isn't.
3. Products X, Y, and Z are packaged in carrying cases, which buyers seem to prefer over product-A packaging.

You will want to research some facts that can be used as sales points for product A. You may find that

1. Although product A costs more, it outperforms and outlasts products X and Z.
2. Product A is not a fashion accessory. Designer colors aren't related to performance.
3. Product A is self-contained and has no detachable parts, so it is handsome and more convenient without a carrying case.

At the same time, your observations and surveys may lead you to develop some theories or hypotheses about your product:

1. We should reduce product A's price to be more competitive with products X and Z.
2. We should make product A available in designer colors to compete with products Y and Z.
3. We should develop a useful carrying case for product A to compete favorably with products X, Y, and Z.

- Evaluate your hypotheses by assigning point values to each or by using another test method. They may all be partially true or false. If your hypotheses prove false, you may have to advance some additional hypotheses to evaluate. In the case of product A, research may indicate that price, a wide range of colors, and a carrying case are the three top buyer criteria.
- Break down the subtopics into sub-subtopics, if this is helpful to get at the real solutions to the problem.
- Gather all the information. This can require personal research, data collection, surveys, or experiments. Business problems usually rely on surveys, scientific problems on experiments. Information problems may be solved using library research. Employ objective, proper, and thorough methods here to avoid invalidating your solution.
- Test your gathered data:

  Is it objective? Keep an open mind and consider all aspects to determine if sources are reported fairly and completely. Guard against bias.

  Do others agree? Use the input of others to question and challenge your interpretation.

  Is it reasonable? Check conclusions with logical thinking and make the surrounding facts support them.

  Does it hold up? Play devil's advocate, taking the opposing viewpoint, and see if your conclusions hold up. Represent them fairly in your report, showing supporting evidence.

  Statistical data and interpretation is key in many reports. But scientific accuracy and integrity must be used in reporting this information. Check this out thoroughly before including it in your report.

- Organize the information into a report format, keeping precise records of sources.
- Write the rough draft.
- Be consistent in tense. Either present or past tenses work well, but use the same tense throughout.

- Be consistent, too, in personal or impersonal viewpoint. The personal "I" or "we" can be as effective as the impersonal tests and facts, but different organizations and disciplines prefer one over the other. Often the informal report will use the personal and the formal report will use impersonal viewpoint. Check your organization's style preference.
- Use effective transition words to begin new paragraphs. This helps keep the reader's attention.
- Make effective use of graphs, illustrations, and charts to make points.
- Enliven your writing by using effective, vigorous action words, but don't overdo it.
- Revise. Cut out nonessential parts, check for stilted words, jargon, inconsistencies, redundancies, and errors in logic. Eliminate any general, abstract, or vague statements. During this process, ask these questions:

  Does the introduction establish the scope and methods to be used?

  Are all the points in the introduction fully developed in the body?

  Is the development of points logical and complete?

  Are there ideas or sections that should be combined or relocated?

  Is there a clear solution to, or a complete discussion of, the stated problem?

  Is there a clear relationship between ideas and facts?

  Does the report flow logically?

  Is information complete for reader understanding?

  Is opinion correctly identified from fact?

  Have all the facts been double-checked?

  Do headings and subheadings properly reflect content?

  Are all grammar and spelling errors eliminated?

- Review and proofread with as many other people as practical. Consider any pertinent reactions, comments, and changes.
- Edit. It is best to give your report a few days on the shelf so you can become objective again before you give it a fresh, last look.

ELIMINATE WRONG MESSAGES

- Don't embellish facts, use them out of context, or misinterpret them to support a point.
- Don't use material without giving proper credit.
- Do not make faulty or illogical cause-and-effect conclusions. Use sound reasoning to be sure of a relationship. And remember, conclusions are not always necessary. Some things are inconclusive. Say so.
- Don't make the mistake of assuming a lack of evidence proves the opposite is true.
- Do not compare apples to oranges. Data must be similar in nature for comparisons to be authentic.
- Eliminate digressions or unfocused material. These can easily derail the report.

SELECT A FORMAT

- To organize the report in a conventional outline manner, use this format:

I. Major or First Level Heading
   A. Minor or Second Level Heading
     1. Subhead or Third Level Heading
      a. Fourth Level
       (1) Fifth Level
        (a) Sixth Level

- To arrange the report by the decimal system, use this format:

1.0 First Level Heading
  1.1 Second Level Heading
    1.2.1 Third Level
      1.2.2.1 Fourth Level

- In typing the report, outline form may be presented:

I. MAJOR OR FIRST LEVEL HEADING
  A. Minor or Second Level Heading
    1. Subhead or Third Level Heading
     a. Fourth Level Heading or Paragraph Heading

- Headings may be typed without numbers or letters:

MAJOR OR FIRST LEVEL HEADING
<u>Minor or Second Level Heading</u>
Subtopic or Third Level Heading
    Fourth Level Heading or
    Paragraph Heading

- Establish a consistent format for all reports.
- Follow an approved and consistent reference system such as shown in the *Chicago Manual of Style* to record footnotes and bibliography listings.

Formal Report

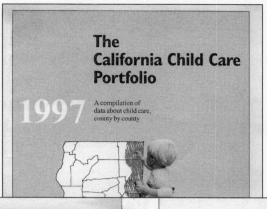

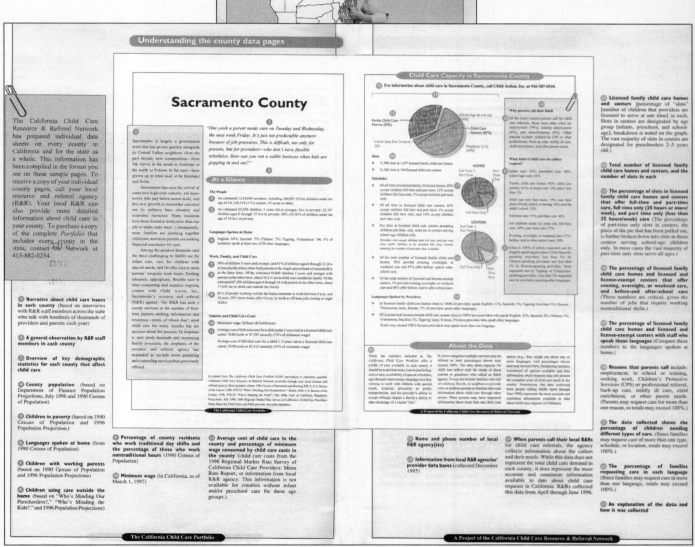

The California Child Care Portfolio, Public Relations Society of America 1997 Bronze Anvil Award–winning special-purpose publication.

21

INFORMAL REPORT

Sound judgment is the ground of writing well:
And when philosophy directs your choices to
proper subjects rightly understood, words from
your pen will naturally flow.

—QUINTUS HORATIUS FLACCUS

The informal report functions to inform, analyze, and recommend. It usually takes the form of a memo, letter, or a very short internal document like a monthly financial report, monthly activities report, research and development report, etc.

This report differs from the formal report in length and formality. It's written according to organization style rules, but usually doesn't include the preliminary (front) and supplemental (back) material (see page 133). The informal report is usually more conversational in tone and typically deals with everyday problems and issues addressed to a narrow readership inside the organization.

Participatory management diminished the role of the informal report, but computers revived it, especially since management team members are frequently in different locations. An informal report is often completed quickly and transmitted electronically.

DECIDE TO WRITE

There are many embodiments of the informal report:
- Progress report
- Sales activity report
- Personnel evaluation
- Financial report
- Feasibility report
- Literature review
- Credit report
- Recommendations and suggestions
- Acceptance or rejection of proposals (see "Acceptance," page 81, and "Refusal," page 186)

THINK ABOUT CONTENT

- Informal reports usually do not include introductory material, but include it if necessary.
- Start by asking yourself, "What does my reader need to know, precisely, about the subject?" Put this into a purpose statement, in a single, explicit sentence. In a memo format, this can be your subject line.

- Use direct order organization. Begin with the most important information, usually the conclusion and a recommendation, for most routine problems. This approach saves your reader time. It offers the important information right up front. Write this down in outline form. For example, if you believe your subordinate Ralph Dolittle should be fired, you would start with this subject line: Recommend Terminating Ralph Dolittle. In the Ralph example you would back up your recommendations with the reasons:
  1. Missed eleven days of work in the past month.
  2. Failed to call in on seven of these days.
  3. Was insubordinate on three occasions.
  4. Was caught asleep on four occasions.
- Or use an indirect approach. Start with general information, review the facts, and end with your recommendation. In the indirect approach, you might start with this subject line: Performance Review for Ralph Dolittle.
- Follow this rule for selecting the direct or indirect approach: When your audience favors your conclusion or recommendation, state it directly, then back it up with facts. When your audience is resistant to your conclusion or recommendation, or knows little or nothing about the subject, give the facts first and state your conclusion and recommendation at the end.
- Organize your information under the subtopics of your report.
- Use a personal writing style—using *I, you, he, she, they,* and *we*—if your organization allows it.
- Write and rewrite until your report is interesting, concise, and flows well.
- Make a conclusion, summary, or recommendation statement at the end, even if it repeats your subject line.
- Check to be sure you have completely answered or solved your subject problem or statement.
- Have others review it and give input, if possible.
- Give your report a little shelf time, then come back and give it one more fresh review.

ELIMINATE WRONG MESSAGES

- Do not assume a level of knowledge your reader doesn't have.
- Using a direct approach does not relieve you of the job of listing all the facts. Be sure all your backup facts are logically listed.
- Don't fire off a report without giving it an objective, second look. With e-mail and online communication, there is a big temptation to send something off immediately. Be sure to give yourself reflective time.
- Don't make your report too long. This is usually a sign that it lacks organization. Keep it under one page for simple subjects.
- Don't automatically begin every report in a direct approach. In our employee example, for instance, if the facts or evidence are not so clear-cut, you may be considered biased, capricious, or arbitrary. When the subject is not on the top of everyone's mind, an indirect approach may work better.

SELECT A FORMAT

Use memo, letter, or formal report form.

SEE ALSO "FORMAL REPORT," PAGE 133, AND "MEMO," PAGE 112.

22
FEASIBILITY REPORT

*Knowledge is the foundation and
source of good writing.*

—QUINTUS HORATIUS FLACCUS

The feasibility report defines a need or proposed idea, then analyzes, compares, and recommends a course of action. When your organization is considering a new location, expansion, or the purchase of new equipment, for example, it's imperative that you look closely to see which course of action is best and if that course of action is likely to succeed. A list of questions should start the process:

- Is it practical?
- What is the cost?
- Will it be profitable?
- What are the advantages and disadvantages?
- What will the impact be? Long term? Short term?
- What legal considerations exist?
- What are the personnel, training, and skill considerations?

THINK ABOUT CONTENT

- Develop a purpose statement. Make this statement as specific as possible. It should include a problem statement if this is part of the reason for the study and report. It must state both the objective and the scope of the report. For example:

  Our present installation technique is too labor-intensive and its service life is too short. This report compares four new installation techniques and recommends one for use by our installers.

- Make a list of all the questions that must be answered. Get the input of all the people involved to develop a complete list. For the example just given, here are some of the questions you might include:

  What are the materials costs of each new procedure?

  What are the training and skills requirements of each new procedure?

  What are the time and labor requirements of each procedure?

What improvement in serviceability and service life does each new procedure offer?

What is the sales impact of each new procedure?

What are the equipment costs to complete each of the new procedures?

What are the projected savings in service calls for the new procedures?

- Turn these questions into criteria statements by which to measure each alternative, such as

The materials cost comparison for Procedures A, B, C, and D

The training and skills requirements comparison for Procedures A, B, C, and D

The time and labor requirements for Procedures A, B, C, and D

The service life comparisons for Procedures A, B, C, and D

The sales impact comparisons for Procedures A, B, C, and D

The equipment costs comparisons for Procedures A, B, C, and D

The comparative savings in service calls for Procedures A, B, C, and D

- Develop a preliminary study and report outline
- Complete the information gathering, tests, investigation, and fact finding and collection.
- Develop the final report outline.
- Write the report, using visually effective graphs and comparison charts to make the information interesting and easy to comprehend. The report should include a precise introduction of the problem, purpose, and scope; a body of detailed evaluations of the alternatives; a conclusion that summarizes the evaluation of each alternative; and a final recommendation.
- Rewrite, edit, and review. Use other people to review, making sure the report is complete, polished, and easy to understand.

SELECT A FORMAT

- Use headings, subheadings, and sub-subheadings to clearly guide the reader.
- Use white space to make the report visually inviting to read.

SEE "FORMAL REPORT," PAGE 130, AND "INFORMAL REPORT," PAGE 138.

23

TECHNICAL AND SPECIAL REPORTS

*Fine writing is next to fine doing,
the top thing in the world.*

—JOHN KEATS

The technical report is a category, not a type. Many industries and disciplines need specialized reports. The contents should be dictated by the audience, the precise purpose, and the particular discipline or industry. But these reports are technical in nature.

For example, the research and development department of an equipment manufacturer needs to write troubleshooting reports, which list possible causes of precise symptoms or problems, tests for these, and possible solutions. These reports may be written for field service personnel or customers who own the equipment. The audience and purpose dictate the content and format.

Within the insurance industry and in police work, there are needs for specialized accident or incident reports. These reports must have precise information recorded in consistent formats. Quite different is the content and format of the investigative report. The staff report, too, could be classified as a technical report, but because its audience is human resources professionals and supervisors and its purpose is to evaluate personnel performance, the content, organization, and emphasis will differ greatly from other technical reports.

What is common about technical reports is the emphasis on the audience, a well-defined purpose, and a consistent format that reflects the needs and conventions of the discipline or industry the report serves. It is important to know the "report culture." Check present and past reports of your organization, industry, or discipline.

DECIDE TO WRITE

Use this communication to report
- Investigative findings
- New facts
- Solutions to problems
- Evaluations
- Statement on problems
- Progress
- Status

THINK ABOUT CONTENT

- Ask detailed questions until you have clarified the problem, purpose, and scope of your report.
- Write a preliminary outline. Then review it with others involved in the process, if possible.
- Complete the information gathering, investigation, testing, and research, making detailed notes,

recording figures, and listing sources.

- Write a final outline.
- Write your report, focusing the content on completely answering, solving, or fulfilling the promise contained in your beginning problem, purpose, or scope statement.
- Rewrite, edit, and review. Get others to help to ensure objectivity and comprehensiveness.

CONSIDER SPECIAL SITUATIONS

- *Progress* reports or *contact* reports emphasize what has happened or changed over time since the last report. One of the most common examples of this is the *sales* report. But a progress report is also used extensively—in a very different format—for government projects, political campaigns, advertising campaigns, construction, and many other industries. This report creates a record and keeps others informed. Straight reporting of information with a minimum of comparison is used for this report, which is usually written for a limited audience.

  Use action headings and make statements concise. Structure your report with an introduction that identifies the project, its director, and the project goals. Include a brief summary of the last progress report; a body listing progress, problems, comments, notable features, and budget considerations; a section that previews expected progress for the next reporting period; and a last section that gives a conclusion about overall progress.

- *Status* reports emphasize the current condition of a project, detailing what exists (rather than what has changed). They are divided into the necessary component parts, and the writer includes detailed observations and some evaluation for a limited audience.

- *Trip* reports and *event* reports are required by organizations to keep other employees informed and establish a permanent record. These reports should be brief, with the emphasis on new information. They are usually done in memo format, addressed to the writer's supervisor and copied to others. The subject line lists the destination and

date. The body gives the purpose of the trip, persons visited, and accomplishments. Include only important events, and use subheads to identify them. End with conclusions and recommendations.

- *Trouble* reports or *accident* reports are usually internal memos dealing with accidents, equipment failure, unplanned work stoppage, or other problems. They create an official record and inform a limited audience. Management uses these reports to determine causes and the need for change to avoid a recurrence. Often these reports are used for insurance and legal purposes, so it is vital that information be factual, accurate, as precise as possible, and complete—without unsolicited opinion statements.

  The subject line should list the precise problem. The body describes the problem. Be sure to answer these questions:

  Was anyone injured?
  Where exactly did the problem occur?
  What happened?
  What was the exact time?
  Was there any property damage? What?
  Was there work stoppage?
  Who witnessed the problem?

  Record accurately the time, date, location, treatment of any injuries, damage to property, names and addresses of witnesses, statements of witnesses, equipment damage, and any other important information. Make the tone objective, and place no blame.

  Conclude with the action taken and future action that will be taken to insure that the problem does not occur again.

- *Investigative* reports may give the results of a survey, marketing study, product evaluation, literature search, or procedure investigation. The purpose of this report is to give precise analysis of the subject and offer recommendations.

  Open with a purpose statement. In the body, first completely define the scope of the investigation. If it is a survey, for example, define the number and composition of those surveyed by age, education, geographical location, occupation, income, interest, opinions, and any other information that impacts your information. Define the limits of the survey technique (see "Survey and Questionnaire," page 149). Then report the findings and their significance. Conclude with recommendations.

- *Literature reviews* and *annotated bibliographies* are literature or printed material summaries on specific topics, published in a specific time period. These reviews offer a complete listing with an evaluation and serve as sources for further in-depth research. For example, a literature review may list all the information published on "e-mail" over the past five years. A literature review or annotated bibliography may also be part of a larger report.

    Literature reviews help professionals—industrial, medical, academic, and other areas—keep abreast of new things in their fields.

    Sources may be listed chronologically, from the earliest source, or they may be arranged by subtopics covered.

    In the heading or brief introduction, give the scope of the subject to be covered, the sources (books, magazine articles and journal articles, computer sources, etc.), and dates of publication or origination. In the body give each listing accurately and completely so readers may easily locate listed sources (follow a stylebook like the *Chicago Manual of Style*). For each listing, give the scope of the work and its value to the reader. Be concise.

- An *abstract* gives a very brief synopsis of a longer report or book. A *descriptive abstract* defines the purpose, scope, and methods used; an *informative abstract* includes this information and the results, conclusions, and recommendations. The abstract should run between 200 and 250 words.

- *Staff* reports are written to document problems, analyze, and recommend solutions. Because this report is usually standardized by the organization, it is easy to develop a macro or merge document on computer or word processor software. The report can then be set up in memo format with sections for the problem or summary, related factors, facts, discussion, conclusions, and recommendations. Standard responses can be part of the software program so that only particular details must be filled in. Because these reports may play a part in some legal action or employee issue, they must be completed in precise, concise detail. Employees involved are usually asked to review and sign these reports if they will become part of the employee's file.

- The *executive summary* may be a separate, brief document, or part of a much longer report. An executive summary is similar in structure to the abstract but usually longer. The objective is to briefly cover all the points of a formal report: the purpose, scope, methods, results, summary, conclusions, and recommendations. It gives enough concise detail to inform executive readers of the entire report contents so they will not have to read the full-length version.

    Write this summary to stand alone. Cover the essential information proportionate to the coverage in the full report. Do not refer to tables, charts, etc., not included in the executive summary. Don't use technical terms unless absolutely necessary. Visuals aren't included unless they are integral to the summary.

ALSO SEE "FORMAL REPORT," PAGE 133; "INFORMAL REPORT," PAGE 138; AND "FEASIBILITY REPORT," PAGE 140.

Navy Team Public Affairs
Crisis Response: Recovery Operations for Trans World Airline Flight 800

<u>Background Research</u>

One of the basic tenets of Department of Defense public affairs is maximum disclosure with minimum delay. Navy Team Public Affairs specialists know that accidents involving a death or serious injury adds a special set of concerns. Personal privacy and sensitivity for victims and their families tempers our response.

We are familiar with crisis operations. Team Public Affairs has responded to the exceedingly challenging environment of crisis ... where initial details are sketchy; first reports are wrong; the demand for information is overwhelming; and satellite-bounced broadcast news slices through the time between accident and first report. But nothing could prepare us completely for the crash of Trans World Airline's Flight 800 in July 1996.

There was almost no time for research. Team Public Affairs relied heavily on lessons learned from the past, even though the past wasn't an exact fit. We quickly decided that a look at the environment Team Public Affairs specialists would face in the wake of such a tragedy was a key to our research effort. People and resources we could use to put a public relations plan into action were catalogued and summarized. And then we had to get going.

Out of this environment of chaos certain lessons from the past turned up once again. These basic lessons or concepts popped out of our research. They would later anchor our plan of attack. We needed to educate target audiences ... audiences who probably knew little about our capabilities. Sensitivity and care for the feelings of the victims' families was paramount. An ongoing investigation limited what could be released and determined when information was provided to the public. Various agencies were involved in crisis response actions, and coordination of public relations efforts was a key to successful communication.

The pressure to produce and release information would be overwhelming at times. Media from everywhere would swoop in on the crash site in large numbers, and they would get and then report bad information. This could shake public confidence. Our lessons learned reminded us that anyone involved in this effort might go from humanitarian status to target for ridicule and blame. We needed seasoned public relations professionals on scene ... and on scene quickly. Our on scene Team Public Affairs professionals would have public information release authority. Because the crash site was remote—and at sea—we needed to bring our own photo and video capabilities. We would be capturing and then releasing the images that the media needed to tell the story.

<u>Planning</u>

We boiled down this quick research effort. Our public relations action plan had to: 1) Build public confidence in the Navy through the dissemination of timely information; 2) Support to the fullest extent possible the many news organizations who appeared at the crash site; and 3) Take into account the welfare of the families of the crash victims. As we devised our plan, we listed the special considerations that anchored our public relations efforts: 1) The navy's role, although significant, was in support of an investigation effort led by the National Transportation Safety Board (NTSB); 2) The crash site was an active investigation scene that could, at any point, be declared a crime scene. Our public relations activities fell under an umbrella of scrutiny designed to prevent possible evidence from being released; and 3) this was a multi-agency operation. While the navy frequently operates in a joint military environment, it rarely operates with such a diverse group of local, state and federal agencies. In many ways this was new territory for us.

Within this framework our mission was to tell the story of Sailors and their specialized skills, and show that the navy was a leader in the skills required to conduct recovery operations. To accomplish our mission the public relations plan focused on three specific, target audiences. First, the victim's families. Second, the American public and the media. Third, our Navy people and their families. We also knew our plan would have to remain flexible and fluid to some extent. We needed to react quickly to a dynamic on scene environment.

The navy's annual public affairs strategy, contained in Playbook 1996, provided a central theme for our communication points and efforts ... "U.S. Navy-Right mix, Right Place, Right Now." From the same book we used the quarterly theme "Citizens First, Second to None" to describe the sacrifices willingly made by our Sailors during this prolonged and righteous operation.

The first part of our plan involved organizing and physically deploying our Team Public Affairs personnel. Our public relations professional from the Navy Office of Information East in New York would lead the way. He was the closest to the crash site and also knew the media in the region. People from the Fleet Hometown News Center, Public Affairs Center, and Fleet Imagining Command, all based in Norfolk, VA., were sent to provide additional people-power and high technology photo and video capabilities.

The second part of our plan involved establishing a Command Information Bureau (CIB). This would become our on scene headquarters.

Navy Crisis Communication Planning and Execution during TWA Flight 800 Recovery Operations in 1996 by Naval Seas Systems Command, as submitted to the Public Relations Society of America for the 1997 Silver Anvil Awards. In chronological order, this special report documents how—under the most difficult of circumstances—the Navy Team Public Affairs handled coordination and dissemination of information during a crisis.

Execution

- We were ready when the Navy was tapped for recovery assistance.

- We established and equipped a CIB at the recovery operation command post.

- We established a Navy liaison at the NTSB public affairs cell in Smithtown, New York.

- Combat camera personnel, all certified to dive, were provided by the Fleet Imaging Command to document the underwater salvage operation. The images provided by these professionals became a key story teller.

- We used the Navy Public Affairs Library (the Navy Chief of Information Website) to communicate to our external audience, many of whom were turning to the World Wide Web for information about the crash.

- We established a clipping service to inform our internal audience, as well as the many agencies involved.

- We selected digital imagery as the best photo format to promptly transmit images to news organizations and our web site.

- We used the Navy News Service, which transmits internal stories by naval message, e-mail and electronically in the form of hard copy newsletter throughout the Navy, to keep our internal audience informed.

- Releases generated by the Fleet Hometown News Center and the Navy Public Affairs Center were used to get more bounce for the ounce. This was the way we got the story of Navy professionalism to hometown newspapers all across the country.

- We provided access to the media via embarks (visits aboard ships at sea), background interviews, and stand-ups.

- Ground rules were established to help us consistently and correctly handle photos and videos gathered at the site.

Evaluation

Diving ended in early November and trawling operations began immediately afterwards. To date, the cause of the crash has yet to be determined. There is no final answer for the victim" families or the many Navy personnel who were involved in recovery operations. The Sailors did their solemn, professional best in a difficult environment. In the final analysis, we succeeded in our mission of telling the story of Navy sacrifice and professionalism to all intended audiences.

- We always kept the feelings of the victim's families in the forefront.

- All media queries were answered promptly and professionally. There were numerous accurate articles and television stories about the tremendous human effort of Sailors in the face of adversity. We met our objective to educate the media and the American public.

- Effective methodology for timely review and release of video and still images helped us show the American public the dangerous working conditions our divers faced.

- The number of "hits" on the Navy Public Affairs Library site on the World Wide Web reached record numbers. Major online news organizations linked their sites to ours, and a number of articles in major newspapers remarked on the value of our site as a resource.

- A strong working relationship was developed with the NTSB and FBI. The FBI recently told ABC Evening News, when they began production of a piece six months after the crash, that ABC "couldn't get the story right" if they didn't include interviews with the Navy divers involved in the operation.

- Our internal audience was kept informed with articles in All Hands, the monthly magazine distributed to the fleet; Navy & Marine Corps News, a weekly program distributed to all Armed Forces Radio and Television overseas broadcasting detachments and simultaneously broadcast on numerous public access channels in the U.S.; and the Navy Wire Service, which operates much like a news wire service.

- Our clipping service received high praise from recipients. It was a tool to apprise leadership and Sailors alike of what was being reported in the press. A natural feedback tool that was distributed daily while the Navy was on the scene.

24
RESEARCH

Seize the subject and the words will follow.

—CATO THE ELDER

How to write it often depends on knowing how to research it. This can be the most exciting part of your writing. The process of in-depth learning about the subject takes some special skills, and it must not be shortchanged. Where and how you begin your research will depend upon the subject matter and where you enter the process. Sometimes you will work from the general to the specific, other times from the specific to the general.

There are two basic ways to get the information you need: primary, or first-hand research, and secondary, or indirect research. Primary sources include both unpublished and original sources, such as organization records and your own experiments, observations, and surveys. Secondary sources are published works such as encyclopedias, almanacs, directories, various kinds of publications, books, and statistical sources.

START WITH SECONDARY SOURCES

Secondary sources are the most accessible, least costly, and most complete. Beginning here is a necessary first step for any researcher. Now many of these sources are available on the Internet, although there may be a subscription required for access.

Where to Start

The New York Public Library Book of How and Where to Look It Up

Encyclopedias

Encyclopedia Britannica
The Encyclopedia Americana
Academic American Encyclopedia

Magazines and Special Publications

Reader's Guide to Periodical Literature (available as Wilsondisc on CD-ROM)
Magazine Index (MI, available on CD-ROM)
The New York Times Index
New York Times microfilm collection
Psychological Abstracts
Social Science Index
Woman Studies Abstracts

More Information

Encyclopedia of Associations
American Statistics Index
The Research Center Directory
Directory of Special Libraries
The Official Museum Directory
American History Sourcebook
Telephone books

Biographical Directories

Who's Who in America
Who's Who in the World
Who's Who in the East
Who's Who in the Midwest
Dictionary of American Biography (prominent
Americans of the past)

Almanacs

The World Almanac and Book of Facts
The Irwin Business and Investment Handbook

Trade Directories

The D & B Million Dollar Directory
Thomas Register of American Manufacturers
America's Corporate Families
Directory of Corporate Affiliation

Government Publications

Monthly catalog of U.S. government publications

Statistical Sources

Handbook of Basic Economic Statistics
Statistical Abstract of the United States
Predicasts Basebook
Standard & Poor's Statistical Service

USE INDIRECT RESEARCH SOURCES

1. Use interlibrary loan services or database
   searches. With database searches—to be material-
   and cost-effective—limit your research by indicating the subject, date, and language. Charges
   are usually based on online time.
2. Use association, newspaper, and corporation
   library sources.
3. Use public relations people in corporations,
   hospitals, and associations.
4. Search public records in the courts, prisons, and
   other public places.
5. Buy the research services of a reference librarian,
   private investigator, or search organization:

People–Lineages, Inc., Salt Lake City
People Finders (Florida)

CONSIDER PRIMARY RESEARCH

1. Interview people.
2. Search organization, library archives, and unpublished sources and records.
3. Conduct an experiment.
4. Set up your own observation.
5. Conduct a survey.

25

SURVEY AND QUESTIONNAIRE

It is not every question that deserves an answer.

—PUBLILIUS SYRUS

Sometimes the best way to get information is to ask questions. But which, and of whom? You will need to establish a survey method and develop a questionnaire, especially if you need information like personal attitudes, opinions, or evaluations.

First you must identify the information you need and eliminate direct and secondary research sources for that information (see "Research," page 147). Next you must decide how to select a representative sample of the people you need answers from, and decide on the format and delivery of your questions. Will you use personal interviews, telephone interviews, or a printed and distributed questionnaire to get the answers you need?

DECIDE TO WRITE

Use a questionnaire or survey when you need special information not available through any of the sources you've investigated.

THINK ABOUT CONTENT

- Select a representative sample of the entire audience. (You may need to study and employ scientific marketing selection techniques to ensure a valid sample that will produce valid results. Check marketing resources.)
- Write a questionnaire based on what you need to learn.
- Make sure the questions are easy to understand.
- Gear the questions toward facts as much as possible, and request quantitative responses whenever possible.
- Create a layout that invites readers and allows adequate space for their responses.
- Try your questionnaire on a pilot or test group first, get feedback, and incorporate any changes they suggest.
- Establish a method for evaluating the results. Remember, you must be able to present the findings clearly and completely, which will require you to objectively interpret answers to questions.

AVOID WRONG MESSAGES

- Avoid leading questions.
- Avoid questions that touch on areas of personal prejudice (unless this is the information you need).

Homeowners' Association Questionnaire

SUNSET HOMEOWNERS'
OPINION SURVEY

Please complete *one survey per household*. This is an opinion survey to help the new Board of Directors. Please read entirely before answering.

Name: _____ Unit #: _____

1. *Concerning the process of decision-making at Sunset, we*
     _____ are pleased with the elective process we have now with the Board interpreting the Covenants and Codes for Community Living.
     _____ would like to see a more direct democratic process, and we pledge to actively participate by voting on decisions.
Other: _____
_____
_____

2. *Concerning the interpretation of the Codes for Community Living, 2.3 Unsightly Articles, we believe the following should apply (Y—yes; N—no):*
     _____ Portable basketball hoops should be allowed in front of homes if they are taken in at night.
     _____ Permanent basketball hoops should be allowed to be attached to the front of homes if kept in good condition.
     _____ Basketball hoops of any kind should not be allowed in front of homes because they are dangerous so close to the street, as well as "unsightly." Basketball play should be restricted to the neighborhood hoop at the clubhouse.

Other concerns or opinions:
_____
_____
_____
_____

3. *Concerning the quality of life at Sunset our family enjoys these amenities (please use O—often, more than once a week; I—infrequently, about once or twice a month; or S—seldom, less than once a month; N—never.):*
     _____ Swimming pool
     _____ Tennis courts
     _____ Jacuzzi
     _____ Clubhouse
     _____ Exercise equipment (in clubhouse)
     _____ Park area
     _____ Enclosed and gated community that eliminates outside traffic during night hours

Other qualities and services we enjoy and want to preserve:
_____
_____

Additionally, we would like to see these changes or additions in these items:
_____
_____

4. *We would like to see Sunset expenditures focus on the following areas (numbered in importance 1—top priority, through 5—least important):*

_____ Extended summer swimming pool hours:
　　　 _____ to _____ Monday through Friday
　　　 _____ to _____ Weekends (Saturday and Sunday)
_____ Beautifying the park area
_____ Creation of a basketball area in the park
_____ Purchase of additional exercise equipment in the clubhouse: _____
_____ Signage and landscaping lighting on Drury Lane at entry

Other: _____
_____
_____
_____

5. *Concerning holiday lighting:*
_____ What we have is fine.
_____ We would like small white lights on the trees at the entry.

Other: _____

6. *We would like to see these activities (Y—yes; N—no):*
_____ holiday family get-together (__ November; __ December)
_____ an active Sunset garden club
_____ book review club meetings at the clubhouse
_____ exercise classes at the clubhouse
_____ swimming instruction at the pool
_____ summer family picnic (__ June; __ July; __ August)

Other: _____

7. *We are willing to organize/volunteer to serve on the following:*
_____
_____
_____

We have these additional comments and suggestions for the Board:
_____
_____
_____
_____
_____
_____
_____
_____
_____
_____
_____
_____
_____

Fold and place your completed survey in the HOA slot to the left of the mailboxes.

VI. INQUIRIES, REQUESTS, AND RESPONSES

26

REQUESTS AND INQUIRIES

…ask, and ye shall receive,
that your joy may be full.

—JOHN 16:24

At the heart of the request letter is the need to effectively communicate what you want. You must ask that your requested information be sent in response or that further direction be sent to help in your quest. Your letter should be brief, functional, and gracious in tone. And be sure of the last. You need to make the reader want to help you.

A letter of request may be labeled "inquiry," though this is sometimes quite different in nature. (Erroneously, too, a query letter may be referred to as a request letter. When a writer corresponds with a publisher proposing his or her composition be published, it is much more a sales letter than a request letter. See "Query," page 161.)

If you are requesting routine information, make your letter as brief as possible, but always make it clear and courteous.

This type of letter is, of course, one of the mainstays of business life. And in this, as in all letters, you will leave the reader with an impression about your organization. Business requests should be made on business letterhead, if possible.

DECIDE TO WRITE

When you are seeking one of the following, you'll use a request letter:

- Advice
- Appointments, interviews, meetings
- Business or personal assistance
- Bids, consultations, proposals, estimates
- Change of status: variance or zoning changes, name changes, changes in marital status, etc.
- Contributions, donations
- Information: copies of credit reports, documents, medical records, instructions
- Interviews and information about job openings
- Loan (see "Credit Inquiry and Providing Credit Information," page 206)

THINK ABOUT CONTENT

- Think through your request before you start writing so that you can state what you want clearly.
- Be sure you understand the protocol of making your request. If you are, for example, requesting a copy of your credit report, you must conform to the particular requirements of the credit company, which usually involve properly identifying

yourself, enclosing a statement or copy of credit denial, and enclosing a check for the report. The processes of requesting your military records, medical records, etc., will have their own special requirements. Find out what, precisely, these are, and comply in your request to get the results you want.

- When addressing an organization that receives large volumes of requests on a variety of topics, use a subject line to immediately aid the reader in identifying yours: "Subject: Report 1996-B."

- If you have several related queries or requests, list them from the most important through the least, so the reader can easily check the items off.

- Be sure your request is so detailed that you get precisely the response you want. This is essential when you're requesting bids, for example, because unless your request contains the complete specifications for the work, the reader will be unable to respond. Also include all sources for further information and all deadlines.

- Make responding as easy as possible for the reader. Enclose a permission form to use copyrighted materials; a sample of the product you need help with; a self-addressed stamped envelope; a postcard; an e-mail address; a fax number, etc. Put yourself in the reader's place and try to make his or her work as easy as possible.

- For long, difficult requests, requests that require much of the reader, and requests that have a response time frame, telephone and give the recipient advance notice before sending your request.

- Introduce yourself, if yours is anything other than a routine request for prepared information.

- Begin with a clear, concise, and courteous statement of your request.

- Be as specific as possible.

- State, if appropriate, the reason for your request and the use you will make of what you are requesting.

- Include a reason why the reader may be interested in responding.

- Let the reader know where to send the information, or how to contact you with questions.

- Include the invitation to call you collect with questions, if this is appropriate.

- Conclude things in the last sentence or two, restating your request briefly, if it is complex; and making a statement of appreciation for the reader's cooperation: "All the specifications and references are listed on pages 11 through 18. We appreciate your company's interest in this project, and we look forward to receiving your bid by April 7. Thank you."

- Express your appreciation for the expected cooperation of your reader.

ELIMINATE WRONG MESSAGES

- Do not use a commanding tone: "Send me your report A-510 by return mail" may make the reader bristle.

- Eliminate, too, an apologetic tone or a tone that does not expect an answer to your letter: "I'm sorry to bother you with this, but I need a copy of the report on early therapy for diabetes" and "If you are unable to send me a copy of the report, I will certainly understand" are too weak.

- Don't bury the items of your request in long paragraphs. Don't write "Please send me your brochures on Model 75-74; Model 610-66; Model 774-23; Pipettes 566-43; and the Analyzer 511-10." Instead, indent so the reader can easily see what your want:

  Please send me your brochures on
  Model 75-74
  Model 610-66
  Model 774-23
  Pipettes 566-43
  Analyzer 511-10.

- Avoid vague requests that may go unanswered or simply be discarded. Do more research in advance so you can make your request specific and, if possible, get the name of the person who will be able to help you.

- Conclude your letter with a statement of appreciation, which may further energize the reader to help you: "Thank you for handling this request."

CONSIDER SPECIAL SITUATIONS

- Make it a policy to put all requests in writing, and always be explicit. A simple "This confirms my request for reservations for the Elks meeting at the Boulderado, May 13" won't do. In this example, your request should include the number of guests for whom you are requesting rooms; the number and time of meeting rooms you'll need, and how each will be arranged; the number of people, time, menus, and service expected for meals; and the charges and fees involved. If possible, use a request form from the hotel. You could also ask for an example of a request for a similar meeting if you don't do this regularly.

- A request to quote should be responded to with a signed permission letter. Include in your request a completed form with the exact quote defined—"I request permission to quote the following:…"—and list the exact source, including book title, author, page number, and the complete information about your publication (including title, author, publisher, price, and the relationship of the quoted material to the whole piece).

- When requesting a change of address, indicate both the old and the new address:

  Please change my address in your records

  from: 315 South Cherry
  Detroit, MI 49334

  to: 776 East Alameda
  Denver, CO 80220

- When requesting that copies of your medical records be sent to another physician, you may be required to sign a special consent form. Check on this first to save yourself time.

- If requesting a speaker to make a presentation to your group, use both special tact and precision. You will undoubtedly want to check on the potential speaker's performance record before requesting his or her services. Include complete information about the date, time, location, setting, audience size and composition, focus and subject matter of the meeting, allotted time for the speech, and a list of suggested topics, if appropriate. There's nothing quite as inappro-priate as having a "famous" writer be the guest speaker at a writers' banquet, for example, then listening to the speaker use the occasion to vent his or her unrelated political ideas, especially if you promoted the speech as "how you can sell your book."

- In making any request of a government agency, check first to learn the required form and protocol for your request. This will save you considerable effort and help ensure the response you want. If, for example, you are requesting a reevaluation of your property tax, you will undoubtedly have to include the legal lot number or other location and description information, and detailed information on values on comparative homes in your immediate area. This is usually done by producing the sales prices of homes in your immediate area, computed into the sales price per square foot.

- In writing to any governmental agency or bureaucracy, use identifying name and numbers for the best chance of receiving a response: "Please send me a copy of proposed *Bill 555-543: City Crime, May 21, by Senator Q. K. Jackson.*"

- In requesting changes in government policy, designated zones, usage, etc., do your research first. You must understand the history of a particular zoning requirement, for example, because your request must be made in terms of the inappropriateness of that designation and the reasonableness of your request. There may be any number of requirements for getting your request into the right form and then obtaining agreement among those concerned. Researching all related matters and complying with form and content requirements will increase the chances of your request being granted.

SELECT A FORMAT

- Simple personal requests for such things as sales literature or a free sample may be handwritten on a postcard, fold-over note, or personal letterhead. For longer, more complex requests, use letterhead and type the request.
- Routine business requests to another company may be made on preprinted postcards, preprinted forms, or letterhead. Longer or complex requests should be made on letterhead. If requests are done on letterhead, they should be typewritten.

WRITE STRONG SENTENCES

▶ As directed by Mr. R. Roberts, I am requesting a copy of *Patient Care 145: Health-care Reform.*

▶ I request a double, nonsmoking room (a king-size bed), on the fourth floor if possible, for Thursday, April 2. I am arriving at 3:10 P.M., on United Airlines.

▶ I think we need to have further discussion on our strategy for the Pepper account, and I request that you let me know if you have an hour available on the afternoon of either the fourteenth or fifteenth so I can set it up.

▶ Jack Adams has done some outstanding work on the job descriptions, and I would like to receive a copy of his report at your earliest convenience.

EDIT, EDIT, EDIT

Eliminate every unnecessary word to make your request crystal clear.

ALSO SEE "CREDIT INQUIRY AND PROVIDING CREDIT INFORMATION," PAGE 206; "COLLECTION LETTER," PAGE 225; "RESPONSE," PAGE 171; AND "QUERY," PAGE 161.

Report Request

(Date)

Dear Mr. Williams:

Ms. Deanna Jobs asked me to request a copy of the report passed out at the last meeting of the Atlanta Water Board of Directors. The subject of the report is projections of water usage in the year 2025.

She will appreciate receiving a copy by the fifteenth. Thank you.

Sincerely yours,

Janet Reems

Request for Order Status Information

(Date)   FAXED

Dear Bob:

REFERENCE: ORDER # 3234

There's some confusion here about the status of our order for retainers submitted on April 29. Margie Stich of your office indicated to our Louise Cole that you are out of several of the sizes we need. Please give me a status report on our order, in writing, immediately. Fax it to my office by 2 P.M.: 440-554-5656.

We must have a number of sizes in here by next Wednesday to keep production going.

Your truly,

Jim Riser

Information Request

(Date)

Dear Ms. Jackson:

I enjoyed your presentation at the Gates Tennis Club and request specific information on rates at Tennis, Inc.'s camp on the following dates:

-April 12 through April 22
-June 17 through June 27
-August 15 through August 25

Please also give me a listing of the advantages (if any) of being a guest at one time over another. I am a level 5.0 USTA evaluated player, and my objective in attending is to raise my tennis skill level to a 5.5 level. Thank you for your assistance. I look forward to your response.

Sincerely,

Walter Gill

> Make sure to give a clear request. Be specific.

> Set off information to make your request immediately apparent.

> Make your reader want to help.

Request for Job Leads

(Date)

Dear Jack:

It was nice seeing you at the National Product Managers' Association meeting in New York. I'm happy to hear that the Simmons' lead from our meeting resulted in a long-term project.

Jack, confidentially, I am casting about for product manager positions in medical instrumentation corporations with a proactive, employee fast-track philosophy. Since you are in-the-know with your consulting work, I wonder if you have any recommendations. Obviously, I will treat any information as completely confidential.

I would appreciate any direction you may be able to give here.

Regards,

Tim Bottoms

Request for Credit Report

(Date)

Dear Mr. Allen:

Reference: Credit Report for Lea Grimes, 10 Lake St., Dayton, OH S.S.# 421-44-5256

As I stated on the telephone, I was denied credit at Crooners Bank on April 10. Mr. Jesus Garcia, Customer Service Representative, said the credit report from your organization indicated a number of late payments and other credit problems.

I've enclosed a self-addressed, stamped envelope. Please send me a copy of my credit record immediately.

Yours truly,

Lea Grimes

Request for Processing of Employee Records

(Date)

Dear Mr. Snipple:

Please process the permanent employee paperwork for Jack Jumper, and issue the following:

- Status 2A clearance
- a telephone credit card
- family medical insurance coverage
- an office key to the production department

Mr. Jumper's permanent employment date is August 14, but he will leave on an out-of-town assignment on August 13. I request all his required signatures, etc., be obtained this week, and he be issued his permanent employee packet on August 12.

Please contact me by Thursday if you are unable to comply, and thank you for your efforts in this matter.

Sincerely,

Denise Diver

27

QUERY

Two sorts of writers possess genius: those who think, and those who cause others to think.

—JOSEPH ROUX

This letter is part request and part sales, a hybrid. The term *query* has been coined by writers and authors to describe the letter they send to agents at literary agencies and editors at newspapers, magazines, and book publishers (also see "Pitch Letter," page 251). It proposes an idea written in such a compelling manner as to pique the reader's interest; then it requests that the reader entertain the possibility of buying the proposed written piece from the writer. The same dual-purpose letter is used, too, by inventors, marketers, and other businesspersons to achieve the same two purposes.

The query letter has a critical and tough job, and it is, therefore, difficult to write. It demands the writer's best skills if it is to succeed. (In addition to these rules, publishers and other organizations that solicit query letters may produce their own set of guidelines, which outline the form the organization requires a query letter to take.)

DECIDE TO WRITE

You may use an effective query to
- Create interest in your idea or product and request an opportunity for a presentation
- Get an assignment to do a magazine article or book
- Interest an agent in representing your book or idea

THINK ABOUT CONTENT

- Request the organization's guidelines, if appropriate. Study these, and use any instructions given.
- Introduce your idea in the first sentence or two in a way that will grab the reader's attention.
- Make reference to any connection with the reader that is in order: "It was a pleasure meeting you at the Manufacturer's Fair. As we discussed, I invented a product that I believe will add $5 million in annual sales to your present product line without adding a single person to your present sales staff."
- Keep it focused.
- Demonstrate your knowledge of the reader's business or point of view.

- Define your approach and the scope of your idea.
- Describe your idea and product's potential benefits to the reader.
- Describe your precise qualifications in relationship to the idea or product you're offering.
- List any extras you can deliver. If this is a writing project, for example, list such things as exclusive information, 35mm slides, illustrations, photographs, charts, etc.
- Keep it short. Edit to one page in length, if possible.
- Attach samples, if appropriate.
- Enclose a self-addressed, stamped envelope for a reply.

ELIMINATE WRONG MESSAGES

- Don't allow a demanding tone to creep into your letter. Remember this is part sales, part request.
- Don't use an apologetic tone or phrases like "If it's not too much trouble, I would appreciate an indication of your interest."
- Don't include more than one idea, unless the organization's guidelines have instructed you otherwise.

CONSIDER SPECIAL SITUATIONS

- Learn as much as possible about the reader and the organization. If you're requesting the opportunity to present an idea to a venture capital group, for example, review the projects the group has funded, learn everything you can about the members of the decision-making board, and try to learn why projects were rejected.
- In writing a query letter for a magazine or newspaper, know the particular type of audience the publisher targets so you can properly slant your query.
- If you are querying a magazine, study the last twelve issues so you will eliminate subjects the publication has just covered; or give the subject a new slant, referring to the piece the publication ran.

- If it's appropriate, you may include a little humor in your query letter.
- When writing a query to a magazine editor, introduce your idea in the first paragraph. The second paragraph should describe your idea in terms that will appeal to the editor. Be sure it reflects your writing skill and voice. The third paragraph should include details of your qualifications and the extras you are offering. Tell how both relate to your idea. Give some market information, too, if possible. The fourth or last paragraph should thank the editor for his or her time and effort. End by asking for a response.
- Address your letter to the correct person. In the case of a magazine, for example, check the current publication masthead or call the publisher and ask for the name of the editor who handles your type of idea or material. In the case of a venture capital organization, research the decision makers. Contact the person you feel will be most receptive to your idea or product.
- For magazine writers it's important to know that editors often generate their own ideas. Be sure to ask about these once you have a working relationship with the publication: "I'd be happy to develop a related idea you may have in mind."
- For the magazine writer, flattering or praising the editor, if you have researched the facts carefully, and knowing, for example, that it was his or her idea to change the cover design or start a new column, can go a long way in getting your idea accepted. As one editor said, "In addressing the editor, informed praise always works, but empty flattery will do just as well!"

SELECT A FORMAT

- Submit a typed letter on high-quality letterhead. Never use less than letter-quality computer printouts.

WRITE STRONG SENTENCES

▶ I propose a research project on a small tribe of Indians almost unknown, the Tlingits.

▶ I propose a 2,000-word piece on increasing your partner's self-confidence, tentatively titled, "You're the Greatest."

▶ I'll divide our report into three sections: problems, solutions, and long-term benefits.

▶ This article will detail how your readers can change basic unhealthy eating habits forever in only fifteen days.

▶ Thank you for considering the idea; what do you think?

BUILD EFFECTIVE PARAGRAPHS

▶ "Don't Leave Home Without It" is the tentative title of a piece I'd like to do for your readers who are getting ready for vacation. Did you know, for example, that each year 95 percent of vacationing families are missing at least five vital items they need while on vacation?

▶ The best deterrent to teenage pregnancies may just be basketball—not handing out condoms in junior high or teaching a pure diet of abstinence. That's what our initial research indicates.

▶ This story and four others will demonstrate how schools are successfully raising the self-esteem of teen and preteen girls. They are creating passions and goals within their disadvantaged ranks, and they're reducing teen pregnancies.

▶ What happens to the rubber that disappears from your car's tires as they wear? No one, including top scientists, has had the answer—until now.

▶ The ozone layer, rapidly disappearing from the planet, may be saved with C.C. Chemical's new "SafeEarth" spray. Recent tests show that using "SafeEarth" three times a week can restore healthy ozone levels in five years.

▶ "In-line skating injuries," Dr. Barnes said in a news conference on Thursday, "represent the number one risk for broken bones in Larimer County." And wearing four pieces of standard protective safety pads "reduces risks by 95 percent."

EDIT, EDIT, EDIT

You must grab the reader's interest and persuade him or her to take the action you indicate.

ALSO SEE "PITCH LETTER," PAGE 251.

Magazine Query

(Date)

Dear Mr. Fitt:

"Fast and Healthy" is the tentative title of a piece I'd like to do on creating favorite munchies that replace fat and additives with healthy substitutes. I will include recipes and nutritional information for Big Mama Soyburgers, Mississippi Sly Chicken, French Favorites, Hot Apple Pies, and Me-Oh-My Chocolate Cake.

May I send you the completed 1500-word piece for your consideration?

Sincerely,

I. E. Wright

Magazine Query

(Date)

Dear Nancy:

Life Lines has done an outstanding job with the new social consciousness pieces. I thought last issue's "The Curse of Freedom" was very thought-provoking.

Along that line, I'd like to suggest "Equal Justice," which could start:

> One frozen December night outside a small North Dakota town, two Hispanic farm boys—brothers—crouched behind a parked car in the yard of their neighbor, Lt. Donald D. Dutton, a narcotics detective on the local police force. When Lt. Dutton turned off his truck engine, got out, and took his first step toward the house, the boys opened fire with shotguns. The detective was dead before he hit the ground.

Inside the house was the victim's young wife, Sarah, 29; a son, David, 5; and a daughter, Jenny, 7.

Months of local and FBI investigation coast to coast failed to turn up a single clue. It was only after a girlfriend of the younger brother told a friend at school,

Lawson/(Date)/Davis/page 2

and that friend went to police, that there was a solid lead in this case.

The brothers confessed to being hired assassins, employed by Sarah, who later testified she'd suffered ten years of physical, emotional, and sexual abuse by Lt. Dutton.

It's a riveting tale, which I'd present in 6,000 words, examining (1) why women don't leave their abusers, (2) steps friends and relatives can take to help, and (3) how we must change our laws and legal and judicial systems.

May I have an assignment? Is there any special slant you'd like?

I've enclosed three clippings of pieces I did for *News Today*, *Life Trends*, and *Women*.

Sincerely,

Kay Benson

Detailed Query Letter After Editor's Request

(Date)

Dear Ms. Brown:

As you requested on the telephone today, here's my idea. I'd just finished reading the rough draft of Crime Award–winner Tom Wick's new book, *Sudden Death*, the day that he and I had lunch.

I watched Wick approach the booth, his narrow face its usual mask, round Polo tortoise rims circling his deep-set gray eyes. His burgundy pullover was open at the neck, his roomy khakis skimmed the tops of his brown loafers. "Well, taking notes and everything." He gave me the start of a smile.

"Yes, and recording the interview if you don't mind," I nodded at my recorder.

"No, not if you can get it in here." He looked around at the boisterous lunch crowd.

We'd talked a number of times during the course of his research on this book, and now there was an electric anticipation, "So, what do you think?"

"Riveting," I said. Immediately we were into character analysis, motivation, and legal details of

this tale of a woman who, after twenty-five years, accused her father of murdering her best friend when the girls were six years old—a case of repressed, and finally recovered, memory. Or was it?

This exclusive interview with Tom Wick will contain the groundwork for what I propose as the unprecedented account of the behind-the-book investigation: "Sudden Death."

The piece will follow Wick—an attorney, a bestselling author, a psychologist, and a sociologist— as he examines the long-accepted psychological treatise of repressed memory and trauma. The woman's father was convicted of first degree murder *solely* on this daughter's "repressed" memory testimony, and the appeal process upheld the guilty verdict.

I'll excerpt Wick's book and include interviews with leading expert witnesses in the case: psychiatrists and psychologists.

I'll also chronicle the explosion this case set off in the psychological community. It has pitted expert

against expert and threatens a revolutionary examination and repudiation of some sacred cows of psychological theory and therapy, such as

- repressed memories are always real memories;
- a single trauma does not precipitate repressed memory, whereas multiple traumas often result in dissociative behavior including repressed memory;
- memories cannot be implanted;
- experts can determine if a repressed memory is true;
- experts can determine the authenticity of repression if given a psychological symptom, even long after the event.

This trial has prompted new in-depth research on trauma, true memories, and implanted or false ones. This piece will examine the question of whether the testimony in this case fits the anatomy of a repressed memory or a false memory. Further, it will address the more basic question: Is there such a thing as a repressed memory, and if so how does this mechanism work in relation to trauma?

I'll examine the two diametrically opposed research

projects now going on and will explore both theoretical bases, including quotes from these experts and others.

I can deliver a complete manuscript August 15. I will include, of course, a complete set of audio interview tapes.

I enjoyed our discussion in Dallas. As I mentioned, I have been a newspaper columnist for *The Rocky Mountain News* and *The Denver Post*, a freelance writer of magazine articles (clips attached), and a nonfiction book author.

Do you prefer a take other than the one I've outlined here? How many words would you like? My fax number, again, is (303) 844-7888; my telephone number is (303) 888-2333; my e-mail address is Fbeals888@online.net.

Sincerely,

Fiona Beals

Magazine Second Query After Editor's Suggestion

(Date)

Dear Sally:

Thanks for your call. Yes, I'll do the piece, and here's what I suggest. In my article tentatively titled "Divorce Mediation—Who Wins?," I'll cover

- How much court time mediation saves
- How much money it saves—more than 50 percent over conventional attorneys' fees
- Other benefits, including privacy (no courtroom debacles); parents maintaining control over their children's destiny; faster, less painful proceedings; and the opportunity for the kids to watch their parents resolve this most devastating situation with dignity and caring.

I will include five dynamite stories, documenting figures, and powerful quotes. I'll also tell your readers why and when it doesn't or won't work.

What do you think?

Sincerely,

Doris Ditchfield

> Grab the reader's attention early.

> Define your approach.

Query Letter to Venture Capital Organization

(Date)

Dear Ted:

As we discussed, my partner and I have perfected a method of revulcanizing rubber, which I believe could greatly benefit the retrofit commercial roofing industry.

Our initial projections indicate that, with a modest infusion of $1 million, we could return 200 percent to investors within twenty-one months.

I'm enclosing a sample of our revulcanized pieces, which have tested without tears or deterioration of any kind after exposure to 120 mile-an-hour winds and ultraviolet rays twenty times more intense than we have at 14,000 feet elevation.

We would like the opportunity to make a forty-minute presentation to your board of directors. I will call you next week to arrange a time. Thank you for your consideration; I look forward to talking with you again about those power workouts.

Sincerely,

Mark Phinney

> Grab the reader's attention. Introduce your idea early.

> Define the scope of your request.

> Make your request, and take the initiative to make the next contact.

28
COVER LETTER

A man of letters, and of manners too!

—WILLIAM COWPER

The cover letter is a personal message to the reader, accompanying something you are sending him or her and taking the place of what you would say to the reader if you were face-to-face. It offers pertinent information about the contents and composition of what it is attached to. (When you are sending a report to a group of readers, a foreword or preface may be used instead of the cover letter.)

If your cover letter accompanies a report, first tell the reader so, then include the goal of the report and refer to its authorization.

The resume cover letter is exactly that. It states who you are and why you're writing and asks the reader for an answer. It should be brief and, most important, it should highlight your resume.

DECIDE TO WRITE

Use a cover letter when you send

- Reports, proposals, contracts, agreements, and other documents
- Applications
- Manuscripts
- Resumes
- Instruction manuals, booklets, or sheets
- Contributions
- Samples, prototypes
- Checks unaccompanied by a copy of an invoice or a statement
- Complimentary tickets

THINK ABOUT CONTENT

- State what is enclosed, attached, or has been sent under a separate cover. If you are responding to a request, name the requesting person.
- If appropriate, give the number of enclosures, or make a brief listing of the contents.
- State the purpose or goal of the contents and who authorized them.
- If needed, explain how to use the contents.
- End on a note of goodwill.

ELIMINATE WRONG MESSAGES

- Don't be verbose or repeat, verbatim, information from the document. The cover letter should not exceed one-eighth the length of the report.
- Do not write a cover letter that is inconsistent with the "voice" and tone of the report. This applies to the form and format, too.

CONSIDER SPECIAL SITUATIONS

- Report cover letters should name the report, tell why it was written, who authorized it, its contributors, and then briefly summarize it.
- Cover letters for manuscripts sent to a publisher or agent are some of the most challenging in this category. Publishers often require that authors describe their manuscripts in one short paragraph that compels editors to read on.
- Routine items are usually self-explanatory and do not require a cover letter. These items include invoices, payments, shipments, or other specialized letters.
- Sample or sales literature cover letters need to be unique and also explanatory (see "Sales," page 231).
- Resume cover letters need to snag the interest of the reader so he or she will read the resume. Use the special techniques in "Resume Cover Letter," page 69.

SELECT A FORMAT

- The standard format is a typed letter on business letterhead.
- For interoffice use, a company memo is the proper vehicle. The memo is sometimes used, too, for clients and for colleagues in organizations with which you have an ongoing working relationship.
- The form of the cover letter should be consistent with the contents of the mailing. When its function is sales and there is an enclosed sample or "gift," an attention-getting note is usually the best choice.

WRITE STRONG SENTENCES

Focus on the content—what you're sending and your objective. Concisely describe both.

▶ I've enclosed copies of check numbers 346, 754, 332, and 987 as you requested.

▶ Your feedback to this initial report will be greatly appreciated.

▶ You may also want copies of our Report #443 on changes in the habitat.

▶ This is your free copy to keep.

BUILD EFFECTIVE PARAGRAPHS

▶ I'm returning the spacer prototypes you sent. We tested these on our neoprene elastomeric roof installation and found the spacers would not withstand the wind uplift. Our installation details, test conditions, and phased results are included in the final report enclosed.

▶ Here's my synopsis and chapter outline for *The Owner's Manual for Retirement,* the humor gift book we discussed. What do you think?

▶ This new Employee Manual A-40 was designed to deal with our current issues of diversity at Cobal. Carefully review each section, especially the summaries, and give me your feedback by April 10.

▶ For everything that goes "squeak," now there's Quiet. Try this sample on your biggest noisemakers, and you'll never go back to wimpy lubricants.

▶ Did you think you'd never find a bandage that would stick? Try this new Bonzo on your next boo-boo.

▶ Thank you for your interest in the Gus Grant Program. Complete the enclosed form and return it to us by September 1 to be eligible for grant funds.

EDIT, EDIT, EDIT

Make sure your cover letter is focused and concise.

ALSO SEE "RESUME COVER LETTER," PAGE 69, AND "SALES," PAGE 231.

Internal Transmittal Memo

Memo
(Date)
TO: Jake Johnson, Ted Tobin, Mary Grey
FROM: Annette Madison
SUBJECT: Annual Report, Draft IV

State contents.

We have incorporated the changes and comments from each of you. In your review please pay special attention to the figures on pages 12, 14, and 17. I believe the new company goals statement and the summary on page 25 are now much stronger.

We will need your final comments by Friday at noon. Thank you.

End on a goodwill note.

Cover Letter for Franchise Agreement

(Date)

Dear Mr. Beemer:

Enclosed is the franchise application, which I have amended according to our discussion. Please carefully review the amendments as well as the insertions on pages 4, 5, 9, and 11. I believe this now represents a fair and equitable agreement with the parent company, Pets, and it is my belief this will be an extremely profitable endeavor for Dog Kisses, Inc.

Please call me if you have any further concerns or questions. If not, please sign the four copies, and return them to me. I've enclosed an extra copy for your files.

Thank you.

Yours truly,

Michael Beers

General Cover Letter for Annual Report

(Date)

Dear Ms. Miller:

I'm enclosing our latest annual report. I hope this contains the kind of information you want on the goals and success of the company, especially in the past two years. You will find those figures and comparisons on pages 5 through 12, precisely. But the entire report gives the complete picture of Cantos expansion and growth.

Thank you for your interest in our company, and please call me if you need any further information.

Yours truly,

Victor Weise

Cover Letter for Photograph Negatives

(Date)

Dear Mr. Mann:

Here are the twelve prints of negatives 24A-C as you requested. We did go back in and touch up the negatives, and I believe the results are excellent.

Thank you for selecting Prints, Inc., for your developing needs. We look forward to serving you in the future. Call on us any time.

Best regards,

Alfred F. Newsman

Cover Letter for Shipment

(Date)

Dear Ms. Betts:

Here's a copy of the new brochure. Under separate cover I'm sending the 450 brochures. The four-color printing is beautiful. It was the right decision to use the fall cover photo. This brochure will be a very effective one for you, I'm sure.

All the brochures will be delivered to the central office Tuesday morning. Don't hesitate to call me if you want some taken to the branch offices. We can easily do that.

We look forward to working with you again.

Sincerely,

Stanley Barker

Cover Letter for Broken Part

(Date)

Dear Mr. Dean:

As you requested yesterday on the telephone, I've enclosed the broken desk handle. I've also enclosed a photograph of the desk with the broken handle in place.

Please send me a new handle as soon as possible.

Thank you.

Sincerely,

Donald Costa

Cover Letter for Report

(Date)

Dear Mr. Able:

Here is the salespeople report on the survey you asked us to conduct last August 15. As you can see, our observations pointed to some specific needs for new and extensive sales training.

Following the procedures we outlined and you approved in September, we have included these needs in a revised curriculum plan that we will submit to your training director, Jim Bacon, on November 10. We are confident this curriculum will help correct the skill level deficits of your sales force.

We appreciate the opportunity to serve you. If you want to review any of the details here, please call me.

Sincerely yours,

Robert Berke

Writing, when properly managed (as you may be sure I think mine is), is but a different name for conversation.

—LAURENCE STERNE

A letter of response, whether business or personal, usually takes less time if written immediately. Procrastination is not only a bad habit, it may affect your business and reputation.

Many successful businesses have been built upon the simple principle of a prompt, thorough response. It says to the customer, "I value you, I understand what you want, and your business is important to me." If you remember that corresponding is like a conversation, you will realize that most communications you receive deserve a timely response.

- An inquiry
- An announcement
- A gift (see "Appreciation and Thank-You," page 55)
- A request (for a contribution, payment, letter of reference, etc.)
- Information
- A note of condolence or sympathy (see "Condolence and Sympathy," page 38)
- An apology
- A complaint

DECIDE TO WRITE

The idea is not to create a communications blizzard. A written response is not required or wise in every situation. Often in business, for example, a verbal "Thanks for the information memo, Bob," is the best response. Common sense and company protocol are the bywords here. Many companies state that outside correspondence always requires a written response; internal correspondence often requires only a verbal one. Consider writing a response when you receive

- An invitation (see also "Invitations," page 48, "Appreciation and Thank-You," page 55, and "Refusal," page 186)

THINK ABOUT CONTENT

- State your business, the reason for the response. This is usually a mention of the communication you received: "Thank you for your letter of July 12 requesting the shipping date of the Wickets."
- Make your response both complete and as brief as possible.
- Be sure you have responded to all the points of the recipient's correspondence. Sometimes it is best to organize your response in the order of the communication you received, e.g., "In paragraph one of your letter…"

- Use indenting, bullets, dashes, and the wise use of white space in long or complicated responses to help make your response clear.
- Repeat vital information like the date, time, and location of a meeting.
- Offer other sources of assistance, when appropriate. Make it easier for an inquirer to follow up by offering additional contact names, numbers, and addresses.
- Immediate acknowledgment is the first and best line of action in your response. Often letters of inquiry, requests for information, complaints, etc., require some work before an intelligent and comprehensive response can be given. Acknowledge the letter and tell the reader you are working on a more complete response.
- A response letter to customers should offer value added whenever possible. Many companies have built a strong and loyal customer base by expending that extra effort to include a pertinent research report or send valuable samples of the product. This does not mean stuffing a huge envelope with unrelated sales information, which is never appreciated. It also doesn't mean dodging the point of inquiry.
- Responses to invitations should match the invitation. If the invitation is in the third person, for example, respond in the third person: "Alex and Mable Wilborough, accept with pleasure Frank and Edna Edmonds' kind invitation for dinner on Thursday, the twelfth of June at eight o'clock." If there is an R.S.V.P., you are obliged to respond as promptly as possible, in writing, or call, whichever the invitation indicates. "Regrets only" on an invitation means you are not required to respond if you will attend. However, if two people are invited and one will not attend, if other commitments require you to be late, or if other special circumstances exist, convey this to the host by calling in a timely manner, or by a response note (also see "Invitations," page 48).
- Invite further correspondence, if appropriate.

ELIMINATE WRONG MESSAGES

- As a rule, do not go beyond the scope of the correspondence you received. (This is a rule sometimes wisely broken.)
- Do not let correspondence go unanswered. A polite response is always in order, even in cases where a rude or unmerited complaint has been received, the wrong company has been contacted, or the request seems ridiculous.
- Rude or insensitive responses are never in order. Don't ever be numbered among those who send a perhaps well-meaning but insensitive response—or one that contains a moral judgment—to someone who has had bad news or has suffered a loss.
- Never let your response start with "Sorry I didn't respond sooner, but…" The proper way to handle this is to respond immediately with something like "I am looking into a solution for your problem…and I will be in touch as soon as I…"

CONSIDER EXCEPTIONAL SITUATIONS

- Complaints require immediate responses. Agree on some point with the writer or thank him or her for writing. Relate the action that has been (or is being) taken, and conclude with a goodwill statement.
- A threatening or abusive letter must be handled very carefully. If litigation is mentioned or implied, it is best to refer the matter to an attorney. If there is a particularly threatening tone, refer the matter to the proper authorities. If it is simply an angry letter, respond as respectfully and objectively as possible, expressing that you are sorry the writer is upset.
- Responses to personal requests for contributions should include an opening statement of why you are, or aren't, donating. Enclose the provided form, if any, and request a receipt, if you need it for tax purposes.
- Respond to invitations to celebrations like birthday parties, anniversaries, Bar or Bat Mitzvahs, etc., in a like manner to the invitation. A commercial greeting card with a personal

message is appropriate, even if you won't attend, and a gift depends upon your relationship to the guest of honor.

- Messages and expressions of condolence and sympathy require a written response. This can take a number of forms: (1) written notes, (2) printed thank-yous with written notes to those who were close to the deceased, ill, or injured person, or (3) a thank-you message placed in the local newspaper for someone who is or was a public figure. Responses certainly may be brief and may be handled by a designated person outside the immediate family. Responses should be sent within six weeks of the event or, in the case of an injured or ill person, as soon as the person is able. (See "Condolence and Sympathy," page 38.)

SELECT A FORMAT

- Business responses should be typed on company stationery.
- With computers, responses to requests you receive are made more simple. Send a personal, sincere response—although it may be almost entirely a "boilerplate."

BUILD STRONG SENTENCES

▶ If I can answer any further questions, please don't hesitate to call or write.

▶ We were sorry to learn that the fishing rod you purchased on October 5 isn't satisfactory, and we are happy to offer you a full credit refund or replacement for the defective rod.

▶ Please accept my apology for the error in your January billing. Your account has now been credited with the amount of $45.87.

▶ You are a valued customer, and we will do everything possible to resolve this problem.

BUILD EFFECTIVE PARAGRAPHS

▶ Here is the research report on the milk contamination in New York. We will put you on our mailing list to receive further reports as they become available.

▶ Your letter concerning a customer service problem in our Englewood store has reached me for handling. I am presently investigating this incident and will be in contact with you within the next two weeks to report what I've learned. I am sorry you had an unpleasant experience in our store, and I will do everything I can to try to resolve it to your satisfaction.

▶ I was very surprised to learn you received two instead of one Model C-120 Monitor. Thank you for returning one. Enclosed is reimbursement for the postage and a certificate for you to use in your next purchase of a Basco product.

▶ Thank you for detailing for me your frustration in trying to return the Wacket Thumper. I will investigate the event in the next two weeks, and then I will be in touch with you again. In the meantime, on behalf of Wacket, please accept our most sincere apologies for an unpleasant experience.

▶ We are shipping you two dinner plates today to replace the two you reported arrived broken. I'm sorry this happened. You should have the replacement plates in three days.

▶ Yes, we certainly will honor our guarantee, and I'm glad you brought it to our attention that salespeople in our store are not aware of the details of this policy. Please return your battery to Steve Watson at Store #31, Yosemite and Arapahoe, and he will take care of it.

EDIT, EDIT, EDIT

Be sure your message is clear and your communication ends on a positive note.

ALSO SEE "COMPLAINT," PAGE 193.

Response to Customer Dissatisfaction

(Date)

Dear Mrs. Lincoln:

I'm sorry the draperies for the yellow room aren't what you envisioned. Of course we'll work with you to come to a satisfactory solution. Our interior decorator did survey the room, and he has three possible solutions:

1. We can repaint the walls, adding white pigment to the original paint you selected;
2. We can add a valance in a Schumacher designer fabric to the draperies which will majestically blend wall and drapery colors and pull the entire room together; or
3. We can refit these draperies for use in another room and start over with another fabric.

I shall call you on Thursday to arrange a time to bring over a number of samples that will make these alternatives visually clear. Mr. Roberts feels you will be extremely satisfied with any of these solutions.

Sincerely,

Gloria Van der Bloom

State your business.

Make your response complete and brief.

Response to Customer for Error

(Date)

Dear Mrs. Wiley:

I'm sorry your request for a change in your payment plan was mishandled. I'm still looking into how you could have received a form letter for a delinquent account, and I will explain it when I learn the details.

I have resolved the other matter, and the terms of your extension and the amount of future payments are detailed on the enclosed contract. Please review it, and call me if you have any questions. We value your business, and thank you for working to resolve this misunderstanding.

Sincerely,

Michael Clinton

Response to Request to Alter Price

(Date)

Dear Mr. and Mrs. Finley:

Thank you for your letter listing the items that need to be repaired on the house at 1010 Statesman Street before you feel you are willing to make an offer. This may be handled in one of two ways: (1) you may request the present owner make these repairs, or (2) you may estimate the cost of these repairs, list them, and total them. The total may then be deducted from your formal offer price.

Thank you again for being so alert, and I will be happy to work with you in any way possible—I have sources for bids on repairing these items—so you may complete your computations. I shall call you next week to learn your decision.

Sincerely,

Ronald Q. Moe

Response to Request for Replacement Product

(Date)

Dear Mr. Brokett:

Your request for a replacement motor for the Decker Docker saw is being reviewed by our service department at the store where you purchased it. Mr. Fred Mamet, the service manager, will need to see the saw to make a final determination, and he requests that you call him between 9 A.M. and 5 P.M., Monday through Friday, to arrange a time to take the saw in.

I'm sorry you had this problem, and we will work with you to get it resolved.

Sincerely,

Mike Bolster

Response to Damaged Product

(Date)

Dear Mrs. Baxter:

Thank you for your immediate letter notifying us that the glass coffee table, The Imperial Fox, arrived with a scratch. We will deliver a replacement table and pick up the scratched one on Thursday, between 2:00 P.M. and 5:00 P.M. If this time is inconvenient, please call the delivery department and ask for Max, at 334-4400.

Thank you again, and I hope you enjoy the new table.

Sincerely,

Thelma Reed
Customer Service

30

CONFIRMATION

... the second rule of communicating is to tell 'em that you told 'em.

—ANONYMOUS

The letter of confirmation is the tool of business record-keeping. Its primary purpose is to retell the recipient what action was taken, to reaffirm the decisions made and terms agreed to.

This letter may certainly have a number of secondary purposes, including acknowledgment, building goodwill, thanks, appreciation, and acceptance.

DECIDE TO WRITE

You may want to use this letter to

- Acknowledge materials, documents, items received, or confirm discussions held
- Reiterate decisions made
- Confirm upcoming meeting information or attendance
- Verify (confirm) reservations
- Create a record

THINK ABOUT CONTENT

- Confirmation letters may easily become hybrids. When a letter confirms the decisions of a meeting between sender and a client, it may go into explanations of the positions, discussions, and changes involved in reaching a decision.
- It is entirely acceptable to include your own confirmation postcard upon which the reader checks an item or pens a brief response. Authors may send self-addressed postcards, for example, to receive an immediate confirmation from publishers that their manuscripts have been received. Grant applications, legal documents, and many other types of notices are treated in the same manner. The postal service offers the same kind of a confirmation of receipt.
- State the points to be confirmed in the context of action taken, discussion, information received, and date, time, place, etc. Brief, complete information is best. Most true confirmation letters are only a few sentences.
- Give any and all pertinent supplementary identifying information, including how to contact you.
- Close with a friendly comment, and thank the reader for his or her efforts.

- Include a signature line for the recipient if the letter is to become a legal agreement or contract.

ELIMINATE WRONG MESSAGES

- Avoid talking down to the reader: "Be sure to make a note to bring your calendar…" Keep the message brief and objective.
- Don't let a simplistic tone creep in.
- Do not go beyond the bounds of confirming information.
- Don't list future, unrelated action items, or try to persuade.

CONSIDER SPECIAL SITUATIONS

- Confirmations for reservations at hotels, motels, the theater, fundraisers, etc., may mean that you are agreeing to pay for the reserved item, whether you use it or not. Confirmation is often made by telephone and involves giving a credit card number. When payment is involved or reservations include special preparation or accommodations, a written confirmation may also be required. In this case, be very specific about date, time of arrival, length of stay, price, accommodations, special arrangements and provisions, specific facilities, and inclusions.
- It is always good to confirm you have received a customer or client order, agreement, change, or special request. Keep the confirmation letter brief, and include a friendly close.
- Confirmation letters are required when the intended recipient is not available to respond. In this case, the designated person should send a brief letter confirming receipt and stating that the intended recipient will respond as soon as possible.
- A confirmation should be sent in response to an invitation if the host requests it. This is often done on an informal fold-over notecard (see "Invitations," page 48).

SELECT A FORMAT

- Postcards, form notes, or letters can be used for routine confirmations to indicate receipt of manuscripts, documents, requests, packages, etc. These may be printed so the sender simply checks the appropriate message:

  ___ We have received your proposal.

  ___ We will get back to you with a response in approximately ___ weeks.

- Business confirmations that must be composed should be typed on letterhead.
- Interoffice confirmations may be done on simple, printed memo forms that allow the sender to check the appropriate response and pen a short note.

WRITE STRONG SENTENCES

Start with the action, and write a concise statement.

▶ Thanks for your call. I'm looking forward to our meeting next week.

▶ This will confirm my reservations for Friday, April 4, through Monday, April 8, for the following accommodations.

▶ The five cartons of computer parts were just sent by air express. [Faxed.]

▶ This confirms our agreement that your company will start the renovation on Monday, April 1.

▶ The Jackson Report arrived in our office this morning, and we will be meeting to review it on Wednesday.

BUILD EFFECTIVE PARAGRAPHS

▶ As we agreed on the telephone, Rounder and Long will be pleased to represent you in the Webster matter. I have set up a meeting on Thursday, October 7, at 2:00 P.M. with Bill Webster here in my office. I shall be in contact with you immediately after that meeting.

▶ We have received your application to be part of the aging study. We have been overwhelmed with applications, and it will require another two weeks for us to process them and select the participants. Please be patient and we will contact you in approximately three weeks.

▶ Thank you for your grant application, which we have now received. The winners will be announced on July 15, and all applicants supplying the requested postcard will be immediately notified.

EDIT, EDIT, EDIT

Make sure your communication is simple, clear, and complete.

Confirming and Documenting Agreement

(Date)

Dear Mr. Beevis:

This confirms our agreement of this morning's telephone conversation. Yes, you may have access to your pastureland by using my private road as long as your conduct causes no stress or threat to my livestock grazing in the adjoining pasture.

Yours truly,

Bea Holden

Confirming Verbal Changes in Employment Agreement

(Date)

Dear Ms. Buhl:

This confirms the changes we made this morning on the telephone to your employment agreement. We will (1) increase the salary to $65,000 per year, (2) the vacation days after one year of employment will be ten, and (3) your bonus percentage will be raised to 7 percent.

Please make these changes in the contract, initial them, sign them, and send them back to me for my signature.

We are so pleased to have you aboard. Welcome! I feel sure your relationship with Conning will be an extremely rewarding one.

Sincerely,

Cheryl Gunliffe

Confirmation of Receipt of Information

(Date)

Dear Mr. Logan:

We have now received your mortgage loan application. Because of the number of credit references, employers, and previous lenders on your application, please allow six weeks for loan processing. → State the point of your letter.

If you have any questions, please contact Bonnie McGregor at 334-7777. → Give contact information.

Sincerely,

Thurston Blocker

Confirming a Speaking Engagement

(Date)

Dear Janet:

I will be happy to accept the January 5, 1:00 P.M. panel slot on your "Where's the Information Superhighway Headed?" panel to be held in the Marker Hotel's Ball Room. I will also teach the two breakout sessions at 2:00 and 3:00 P.M. as you requested.

My secretary will confirm my hotel reservation. I understand you will confirm the room setup, and make sure that the computer, overhead projector, slide projector, and microphone are provided, set up and ready to go in my classroom.

I look forward to being a part of your program.

Yours truly,

Donna Zickermann

Confirmation of Nomination

(Date)

Dear Alice:

I will accept the nomination to serve as next year's president of Hers, as long as you agree to be vice president.

It should be a great opportunity to work together. I look forward to it.

Sincerely,

Valerie Sower

Confirmation and Agreement for Speaker

(Date)

Dear Silvia:

We at Business Women are so pleased you have agreed to be our premier speaker at this year's Convention banquet at the Peachtree Hotel on June 5.

State your business.

The setting for our meetings will be informal, starting with a cocktail hour at 6:30 P.M. in the Blossoms Room. Dinner will be served at 7:30. You will be introduced by Janet Rewfrow at 8:30 P.M., and we have allowed thirty minutes for your presentation, with another fifteen minutes for a questions-and-answers period to follow immediately.

Business Women will pay you $2,500 for your participation, plus we will cover the cost of your flight, room, and meals on June 5.

Give all the pertinent information.

The audience, an expected 400, will be composed of member professionals who will be well-versed in sexual harassment issues. Their questions, I expect, will center around cases and verdicts, outcomes in terms of financial settlements to plaintiffs, and future legal trends. We will be set up with an overhead projector and lapel microphone ready for you. Please plan to bring any handouts because getting

Radwitz/(Date)/page 2

copies made was a problem last year. As agreed, you may bring copies of your book for participants to purchase. We can furnish a volunteer to handle book sales if you like.

Rudy Wilkes, who will be carrying a sign with your name on it, will meet your flight: United #221, arriving in Atlanta at 7:30 P.M. on June 4. If there is any change in your plans, please call Rudy at (404) 677-9888.

I will arrive at the Peachtree on June 4 at about 4:00 P.M. I have reserved room 433. Please leave me a message after you arrive.

If there is any additional equipment you want for your presentation, please contact Sally Dithers at our offices, extension 256, as soon as possible.

Close with a friendly statement.

We are so delighted you will be joining us this year. Please sign both copies, confirming you agree to these terms, and return one copy to me.

Yours truly,

Sadie Hawker

_____   _____
Silvia Radwitz   Date

31
ACCEPTANCE

What comes from the heart goes to the heart.

—S. T. COLERIDGE

A letter accepting a dinner invitation is easy. Just express your gratitude and anticipation of the dinner. For formal invitations responding may be even simpler because there may be an R.S.V.P. acceptance card, which must only be filled in and returned.

Accepting a job offer or an invitation to be a seminar speaker is more difficult. Your letter may be the only documentation of the agreed-upon terms. Be sure of your decision to accept, then write in a timely manner.

DECIDE TO WRITE

Use this communication to respond to
- An invitation to a wedding, dinner, party, meeting, seminar, conference, or hospitality
- A job offer
- Proposal, bid, contract, or change to these
- Request for contribution, donation, favor, help, or recommendation
- Membership approval or invitation to join a club, association, organization, committee, or commission

THINK ABOUT CONTENT
- Consider the person issuing the invitation, especially in the case of a dinner or party.
- Address your acceptance to the person from whom the invitation came.
- Thank the reader for the invitation.
- State your acceptance, expressing your pleasure at being able to accept.
- Confirm the time, place, and details, if appropriate.
- End with a statement of anticipation or your expectations for the event. (If you find this difficult, it may be better to decline the invitation.)

ELIMINATE WRONG MESSAGES
- Don't digress into unrelated business.
- Avoid placing conditions or qualifications on your acceptance. Your acceptance should not place conditions or additional demands on the host.

CONSIDER SPECIAL SITUATIONS
- Timing is always important. Send your acceptance within a day of receiving it, or as soon after as possible.
- If you have questions, call the host or designated person for clarification.

- When the acceptance is for one of an invited couple, check with the host, if appropriate, to make sure this does not present a problem.
- In accepting a television interview or seminar speaking invitation, be sure you understand all the requirements and details. The first paragraph of your letter—after you state your acceptance, the time, date, and place—should include any details or questions to be addressed before the event. And be sure the topic is mutually agreed upon in writing. There is no such thing as an "open-ended" interview.
- Teach children early to write acceptances.
- If something comes up after you have accepted, call the host immediately and explain.

SELECT A FORMAT

Make your reply consistent with the invitation. A typed invitation on a business letterhead requires a typed acceptance on a business letterhead; an informal handwritten invitation requires an informal acceptance, usually a telephone call. The exception is if you receive an engraved invitation, and there is no enclosed, engraved reply card. Send a handwritten reply on a card or fold-over note using the same words and layout as the invitation:

> Mr. Horacio and Ms. Katherine Phinney accept with pleasure the kind invitation of Mr. Peter and Ms. Nancy Kowaleski for dinner on Saturday, the tenth of December, at eight o'clock.

WRITE STRONG SENTENCES

▶ We respectfully accept the invitation to attend the State dinner.

▶ Yes, I would be pleased to present the "Stock Watch" portion of the Investors' Program on March 12, 2:30 P.M. at the Bellview.

▶ Please count on me for the Board of Directors Meeting, January 12, at 7:00 P.M. at the Club House.

▶ We certainly wouldn't miss the opening game of the Tigers, and we accept your kind invitation for the tailgate party at 2:00 P.M.

BUILD EFFECTIVE PARAGRAPHS

▶ I am extremely pleased to be voted into the Businesswoman's Hall of Fame. It is truly an honor. I shall look forward to the banquet on February 15, 7:00 P.M., at the Turner Center.

▶ We are pleased to inform you that your bid for the reroofing of the sports center has been accepted. Please call me to arrange a time to sit down and discuss the start date and other details.

▶ Jenny and I will be delighted to come to your Halloween party. I bet you won't guess who we are.

EDIT, EDIT, EDIT

Use clear and concise language.

ALSO SEE "INVITATIONS," PAGE 48, AND "REFUSAL," PAGE 186.

Acceptance to Appear as TV Interviewee

(Date)

Dear Anne:

Thank you for your invitation to be a guest on *Business Talks*. I will arrive at the 4News studios at 1:00 P.M. on Thursday, June 5, for the preparation before taping the segment. I understand the topic is "Starting a New Business," and I will be prepared to go through the basic steps. I shall bring five four-color charts with bulleted items. I will be prepared to answer your questions about accounting, legal counsel, banking, and consultant resources for new entrepreneurs in our community. I would also like to know the names and organizations of the other two guests who will appear on the program, and their exact topic areas.

I have been instructed by my wardrobe people not to wear white or large prints. If there are any other cautions or directions in this area or tips on preparing for the make-up session I should know before I arrive, please contact my secretary, Biddie Brindle.

I look forward to it.

Sincerely,

Denise Copperfield

> Thank the reader for the invitation.

> Confirm the details.

> End with a statement of anticipation.

Acceptance of Proposal

(Date)

Dear Mr. Hill:

Congratulations. Your proposal to provide public relations counsel for the Celebrity Tennis Tournament has been accepted.

We will want to amend the proposal, as discussed, to include the handling of our brochures, press releases, the annual report, and other written communications.

The telephone surveys and letters will be handled by our public affairs department. Mr. Corey Kettle will be in charge of these activities, and he will also be the person to whom you will report.

Please make the above changes in the contract, and call me to arrange a time for all of us to get together. We all look forward to working with you.

Sincerely,

Donahue Bugle

College Acceptance

(Date)

Dear Byron:

We are happy to announce that you have been accepted to Smuthers for the fall semester. Congratulations! A complete schedule of orientation activities and events is enclosed.

Most of your classmates will arrive here on August 28. We request that all new students go directly to Haver Hall to check in, and there you can set a time to meet with your counselor.

We look forward to having you at Smuthers.

Sincerely,

Jimmie Dithers

Accepting a Wedding Anniversary Invitation

(Date)

Dear Satchel:

Rachel and I accept with pleasure your kind invitation to attend the twenty-fifth wedding celebration for your parents, James and Demi Whittman, on July 7, at the Grange Hall, 4:00 P.M.

Sincerely,

Darrel Demming

Formal Acceptance for One

Ms. Catherine Bauer
accepts with pleasure
Robert Q. Jackson and Lila Simpson's
kind invitation to a dinner
on the tenth of August at 7:00 P.M.
but regrets that
Howard Philpott
will be unable to attend.

Accepting a Request to Write a Recommendation

(Date)

Dear Darin:

I am delighted to accept the invitation to write a letter of reference for you to the Dean at Bowens. I shall sit down and do it right now.

I'll be eager to hear how it turns out, and I'll keep my fingers crossed. I could never tell you before, of course, but you were always one of my favorite students.

Cordially,

Bernie Hill

Acceptance of Informal Business Meeting Invitation

(Date)

Dear Melvin:

I was pleased to receive your telephone call and letter of invitation to attend the Germ Inhalant Committee initial luncheon meeting on September 16 at noon at the Regency in Denver. I will fly in the evening before and stay at the Regency overnight. (My secretary will make all those arrangements.)

I will bring twelve copies of the Sneezer's Report and information on conference facilities in Tahoe.

Thank you for arranging this first meeting. I'm pleased and eager to work on this worthwhile project.

Sincerely,

Conrad Greeves

Accepting an Informal Invitation with Substitution

(Date)

Dear Nina:

Thank you for extending the invitation for me to represent Nickors at the annual Fireman's Banquet in New York on October 10, but I will need to modify the topic area you request, as I discussed with you, from "Trends in Inhalation Techniques" to "Equipment for the New Century." I've enclosed a copy of the presentation I made last week in Los Angeles.

I will be pleased to make the presentation in the 40-minute format, and all the equipment you have listed in your letter of August 12 will be needed. The accommodations you have described are fine.

Please call me with any additional details as they become available. I'm looking forward to attending the banquet and believe the audience will be especially pleased with the new developments I will describe.

Sincerely,

Ezra Newton

32

REFUSAL

It is not the hand but the understanding of the man that may be said to write.

—MIGUEL DE CERVANTES

The refusal letter has two main goals: to say no and, at the same time, to promote goodwill. The bad news may be preceded by a positive statement, or, if you know the reader prefers directness or will receive the bad news routinely, use a direct approach. In either case, end with a goodwill statement.

DECIDE TO WRITE

Use this letter in responding to
- Credit applications (see "Credit Inquiry and Providing Credit Information," page 206, and "Credit Approval and Refusal," page 212)
- Requests for volunteer participation, financial contributions and donations, letters of reference, loans, bids, raises, appointments, meetings, and interviews
- Adjustments (see "Credit—Requesting an Adjustment in Payment," page 218)
- Returns
- Gifts
- Sales
- Invitations to social events, dinner parties, fund-raisers, weddings, etc. (see "Invitations," page 48)

THINK ABOUT CONTENT

- First be sure you understand the request or problem.
- Determine a logical explanation or reason for your refusal, making an effort to empathize with the reader during this process.
- Open with a sentence that sets up the explanation. It may be a thank-you, it may agree with the reader on some point, or it may combine an agreement and an apology. This helps set a positive tone for the letter and helps to gain the reader's cooperation. Begin with a neutral response to the request, to help set up your next statement: "Your efforts to establish the Young Authors' Scholarship Fund are very commendable. I wish you success in this worthy endeavor." This is preferable to opening with "We cannot contribute to the Young Authors' Scholarship Fund."

- By using an indirect approach the reader is ushered through the logic or reason for your refusal before he or she reads the refusal itself. This allows him or her to gain more understanding of why you are saying no: "We at Great Water value promoting young literary talent. That's exactly the reason we budget five percent of profits each fiscal year to support such causes."
- Stating your case in positive terms can make all the difference:

  > We have already committed this year's budgeted funds, but we will place your request in our file for consideration for next year. Please contact me again in December with updated information about your needs for next year.

- Always be tactful, even in the face of an outrageous request, and make your refusal devoid of personalities and comparisons.
- Make your refusal clear, unequivocal, and positive.
- Include a counterproposal, compromise, or a suggestion if possible: "Ms. Susan Sloan is a very qualified speaker who has won several awards for her presentation skills. She would do an excellent job."
- Close with a goodwill statement, such as best wishes, or an unrelated compliment: "Best wishes for the success of this year's Young Authors' Fund project. I look forward to hearing from you in December."

ELIMINATE WRONG MESSAGES

- Don't make negative statements.
- Don't offer excuses.
- Avoid unconvincing arguments or opening opportunities for the reader to debate the matter further.
- Don't be harsh.
- Lying is not a good approach.
- Never blame others for your refusal.

CONSIDER SPECIAL SITUATIONS

- In the case of an invitation, the refusal letter sometimes becomes an apology (see "Invitations," page 48).
- In refusing an invitation, send your letter or note to the person listed under R.S.V.P. or the first host, and mention any others listed on the invitation.
- Explanations for refusing an invitation will depend upon the type of event, the number of attendees, your relationship to the host, and your function at the event. If you are invited to be an attendee at a large convention, seminar, or conference, you may not be obliged to respond, or you may make only a cursory refusal: "I will be unable to attend… " If you are scheduled as the keynote speaker at an International Banquet of 2,000 clients, your refusal—especially if you initially accepted and are now refusing—should be a detailed explanation. You should also, if possible, make suggestions about a replacement.
- When you decline to do a favor such as a letter of reference, an introduction, or setting up a meeting, you are not obliged to explain yourself.
- The adjustment refusal letter should begin with a neutral statement that sets up your next statement of strategy but does not give away your decision. The next statement should be a positive and factual explanation. You must then refuse clearly and positively and, if you can, offer a counterproposal. Remember to make your statements in positive terms. Conclude with a complimentary, encouraging, or upbeat message.
- When you use a direct refusal, be sure to start with a warm greeting or neutral opening: "Thank you for your letter of May 20 asking me to volunteer as scout master." In the case of a personal friend, the refusal can open casually: "It was great to hear from you." State your refusal in positive terms: "My commitment to the Safe Neighborhoods Project this year demands all my spare time."
- Be sure to completely identify the request you're refusing by naming the project, date, and time.
- Direct your letter to the proper person.

- Remember that your objective in refusing business credit and adjustment requests is to keep the customer or client. Offer an alternative solution or counterproposal whenever possible. It is especially important here to set up the logic of your explanation and lead the reader through it in an effort to appeal to his or her sense of fair play. It is also important to be firm and positive in tone: "We extend a line of credit to businesses that have operated in this location for over one year. We would invite you to reapply to Mr. Albert Green in November with the references listed on the enclosed sheet, and we sincerely hope to do business with Sun Screens at that time. In the meantime, please consider the advantages of setting up all your company checking on First Bank's 'System One Plan' as a preliminary step."
- Refusing inducements and gifts can be done by thanking the reader and then stating a firm policy of turning down all such offers or items.
- In refusing bids for a job or project, be as helpful and informative as applicable regulations will allow. The bidder probably expended a considerable amount of time, energy, and, perhaps, funds in an effort to get your business. He or she deserves as much courtesy and support as you can offer. Also remember the reader may be a future supplier. List areas or items where the bid did not meet specifications or guidelines, and, if possible, list why the winning bid was awarded the work. Close on an upbeat note.
- Keep blame out of your refusal letters. When terminating business or personal relationships, objective information and taking participant responsibility are the best approaches. Honesty, tact, and kindness are the principles here, and it is wise to avoid detailed explanations. Your decision should be briefly stated, firm, and clear.

SELECT A FORMAT

- Personal refusals are often handwritten.
- Business refusals should be typed on the proper letterhead.
- To make form refusals as individual as possible, use a word processor or computer and insert an inside address and salutation to the reader.

WRITE STRONG SENTENCES

Start with a strong, positive verb and build your sentences carefully.

▷ I must cancel my conference reservation.

▷ I appreciate you asking me to join the Jumpers' Club.

▷ We have selected a bid that more closely meets our specifications for the number of workers to be on-site during the contract period.

▷ Please call me next year.

▷ We appreciate all the work that went into your preparation of the Crichton proposal.

BUILD EFFECTIVE PARAGRAPHS

▷ Thank you for submitting your proposal for the Wayland Project. We felt your graphics were especially strong.

▷ I enjoyed talking with you on May 10 about the product manager position at Harper. Our selection task was made very difficult by having over twenty-five extremely qualified applicants.

▷ I am honored at your invitation to speak to the Farmers' Association. I am aware of all the good work the organization is doing.

▷ Thank you for your letter of March 19 describing the problem with the golf clubs. You are correct in assuming that we want to hear about any sales problems.

▷ I have carefully reviewed your letter of June 7 describing the problem with the evening gown. I know that as a twelve-year Marks customer, you know we make every effort to satisfy our customers.

▷ We have received your notification that you will be unable to attend day two of the Martinville Conference. Our policy is that we must charge attendees the total conference fee since our costs for the accommodations remain the same.

EDIT, EDIT, EDIT

Be sure your message is clear, firm, and ends on a good note.

Refusing to Be Club Officer

(Date)

Bob,

  I'm flattered at the suggestion I would make an excellent president of the Futures Club, but I have committed all my free time for next year to Jamie's Scouts and Jennie's Little League.

  I would certainly consider it next year, and I appreciate your vote of confidence.

             Sincerely,

             Douglas Viders

> State your refusal in a positive manner.

> Close with a goodwill statement.

Refusing an Employment Candidate

(Date)

Dear Martin:

It was a pleasure meeting you and discussing how your qualifications might fit the position of sales manager at Basco. You have especially strong leadership skills.

Our needs, I believe you'll agree, aren't the right match for you. All of us here—Jack Mason, June Lockham, Alice Kardon, and Jim Duke—wish you the best in finding the right situation.

Thank you for your interest and time, and our best wishes for your future success.

Sincerely,

Joe Wagner

> Use indirect order for bad news to someone you don't know well.

> End with a positive statement.

Refusing Customer's Request to Accept Return of Damaged Goods

(Date)

Dear Mrs. Whitmore:

Thank you for your letter of April 2 describing the problem with the red ball gown. As you know, we at Bates try very hard to satisfy our customers.

Three of us in customer service reviewed the problem after you brought the gown back to the store on April 10. I have also discussed the situation in detail with the manufacturer's representative to try to come to a solution.

Since the gown was worn and stained, we cannot, of course, sell it as new merchandise. And, as the manufacturer explains in the enclosed letter, the staining problem is a characteristic of the silk fabric, and not a defect in design or construction.

I am returning your gown to you. Both the manufacturer and I suggest you may want to contact Lace's Dye in Evanston to see if they can dye the garment.

Whitmore/(Date)/page 2

On behalf of Bates, I would like to offer you, as a long-time, valued customer, the enclosed gift certificate for $25 to be used in any of our stores anytime within the next year.

We look forward to serving you in the future.

Sincerely,

Judi Wolf

Refusing an Invitation

(Date)

Dear Jack and Joan,

How very nice of you to invite us to the reception for Susan on June 10. We have, unfortunately, committed to be adult sponsors at Gary's Young Republicans' party that night.

Please do give Susan our best. We look forward to getting together soon.

Sincerely,

Mary and Jack Burrus

Refusing Order Due to Past Credit Problems

(Date)

Dear Mr. Vilas:

Thank you for your order #3423, of March 10, for Marker Tools.

You may recall that your last purchase in 1997 resulted in our taking collection action for payment through Action Collection.

To establish a new working relationship, we request that you send payment for this present order in the amount of $1,582. We will immediately respond by rushing you the tools within forty-eight hours.

Thank you for considering us again, and we hope to hear from you soon.

Sincerely,

Holly Parker

VII. PROBLEMS

33
COMPLAINT

Come now, let us reason together.

—ISAIAH 1:18

The complaint letter has a single objective: to get a positive result. To accomplish this, try to take the place of the recipient so you can make a simple list of what he needs to know in order to take corrective action. Then use a direct approach and state the complaint in brief, clear, and, whenever possible, polite terms the recipient will understand.

It is often most effective to use a list form and simply state the facts—what is wrong—in just enough detail to enable the reader to take action. Include pertinent information like dates and persons involved, and refer to relevant documents by identifying numbers wherever possible.

If you are angry about a problem, it will be necessary to calm down before you write. Or, you can write your angry letter, read it, then throw it away. Then start your real letter of complaint.

Your tone should be rational and imply that you fully expect the reader's cooperation.

State an acceptable solution or a requested action, and be firm, positive, and polite. End on a positive but firm note.

Attach copies—keep the originals—of any pertinent documents showing the item, situation, date of transaction, place of transaction, and cost—for example, a sales receipt, invoice, original request, and original inventory certificate.

DECIDE TO WRITE

You may need to write this letter for one of the following situations:

* A purchase that is wrong, damaged, defective, delivered too late, spoiled, broken, has missing parts, no instructions, or no warranty
* Neighborhood, friend, personal, community, or workplace problems of a personal nature
* School problems
* Pet problems
* Social, club, and community problems
* Errors in billing, order, financial statement, minutes, or a collection procedure that has been initiated against you
* Employee problems of payment, productivity, attitude, incompetence, or sexual harassment
* Whenever legal problems are suspected
* Illegal activities such as the sale of drugs in your neighborhood or workplace, fraud, or false advertising
* Misrepresentation
* Legislative problems or disagreements
* Business policies and practice disagreements

THINK ABOUT CONTENT

- Gather and review all the facts of the situation so you have them firmly in mind and in logical order.

- A written complaint shouldn't always be your first course of action. If, for example, the neighbor's dog barked all night, a telephone call is a better response than a two-page letter. As a matter of fact, a telephone call should be the first line of complaint for most problems.

- Social, personal, pet, and school complaints are usually best resolved with a face-to-face conversation with those involved. Review the rules and policies, and try to state your complaint in terms of infractions.

- Emphasize the solution or corrective action. Stay away from "I" statements like "I want," "I feel," "I need." Use statements like "To correct this problem…"

- Make a written record of all the facts, persons, contact addresses, and telephone numbers involved in your complaint and add to it each time something new happens. This will allow you to be accurate, precise, and complete. Include in your information the date, time, and any person spoken to, and the content and outcome of each conversation.

- Keep all original documents, and make copies to send with your letter. Also keep all subsequent correspondence and documents in a file.

- Offer additional documentation like photographs of broken merchandise whenever possible.

- Write your letter in a timely manner. Although you may need time to get over your initial anger before writing, it is important to write as soon as you have documented all the facts of the problem. Not only will your letter be stronger, but your chances of getting the corrective action you desire will be greater.

- Begin by using positive statements like the fact that you chose the product because of its reputation, and write in the full expectation that the reader desires to take corrective action.

- Unless you are stating a number of items that point to a central problem, use the one-complaint-per-letter rule. If, for example, you are complaining about the lack of service at a department store and you state three examples of this that took place during your last visit to the store, you should list them very briefly. If you want to complain about three different policies that your senator endorses, use three letters.

- Cover the problem completely, even though you discussed it with the reader and he has some knowledge of the facts. You might start, "As we discussed, I received…" Remember, your letter may be referred to someone else within the organization.

- Address your letter to a real person. This may require calling to determine the person in charge.

- Whenever possible, be sure you are complaining to the person with the authority to take corrective action. Otherwise, much time and effort can be wasted, and the problem can be exacerbated by dealing with the wrong person.

- Use a "Reference:" or "Subject:" line, if appropriate, to focus and direct the reader's attention to the problem. State the problem here or in the opening sentence of your letter.

- Begin directly, and state specifically what is wrong.

- Present the facts briefly, clearly, using any reference dates, persons, invoice numbers, inventory numbers, order numbers, prices, and specifications that are applicable. State these in logical or chronological order.

- Use bullets, numbers, and indentation to emphasize your points, and to make it easier for the reader to note and respond to them. This works especially well if you have points to list or chronological events to note.

- Tell the reader why your complaint needs to be taken care of.

- State the specific adjustments, corrections, or action you are seeking. If possible, include a couple of choices for the reader.

- Be polite. The person to whom you are writing is often—if not usually—not the person who created the problem.

- Use third-party experts if an objective opinion or evaluation is needed, and mention this person in your letter. If the person offered a written opinion, refer to it, and enclose a copy. (Indicate the enclosure on the copy line of your letter.)

- Give the reader a time frame for taking corrective action.
- Close on a positive but firm note. State your confidence that the matter will be taken care of as you are suggesting.
- Attach copies of any pertinent documents that support your letter.

ELIMINATE WRONG MESSAGES

- Do not use harsh, accusatory, sarcastic, abusive, blaming, or unfriendly terms.
- Never let your letter wander into side issues or nonissues.
- Don't be vague.
- Do not leave the course of corrective action or the response date up to the reader.
- Do not threaten to sue. It is far better to send a positive letter and indicate a cc: to your attorney with the title of "attorney at law" listed after her or his name. You certainly may—if you are prepared to do so—state, if applicable, that if you do not receive a satisfactory reply by a specified date you will take the matter to small claims court. But be sure you have exhausted every possibility of negotiating first.
- Do not use unreasonable or out-of-line suggestions for corrective action.

CONSIDER SPECIAL SITUATIONS

- Many complaints must take a certain form. First call the organization and talk to customer service to get any complaint form that may be required. Get the correct name and title of the person to send it to, the information to be included, etc. A primary example of this is a complaint of a problem with your credit statement.
- In disputes about purchased merchandise that you have charged on your credit card, you must immediately let the credit card company know there's a problem. Call the 800 number first to make sure you follow their complaint procedure.
- For airline problems, state the flight number, departure and arrival locations and times, where and when the problem occurred, a description of the problem, the names of airline employees involved, and the course of corrective action you suggest.
- Often wrongs exist on both sides of a complaint. Take responsibility for your part of the problem, apologize if appropriate, and suggest a mutually beneficial solution whenever possible.
- There are usually several possible solutions to a problem, so be ready to negotiate and compromise.
- Complaint campaigns to political figures and corporations should be made by each person sending an individual letter. But the other approach of one letter or petition with many individual signatures may be preferable on some issues. Check this out before deciding.
- When merchandise arrives damaged by a second-party shipper, you should immediately notify the shipper and follow the procedure for making a complaint. It's always helpful to take photographs.

SELECT A FORMAT

- Your complaint should look official. Type it on business letterhead, personal business letterhead, personal letterhead, or quality bond stationery.
- Complaint or claim forms are often required. Type these or print very neatly.
- If your letter must be handwritten, make it neat and clear.

WRITE STRONG SENTENCES

▶ I am writing regarding your invoice #7556, dated May 17, 1998, for the Model 1664 Adapters.

▶ I am depending on your expertise to solve this problem in one of two ways.

▶ I certainly don't want our working record blemished by such an error.

▶ Please get these parts to me by Friday.

▶ I suggest we simply settle the matter by your issuing Bonders a $500 credit for the broken parts.

▶ Please send a corrected invoice by May 20.

▶ May we please resolve this situation by June 14?

BUILD EFFECTIVE PARAGRAPHS

▶ I am returning for credit the three dozen ceramic yellow bumblebees, which I did not order. Please refer to my attached order #3210, which lists three ceramic yellow bumblebees and two dozen little foxes.

▶ My fall sale begins September 20. I must have the corrected order by September 15.

▶ This is the fourth time our shipment of paper bags has been late. As you know, we cannot operate our store without them.

▶ I have not received a return telephone call to my letter dated April 10 and addressed to you (copy attached). The assembly line gears supplied by Gears, Inc., are not performing to specifications. I need your immediate response to get this problem solved. We are losing 20 percent of our production each day. [Faxed.]

EDIT, EDIT, EDIT

A cool, clear communication will help win the day.

Complaint Offers Two Alternatives

(Date)

SUBJECT: Cool Daze Air Conditioner, Model 1755A, Serial No. 3745, Purchase Order #6654

Dear Mr. Ricks:

The air conditioner I ordered from Cool Daze on April 1 is not performing according to specifications (see purchase and delivery documents attached). After I called your 800 number, your Mr. Wally Cranks came and inspected the unit. He determined the problem is an internal defective seal, and he recommended replacement with a new unit (see the copy of his report attached).

When I called your office, Mr. William Chatter said you have no units in stock and don't have any scheduled for production until fall. He said you do have several Model 3755As available at $500 more. Since the weather is already heating up, I suggest we settle this one of two ways:

Complaint of No Credit for Returned Parts

(Date)

REFERENCE: Account # 19778

Dear Mrs. Calvin:

Our monthly statement dated October 30 still shows item #33 for the three dozen computer parts that we returned on August 10. I'm enclosing another copy of the receipt your Mr. Bill Denson marked and signed when he received the returned parts.

Please send a corrected statement showing that we have been credited with the $89.99 for the computer parts, and we will remit a check for the balance owed.

Thank you.

Sincerely,

Sue Atkinson

Ricks/(Date)/page 2

(1) Cool Daze supplies and installs the Model 3755A at no additional cost, or
(2) you remove the air conditioner from our roof by May 1 and immediately refund our money.

Please respond by April 23.

Thank you.

Sincerely,

Kim Beerli

Returning Product for Refund

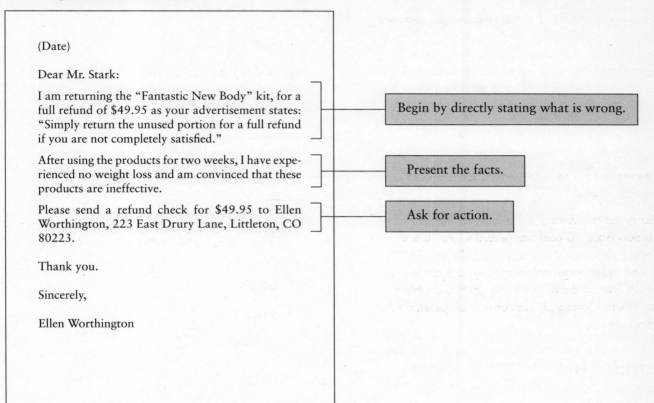

(Date)

Dear Mr. Stark:

I am returning the "Fantastic New Body" kit, for a full refund of $49.95 as your advertisement states: "Simply return the unused portion for a full refund if you are not completely satisfied."

> Begin by directly stating what is wrong.

After using the products for two weeks, I have experienced no weight loss and am convinced that these products are ineffective.

> Present the facts.

Please send a refund check for $49.95 to Ellen Worthington, 223 East Drury Lane, Littleton, CO 80223.

> Ask for action.

Thank you.

Sincerely,

Ellen Worthington

Complaint About Workmanship in Contract Work

(Date)

SUBJECT: Installation of Exposed Aggregate Walkways, Sun Club Resort, May 15

Dear Mr. Bailey:

When our maintenance man reported a series of cracks in the new exposed aggregate you installed two weeks ago, I asked him to check the thickness. He reported that the sidewalk is 2" thick in most places and 3" thick in others throughout the 150-yard length.

Since the specifications (see attached, line 15) call for a 6" uniform thickness, I must insist this installation be corrected. I suggest either

(1) Maco Concrete completely remove the existing exposed aggregate and reinstall a new walkway according to the specifications, and under the supervision of Mr. Ted Walker, our maintenance engineer, or

Bailey/(Date)/page 2

(2) Maco immediately refund the payment of $4,500, plus a removal charge of $1,000.

Please call me by April 15 with your decision, so we may avoid seeking a legal remedy.

Sincerely,

M.B. McDermott

Complaint to Moving Company

(Date)

REFERENCE: Move on August 20, from 110 West Trinchera Peak to 2340 Sundown Mountain Drive, for Walt and Mary Downs

Dear Mr. Richman:

As I stated on the telephone, there were a number of problems with our move by Westward Ho:

(1) The packing sheets were changed to indicate scratches and dents that were not on the original sheets (see the two sets of sheets enclosed),
(2) there is a missing drawer that belongs to the antique credenza (see photo),
(3) the Chinese screen was somehow crushed, ruining the surface, and
(4) the white brocade sofa has a number of stains that my cleaning consultant, Mr. Wayland Coils, says will not come out.

Mr. Richman, as I told you, these damages amount to over $12,000 (see the value, repair, and cleaning statements and estimates enclosed). I have also

Richman/(Date)/page 2

enclosed statements from two antique authorities who saw the items the day Westward Ho packed them and have since examined the damage.

Please fax me the damage claim form, and I will immediately complete it and fax it back to you today. I'm sure you will agree that coming to an equitable settlement by October 15 will be an advantage to both of us.

Thank you.

Sincerely,

Mary Downs

Complaint About Neighborhood Dog

(Date)

Dear Mr. Backus:

I'm writing after leaving several messages on your telephone answering machine over the last five days. As I stated, I have a real concern about the safety of our children given the fact that your dog, Bunky, has jumped the fence to your yard several times and displays a vicious nature. My daughter, Karen, who is five years old, is terrified to pass your yard because of Bunky's fierce barking and efforts to jump over the fence.

Please call me this evening after 6:30 P.M. to discuss this. I'm sure you'll agree this matter needs our immediate cooperative attention. Surely we can come up with a satisfactory solution.

Sincerely,

Annette Korslund

Complaint of False Charge Card Billing

(Date)

REFERENCE: Bank Credit Card # 34-34456-4445, Expiration Date 5/10/2005

Dear Cutomer Service Manager:

The charge #23 for $95 that appears on my current statement (see attached) is in error, and I hereby dispute it. As you will notice, the next item, #24, is a charge for Scissors Salon services in the amount of $78. The clerk overcharged me for a "sparkle" and hair cut, and then rewrote the charge slip, but obviously failed to destroy the errant one. (The charges are for the same date and time.)

Please remove this charge. I am enclosing the proper payment (less the $95).

Thank you.

Sincerely,

Brenda Schaak

VIII. ORDERS, CREDIT, AND COLLECTIONS

34

ORDERS

Reason is the mistress and queen of all things.

—CICERO

Orders, whether they are placed over the telephone, on a printed order form, face-to-face with a salesperson, or transmitted electronically, require specific and clear information. There may still be occasions when it is necessary to submit an order letter for items you wish to purchase. The keys to successful orders: be concise, include complete information about what you want and how you will pay for it, list any order conditions, and provide a contact name and shipping information.

After an order is placed, any number of problems may require you to compose a letter. Using concise, clear, complete information is always the best approach for resolving problems and keeping customers informed about the status of their orders.

DECIDE TO WRITE

Use this communication to

- Order
- To confirm an order received
- Request additional information
- Cancel or change an order
- Inquire about the status of an order
- Clarify payment questions or problems
- Accept or refuse changes
- Refuse or return an order

THINK ABOUT CONTENT

- Cut to the chase in ordering: "Please send me" or "This is an order for" is the best way to start.
- Arrange items with identifying information—quantity, catalog identification code or number, name, description, unit price, and total price.
- Set the order out by indenting:

  3 copies   Melvin Batcher, Clear Thinking,
              2nd Edition, 1995 @ $29.95 each
                                    ....$89.85

- State any conditions of your order clearly. If you must have the order by a certain date, for example, or if you will accept no substitutions, these conditions must be part of your contract agreement.
- Cover tax, shipping information, time frame, any special instructions, and method of payment.
- Make sure your information is complete and the reader has a way to contact you.
- Conclude with a friendly comment.

ELIMINATE WRONG MESSAGES

- Don't confuse the order with unnecessary information.
- Be singular in purpose; don't include other business.
- Don't bury the order in a paragraph.

CONSIDER SPECIAL CONDITIONS

- When writing about an order that was previously placed, always completely identify it by order date and your purchase order number, if possible. Also transmit a copy of the order, if possible.
- If you will accept substitutions, state these clearly.
- Emphasize any deal-breaking information. For example, if your order is only good if the product can be delivered by the fifteenth, say so: "ORDER GOOD ONLY IF PRODUCTS ARRIVE BY JANUARY 5."
- If your order has been lost, emphasize you are submitting a "DUPLICATE ORDER" in the event the first is found.
- Canceling: First, state clearly that you are CANCELING your order. Repeat all identifying information. If you paid by check, ask for a refund; if you charged the item, ask to have your account credited.
- Changing: Start by stating you are issuing an "ORDER CHANGE." Include the original order information.
- Confirming: Telephone orders, especially complex ones over a certain dollar amount, should be confirmed by the supplying organization. If orders will be delayed or must be backordered, the supplier should call the customer and should send a letter that states this fact. A backorder letter should include an apology for the inconvenience and end with a brief statement of goodwill.

SELECT A FORMAT

- Official printed order forms are best. But if a letter is used, be sure to include customer name (with title), business name, address, zip code, purchase order number (if you have one), customer number (if you have one), and contact telephone and fax numbers with area codes. Order information should include a catalog number (if available), description of the items ordered, catalog page number (if available), size, color, type (design, motif, etc.), quantity, unit price, and total price. Where applicable, sales, shipping and handling, place and method of delivery, and payment information—charge, C.O.D., credit card payment, or payment by check—should all be noted. Include and emphasize any conditions or restrictions, such as delivery deadline and the acceptability of substitutions.
- Type letters concerning orders on organization letterhead or personal stationery. A handwritten letter is also acceptable.

ALSO SEE "CREDIT ADJUSTMENT LETTER," PAGE 221; "COLLECTION LETTER," PAGE 225; "COMPLAINT," PAGE 193; "CONFIRMATION," PAGE 176.

Customer Ordering Supplies

(Date)

Jasmine Flowers
Sales Manager

Dear Ms. Flowers:

I am ordering the following from your June 15
price list:

20 boxes	Neenah Parchment bond paper, Dove Gray, 25% rag, 8½" x 11", 20-pound, @ $15.50	$310.00
14 boxes	Neenah Parchment bond, envelopes, Dove Gray, 25% rag, 20-pound, size 10, @ $35.00	$490.00
5 dozen	Printer cartridges, #20A, black @ $22.50/box	$112.50
5 each	Stanza computer stands, #1233, Model K in blaczk @ $298.99	$1,494.95
	TOTAL	$2,407.45

Flowers/(Date)/page 2

Please ship by prepaid parcel post to 540 East
Bayaud, Suite 7, Lincoln, Nebraska 20423, and
charge the amount on the usual 2/20, net 60 terms
to The Barker Account #34456.

Jasmine, I'm nearly out of these supplies and would
appreciate your getting these out by Friday. Thanks,
and call me if there's any problem.

Sincerely,

Joan Thrush

Customer Order Confirmation

(Date)

MaryLou Manners
Sales Manager

Dear MaryLou:

This confirms my telephone order, our purchase
order #44556, for 435 five-gallon Happy Juniper
Shrubs, @ $20.00 . . . . . $8,700.00.

As agreed, you will guarantee that any of these
shrubs that die or fail to thrive within the first year
will be replaced free of charge.

As also agreed, this order is conditional upon these
shrubs being delivered by March 15 to 8220 East
Dartmouth Avenue, #55.

No substitutes will be accepted.

Thank you for your help on this.

Sincerely,

Henry Wilkins

Customer Received Broken Merchandise

(Date)

Richard Munch
Customer Service

Dear Mr. Munch:

I just opened the two custom speakers, Model
ZZXs, that Stereo Parts made and shipped to me
July 2. Two of the membranes over the speaker
openings are punctured. As you directed me over the
telephone, I am returning the damaged speakers to
you for repair or replacement.

I will expect the speakers returned to me by July 15,
as agreed. Thank you for your attention to this
problem.

Sincerely,

Jack Reynolds

Customer Ordering Services

(Date)

Martin Schine, President

Dear Martin:

I would like to order the following services from your December 15 proposal:

1) Prepare the site, including, but not limited to
   a. remove and dispose of existing junipers
   b. grind out pear tree stumps
   c. remove lowest branches on existing Austrian Pines
   d. remove and dispose of existing rock mulches $935
2) Furnish and install 5 yds. compost . . . 440
3) Furnish and install 110' steel edging . . 145
4) Rebuild rock wall at west of garage . . . 430
5) Remove and dispose of existing exposed aggregate. 460
6) Remove and dispose of existing cobblestone 460
7) Furnish and install flagstone step stones 290

TOTAL $3,160

Schine/(Date)/page 2

I agree to the terms of payment in your proposal: 50 percent upon starting and the balance on satisfactory completion. Your "General Conditions" for performance will also be part of our contractual agreement. I do wish to take advantage of the winter discount of 10 percent, or $316, that you offered for beginning the work immediately.

Our agreed completion date is February 15, after which there will be a penalty of $25 per day taken off the price if the work is not complete.

I look forward to having your company complete this project. Please call me if you have any remaining questions.

Sincerely,

Gladys Poundstone

Supplier Notifying Product Arrival

(Date)

Mr. David Kowaleski

Dear Mr. Kowaleski:

It's a beauty! The BMW 735i you purchased through our Munich European Delivery Program has arrived, it has been serviced, and is ready for you to pick up. Please call me at 979-3400 so I can arrange a time for you to complete the paperwork. My hours are 9 A.M. to 6 P.M. Monday through Saturday.

It will take about twenty minutes to complete the transaction and make any adjustments you may request. You will need to bring the folder of paperwork you received in Munich at the time of purchase and your photo I.D. (driver's license).

I look forward to hearing from you. You'll be the envy of Englewood.

Sincerely,

George Crawford
Customer Service Manager

Supplier Filling Partial Order

(Date)
Virginia Trout

Dear Ms. Trout:

Thank you for your order (PO #3455), which we just received. We can fill all your order within the next forty-eight hours, except for thirty-two of the sixty-five pairs of Deep Freeze mittens, which we will backorder and ship to you in two weeks.

You will receive your first shipment of the items on the attached invoice within five days, the remainder within three weeks. Thank you again. We look forward to serving you in the future.

Sincerely,

Nighthorse Walker

**Supplier Concerning Backordered Equipment
Being Shipped**

(Date)

Dr. Peter Hanson, M.D.

Dear Dr. Hanson:

We have received the autoclave you ordered (your purchase order #9984) on January 10, which was on backorder. I am shipping it to you by air service (shipment #44-C-1390), and it will arrive in your office on the thirteenth.

> Cut to the chase. Give complete identifying information.

Thank you for being so patient, and as I said on the telephone, our service representative will call you to arrange a time to come by and check the unit thoroughly.

> Conclude with a friendly comment!

We look forward to serving you in the future.

Sincerely,

Ronald D. Servos

35

CREDIT INQUIRY AND PROVIDING CREDIT INFORMATION

If you want the time to pass quickly,
just give your note for ninety days.

—R. B. THOMAS, *FARMER'S ALMANACK*

Credit information—your own and others—must be handled in a straightforward, diplomatic, and confidential manner. Computer records are threatening confidentiality, and this is an area where people and organizations may be quickly offended. Worse, their ability to do business may be impaired if information is mishandled.

Those who provide credit information have a solemn obligation to be sure it's accurate. They must make sure that the information has been properly requested and give their response with no judgments or advice on whether the reader should extend credit. Do not offer unsolicited information, opinions, or facts you can't back up.

DECIDE TO WRITE

Use the credit inquiry to
- Learn why credit has been denied
- Learn the status or rating of a credit record
- Clear up a credit blemish
- Correct credit report misinformation or mistakes

THINK ABOUT CONTENT

When requesting credit information
- Call first to learn why credit was denied and to learn the name of the agency that issued the credit report.
- Be direct and to the point.
- Give all the necessary, identifying information: name, address, telephone number, purchase date, item, purchase amount, account number, place of purchase, etc.
- For another person's or organization's credit information, reference the request of the party involved, give any identifying background information, assure the reader all remarks will be kept confidential, and conclude with a statement of goodwill and an expression of appreciation.

- For a copy of your personal credit report, write to the bureau that issued it. There are three major bureaus:

    TRW Credit Data
    505 City Parkway West
    Orange, CA 92668
    1 (800) 392-1122

    Trans Union Corp.
    Consumer Relations Dept.
    P.O. Box 119001
    Chicago, IL 60611
    1 (800) 851-2674

    Equifax Credit Information Services
    1600 Peachtree St. N.W.
    P.O. Box 4081
    Atlanta, GA 30302
    1 (800) 453-3977

TRW will supply one free credit report copy annually; Trans Union and Equifax charge between $12 and $25 for each report. You are entitled to a free credit report copy within thirty days after you have been *refused* credit. Call the toll-free number if you have questions, then write and mail a copy of the refusal letter with your request. Make it a practice to write for a copy of your credit report once a year—problems or not—to check that your credit record is accurate. Enclose a self-addressed, stamped envelope.

When providing credit information
- Respond to the exact information requested.
- If the response is one simple answer, give it. If the response consists of more than one answer, start with the major answer.
- Arrange your answer logically. Make clear, concise statements, visually setting them off if possible.
- Be tactful but truthful. Give the points of information with appropriate emphasis.
- End with an appropriate goodwill statement.

SELECT A FORMAT
- For a credit inquiry, type on personal stationery or letterhead. A neatly handwritten personal letter with return address may also be used for your personal credit report.
- When providing credit information, use standard forms where appropriate or type your response on company letterhead.

EDIT, EDIT, EDIT
Your challenge when inquiring about credit is to include all the necessary information in a very clear and straightforward manner. When providing information, be sure to comply with local and state credit-reporting regulations.

> ALSO SEE "CREDIT APPROVAL AND REFUSAL,"
> PAGE 212; "CREDIT ADJUSTMENT LETTER,"
> PAGE 221; AND "COLLECTION LETTER," PAGE 225.

Request for a Copy of Your Personal Credit Report

(Date)

Mr. Bob Kind, Credit Manager

Dear Mr. Kind:

On September 21, I applied to open a bank account at 1st Bank, 540 West Applegate, in Dallas. I was told that there are three negative items on my credit report, and Mr. Jim Bob Aires in the customer service department refused to open the account.

I have lived at my present address at 540 Locust in Dallas for five years. Prior to that I resided at 434 East Windsom Drive in Dallas for nine years. I have worked for Lone Star Graphics, 200 Long Horn Trail, in Dallas, since 1993.

Please send me a copy of my credit report. If you have any questions, I may be reached at (214) 780-9900.

Sincerely,

Suzanne Richardson

> Be direct and to the point.

> Include all the pertinent information.

Request for a Personal Credit Reference

(Date)

Delbert Donavan
Manager, Credit Department

Dear Mr. Donavan:

Regina Merriweather, account #44567, listed your store as a credit reference on her application for a More Credit account. Would you please supply your creditor information on Ms. Merriweather regarding

- length of credit relationship
- monthly and annual billed amounts
- payment record

We will keep the information confidential.

I have enclosed an envelope for your response. I appreciate your prompt attention.

Thank you.

Sincerely,

Harold M. Miser
Credit Manager

Request for a Company Credit Reference

(Date)
Dawson Everett
Credit Manager

Dear Mr. Everett:

Stanley Adkins of Shear Designs in Grand Haven has listed your company as a credit reference. To process their application, we require a detailed credit history. Would you please complete the enclosed credit report, or supply one of your own, detailing

- length of your relationship
- amounts billed annually
- payment history

As I stated on the telephone, your response this week will allow us to process Shear Designs' application, so we can fill an order they have pending. All information will, of course, be kept confidential.

Thank you for your cooperation.

Sincerely,

Eartha L. Jones
Credit Manager

New Company Credit Inquiry

[faxed]
(Date)
Allen Alexrod
Credit Department

Dear Allen:

As I explained on the telephone, High Country Duds has just placed a large order, requesting delivery the first of the month. Their purchasing director, Bob Adler, gave your company as a credit reference.

I realize this company is new, but I'd appreciate any information you have and your recommendation regarding an extension of credit. Your comments will be kept strictly confidential.

I appreciate your help and cooperation and willingness to fax your response.

Cordially,

Nathan Spratt
Sales Manager

Requesting Additional Credit References from a Company

(Date)
Mr. Malcolm Meeker
President

Dear Mr. Meeker:

We are pleased you have decided to purchase our computer system. To complete the sale, we will need some additional information concerning credit references. Please fax me the following information:

* last quarter's profit and loss statement
* copy of certificate of incorporation
* a listing of corporate officers
* the completed attached Form A-345 listing credit references and banking affiliations

I will expedite your order as soon as we have this information. It will, of course, remain confidential.

We look forward to a long and mutually profitable relationship, and thank you for selecting Ace Ware.

Sincerely,

Jack Jenville

Renewing Credit Relationship with Former Customer

[faxed]
(Date)
Ms. Mable Bugg, President

Dear Ms. Bugg:

I'm preparing my confidential credit file on your company for extension of a credit line with us before our visit to your plant next week. I noticed that your financial statements and references date back two years. Our policy for increasing credit lines requires that all such information be current.

Please supply me with updated information for the attached:

* last quarter's profit and loss statement
* five current credit references
* current banking affiliation

All this information will be kept completely confidential.

Please fax your response to my attention by Wednesday so we can keep our appointment for next week.

Bugg/(Date)/page 2

We look forward to again working actively with Grasshopper as we did in the past. Thank you, and please call me if you have any questions.

Sincerely,

Georgina Kettering

Request for Business Banking Credit Reference

(Date)

Dear Mr. Breck:

John Reifer has listed you as the contact person at Manufacturer's Bank for Roller Derby, Inc. (see the copy of John's permission to contact form enclosed). In order to establish a line of credit for Roller Derby, we need an indication of their credit performance, as well as any comments you can make about their operation and management.

The information you submit will be held in the strictest confidence, and it will be used for credit purposes only. We, of course, welcome the opportunity to reciprocate at any time.

Account Opened On: _____
Highest Credit in Last 12 Months: _____
Present Balance: _____ as of: _____
Amount Past Due: _____ as of: _____
Number of Late Payments in Last 12 Months:

Breck/(Date)/page 2

Comments:_____
_____
_____
_____
_____

Please return this letter in the enclosed envelope. Your prompt response will be appreciated.

Sincerely,

Bill Babcock

Positive Business Credit Reference

(Date)
David Jensen
Credit Manager

Dear David:

In response to Bob Adams's request of July 8 to supply you with credit information on BYK, 870 Adair St., Detroit: We have enjoyed a mutually beneficial relationship with BYK for seven years. All the company's payments have been received on time, and we have extended our credit line with the company from an initial $5,000 monthly limit to a present $25,000 line. Annual purchases by U-Ties have increased from approximately $4,500 to $125,000.

If you require any additional information, please call me.

Sincerely,

Jim Backus
Credit Manager

Negative and Positive Business Credit Response

(Date)
Mr. Simpson Alexander
Credit Manager

Dear Mr. Alexander:

Here is the reference requested by Bryant Daniels, your credit applicant, of Flatlanders, 777 West Aberdine, Fort Worth:

- Customer from June, 1997.
- High Credit Balance: $4,520.
- Payments were slow from June to December of last year.
- Comments: The company underwent a loss of customers and cash flow during that period but has resumed prompt payment.

We are currently doing business with Flatlanders in a satisfactory manner.

Sincerely,

Joyce Evers
Credit Manager

Positive Personal Credit Reference

(Date)
Mr. Jim Bates
Credit Manager

Dear Mr. Bates:

This is a response to Alice Mayfield's request to submit a credit reference:

* Average checking balance over the past year was $1,450.
* Average savings balance over the past year was $7,800.
* Car loan payments have been on time, and the present balance is $6,732.

Happy to be of service.

Sincerely,

Arthur Crumb
Customer Service

cc: Alice Mayfield

Negative Personal Credit Reference

(Date)
Anne Weinburg
Credit Manager

Dear Ms. Weinburg:

RE: Confidential report on Ingrid Halloran

Here is the credit information you requested:

Ingrid Halloran
223 West Primrose Lane
Denver, CO 80234

has been a customer for seven years. Her high credit balance was $5,675 last December. Payments have been slow for the past seven months.

I hope this information is helpful.

Sincerely,

Roger Bonds

36

CREDIT APPROVAL AND REFUSAL

The strongest memory is weaker than the palest ink.

—PROVERB

When the decision to extend credit is made—after all the credit information has been collected and analyzed and the applicant has been approved—you are sending a good news message to the individual or organization.

There is no easy way to refuse credit because this sensitive area is closely tied to character, integrity, and social acceptance. Both an indirect approach (see "Refusal," page 186) and an extremely tactful strategy are necessary. Your final strategy will depend to a certain degree on why you are refusing credit. If the economy or the segment of the economy that affects the applicant's ability to pay are weak, the job is not as difficult as a refusal based on an unexplained non-payment of debts. However, never cite exact "bad" credit references; invite the applicant in to discuss these, if desired.

Offer the applicant an alternative plan or a hope for a future credit relationship, if either is feasible. People or businesses with weak credit often become good credit risks in the future. End, if possible, with a statement of goodwill, but don't make promises about the future.

There may be local, industry, state, or federal regulations and standards that apply to these situations. Follow these carefully.

THINK ABOUT CONTENT

Offering Credit:
* State the good news immediately and cordially welcome the credit customer.
* Define any limitations and follow with a brief statement about expanding credit limits.
* Close with a goodwill statement about the future of the relationship.

Refusing Credit:
* Begin with words that set up your strategy and explanation, but are neutral as to the decision.
* Give the explanation.
* Make the refusal statement tactfully, including a statement about a future relationship, if possible.

212

ELIMINATE WRONG MESSAGES

When extending credit, do not include doomsday or negative statements about possible delinquency, late payments, or credit exceptions. If this information has not been conveyed, enclose an explanation and reference it in the letter.

SELECT A FORMAT

Use a business letterhead, typewritten.

EDIT, EDIT, EDIT

Be sure your letter is simple, clear, and sincere.

ALSO SEE "CREDIT INQUIRY AND PROVIDING CREDIT INFORMATION," PAGE 206, AND "RESPONSE," PAGE 171.

Individual Approval for Department Store Credit

(Date)
Sarah Wasserstein

Dear Ms. Wasserstein:

It is with pleasure that I welcome you as a preferred credit customer at Oren's Department Store. As a new credit customer you will have an immediate credit limit of $500.

We believe you will enjoy the convenience and value of our products and services, as well as the special benefits of being a preferred credit customer entitled to special sales and discounts.

Please validate your new enclosed Oren's charge card by signing the back in ink. It is good in any of our stores or for any of our services. Enclosed is a copy of our credit terms specifying how you will be billed each month.

Again, we welcome you as one of Oren's preferred credit customers.

Sincerely,

Marilyn H. Houser
Customer Service

Organization Credit Approval

(Date)
Mr. Harold Appleton
President

Dear Mr. Appleton:

After reviewing all the references listed on your application, we are happy to extend to Harold's Way a $5,000 line of credit on a thirty-day billing cycle (2 percent, ten days). You may make as many purchases of any quantity throughout the month, with no minimum order. Just identify the account with your company name. We will provide you with free, same-day delivery.

We know you'll find an account with Bucko's both convenient and economical, and we look forward to serving you.

Sincerely,

Horacio Blackburn
Customer Service

Offering Limited Commercial Credit

(Date)
Lucille M. Foster
President

Dear Ms. Foster:

We appreciate your credit application. We have now received and reviewed all the responses from the creditors you listed. We would like to offer The Silver Slipper an immediate line of credit for $5,000 based upon our present credit policy.

We will certainly be happy to review and raise this limit to the amount you requested after one year.

We look forward to being of service, and I shall await your first order.

Cordially,

Samuel R. Wright

Commercial Refusal—Additional Information Needed

(Date)

Kevin Doerr
President

Dear Mr. Doerr:

Thank you for your interest in RayGlows and your application for a line of credit. We have now reviewed it thoroughly.

Our policy requires three more references than you have supplied. If you have these references and current financial statements, please return them to me, and we will be pleased to reprocess your application.

In the meantime, we welcome your business on a cash basis and offer you a five percent discount on all product lines.

Sincerely,

Lane West,
Credit Manager

Personal Retail Credit Refusal— Residency Requirement

(Date)

Gwen Longfellow

Dear Ms. Longfellow:

Thank you for your interest in a Homestead House credit account. We are pleased you find the quality and variety of our home furnishings fit your lifestyle.

Begin with a positive statement that sets up your explanation.

Our policy on new accounts requires that applicants have a minimum of one year living in the area, so we are not able to open an account for you at this time. As a newcomer, however, we would like to welcome you to the community with the enclosed certificate. It gives you a five percent discount on your next purchase in one of our seven area stores.

Give a tactful refusal.

We certainly hope you will continue to shop at Homestead House, and we would welcome the opportunity to reconsider you as a credit customer next summer. Please submit an application at that time.

End with a goodwill statement.

Sincerely,

Rhonda Weaver
Customer Service

Commercial Credit Refusal—Lack of References

(Date)

Dick Chancey
President

Dear Mr. Chancey:

Thank you for your order and application for credit. Woods Supplies has long been a friend of new businesses.

We require five credit references of over two years in order to open a charge account for over $2,000. If you have established the additional two references, please submit them to me.

If not, Woods Supplies will be pleased to reconsider a credit arrangement with New Waves after you have been a cash customer with us for one year. Cash orders at Woods Supplies have one great advantage: We offer a 5 percent discount.

Please complete the enclosed order form. I'll look forward to receiving it.

We wish you great success in your new endeavor.

Yours truly,

Roger Crocker
Credit Manager

Personal Refusal—Lack of Work References

(Date)

Mr. Raymond Wayward

Dear Mr. Wayward:

Thank you for your interest in Bowlands and your application for a personal credit card.

Our policy on issuing credit cards requires a minimum of one year, full time, at your present place of employment. Your six months of part-time work record at Shelby's prevents us from issuing you a credit card at this time, but we will be happy to reconsider your application if you will resubmit it when you meet this requirement.

Thank you again for your interest in Bowlands. Enclosed is a 15 percent certificate to use when you make your next purchase.

Yours truly,

Charlene Childs
Credit Manager

Personal Refusal—Slow Payment History

(Date)

Jerald Pearlmutter

Dear Mr. Pearlmutter:

Thank you for applying for a Bullock's credit card. A careful review of your credit references precludes us from offering you credit at this time.

We would like to encourage you to resubmit your application when your credit track record indicates timely payments on your present debts over an eight-month period.

We look forward to the possibility of serving you now with cash sales and in the future by offering you a credit card.

Sincerely,

Jack Bolden
Credit Manager

Corporate Refusal—Bad Credit Risk

(Date)

Marshall Feedler
Controller

Dear Mr. Feedler:

We appreciate your interest in establishing an account and line of credit with Whimple & Sons.

We have now completed our review of your application and have made the credit checks you authorized. We have determined that we can offer Wild Things only a cash arrangement at this time. But, as you realize, cash purchasing here means a real economy with our additional two-percent discount.

We hope you continue as a Whimple & Sons customer. We look forward to serving you.

Yours truly,

Marvel White
Credit Manager

Corporate Credit Termination

(Date)

Sidney Boyer
President

Dear Mr. Boyer:

A review of your account indicates that you have an outstanding balance of $5,678.20, and that no payment has been made on your account in sixty days. We must therefore cancel your line of credit, effective immediately.

Please submit your check for the overdue amount, or contact me to discuss alternative arrangements. We hope you will bring your account current so we can reinstate your line of credit.

Yours truly,

Archie Bufford
Credit Manager

Corporate Refusal, Offering Alternative Payment Methods

(Date)

Doris Misewire
President

Dear Ms. Misewire:

Thank you for your interest in using Formed Container's new line of pop-up packaging for your products. It does make an extremely handsome and marketable combination.

We share your enthusiasm about this venture, and after extensively investigating the credit references you provided in your application, we offer you two initial alternatives for beginning a credit relationship:

- you may pay for the containers in advance of shipping, or
- we will ship containers to you C.O.D.

With either arrangement we will offer you a four-percent cash discount. And after six months we will reconsider establishing the requested line of credit.

Misewire/(Date)/page 2

We hope to have the opportunity of working with you to fulfill your packaging needs.

Sincerely,

Stanley Shakely
Credit Manager

Corporate Credit Cancellation

(Date)
Mr. Sheldon Ryder
Credit Manager

Dear Mr. Ryder:

Our records show that during the past twelve months your account balance has remained above our agreed credit terms. As of today, your balance is $2,100.54, and the sixty-day, past-due portion of that amount is $1,143.56.

In keeping with our credit policy, we must convert our arrangement to a cash basis. Please make an appointment with Mr. Alex Stitwell this week to review your account and work out a more suitable payment schedule.

If our records are in error, please bring your documentation to your meeting with Mr. Stitwell. We look forward to getting this satisfactorily resolved.

Yours truly,

Norman Nicely
Credit Manager

37

CREDIT—REQUESTING AN ADJUSTMENT IN PAYMENTS

It never hurts to ask.

—ANONYMOUS

When a payment schedule or commitment cannot be met as agreed, it is vitally important to take the initiative, immediately, and contact the creditor. Usually face-to-face or telephone contact is the best first course of action. At that time, or immediately afterward, make a written request for, even suggest and outline, an alternative plan for payment. Remember that the creditor holds the power to damage your credit record. Be as tactful as possible.

Be realistic about the plan you propose. Think carefully before you suggest an altered payment plan. Enclose some payment with your letter. And by all means, keep your altered schedule of payment.

DECIDE TO WRITE

Use this communication
- As soon as you know you will be unable to keep the original agreement
- To renegotiate your payment agreement

THINK ABOUT CONTENT

- Examine every aspect of your agreement and find out everything you can about the practices of the creditor before making an alternative payment proposal.
- Refer to any appropriate account or customer numbers.
- Use the indirect (bad news) approach: Make a positive statement that sets up the problem.
- State the problem and, as succinctly as possible, give the explanation for the necessity to alter the payment schedule.
- Give the altered plan details.
- Assure the reader you will pay the bill in total.
- Remind the reader of your past positive performance, if possible.
- State that you have enclosed a check, and list the amount of the partial payment enclosed. (Always enclose a partial payment.)
- End with a goodwill statement about a continued positive relationship, and ask for the lender's cooperation.

ELIMINATE WRONG MESSAGES

* Do not start with a negative statement.
* Do not fail to include an altered plan for payment.
* Do not fail to enclose a check as a statement of good intentions.

SELECT A FORMAT

* Use a business letterhead; for a personal loan, use a standard 8½-by-11-inch sheet with return address.
* Type for business; type or use neat handwriting for a personal letter.

EDIT, EDIT, EDIT

Your request for a credit adjustment must be clear and concise.

Payment Withheld Because of Creditor Error

(Date)

Suzie Stith
President

Dear Suzie:

I'd like to pay the outstanding balance on our account RR-440, but I haven't gotten a response to my letter of March 10 requesting that you check the balance and correct the error in your bill dated February 15 (see copies attached).

I will gladly pay the corrected balance of $765.20 in full when I receive a corrected statement. Thank you.

Sincerely,

Jennie Garrison

Request for Thirty-Day Extension, Slow Receivables

(Date)

Alexander Fishbein
Collections

Dear Alex:

I'm enclosing a check for $200 instead of the $1,300 balance due because, as I detailed in our conversation yesterday, we have, unfortunately, had a delay on several large units. Those have now been shipped, but the accounts receivable pipeline hasn't been replenished.

I am sorry about this reduced payment and certainly do not want to blemish our ten-year, excellent credit record. We'll be back on track and pay this in full in thirty days.

We ask for your patience with this delay. Thank you.

Best,

George Buckingham

Request to Restructure Payments

(Date)

Mr. Fred Aster
Accounts Receivable Manager

RE: Account TR-4578

Dear Mr. Aster:

Following our discussion, I am enclosing a check for $450 to be applied toward our account number TR-4578. This is, of course, less than the scheduled payment of $1,800 designated in our payment booklet. We have had a temporary, marked downturn in business because our customers, who are farmers, have experienced severe flooding, as I'm sure you've heard on the news.

We will need to adjust our payments to $450 a month for the next twelve months, since farmers will not be purchasing and planting this season. We plan to be able to pay our account in full in April of next year.

> Identify the account.

> Begin with a positive statement that sets up the problem.
>
> State the problem as simply and concisely as possible.

> Give the altered plan details.

> Assure the reader you will pay.

Aster/(Date)/page 2

We will appreciate your cooperation in this difficult time. We have enjoyed a long and satisfactory relationship with your company, and we look forward to resuming a mutually profitable one next season.

Sincerely,

Jacob Stern

> Ask for the reader's cooperation.

38

CREDIT ADJUSTMENT LETTER

It takes two to speak the truth—
one to speak, and another to hear.
—HENRY DAVID THOREAU

When you are offering a product or service and something goes wrong, it's your responsibility to take the necessary corrective steps to maintain the goodwill of your customer.

Quick action increases your chances of maintaining a positive relationship and the esteem of the other party. In the ideal situation, of course, your follow-up is so impeccable that you are aware of a problem before the customer has registered a complaint. That often is not the case, of course. But do act immediately. This is when your efforts will be most effective.

Communicate directly, resolve the problem fairly, and work toward complete customer satisfaction, if possible. The critical factors in the adjustment letter are the tone of the letter and the emphasis. Be both respectful and positive, regardless of the factors involved, and emphasize customer satisfaction.

DECIDE TO WRITE

Again, timing is vital. Write this communication immediately when

- An error has been made in the delivery of your services or products
- A customer registers a complaint
- A damaged product has been received
- An exchange is requested
- A refund is requested
- There has been a change in payment terms or amounts
- There has been a billing error

THINK ABOUT CONTENT

- Open directly with good news the customer or other party will want to hear. Focus on a positive solution. In a simple situation this may be the granting of an adjustment. In other situations it may be acknowledging the customer was right.
- Quickly identify the complaint you are responding to. Do not go into a lengthy explanation of the negative aspects of the complaint or problem.
- Briefly, and in positive terms, explain what caused the problem if this is essential to restoring the reader's confidence in you and your organization.

- Explain exactly how you will correct the situation. Make your statement sound eager, not begrudging. Give any steps you will take to prevent the problem from recurring, if this is appropriate.
- Thank the customer for bringing the situation to your attention, if this is appropriate.
- Close with a friendly, positive statement that will help to reestablish rapport, but don't apologize again.

ELIMINATE WRONG MESSAGES

- If the customer or other party was at fault, do not state this outright. Rather, let it be known by implication or understatement.
- Do not over apologize or overemphasize the problem.
- Do not make statements that could be construed as you accepting liability beyond the scope of your responsibility or admitting that you acted in a negligent manner.
- Do not place blame. Keep your statements, whenever possible, objective, brief, and simple.

Incorrect Billing Information

(Date)

Mr. Edward Fishwhacker
President

Dear Mr. Fishwhacker:

Thanks for your call this morning concerning the error in your bill dated April 12 for $2,456. In investigating, I found that due to a computer entry error, your check #8998 was credited to the wrong account. Please accept our apologies. The correction has now been made showing your account paid in full (copy enclosed).

Would you please review your company listing to ensure that we have the correct information:

Customer:	Whaler's Cove
Address:	1 Main Street
	Worthy, MA 01075
Telephone:	(617) 988-9009
Account #:	55420-98

CONSIDER SPECIAL SITUATIONS

In all situations where there are serious issues of neglect or liability, consult your attorney on how your letter should be worded.

SELECT A FORMAT

Use a standard letterhead, typed.

EDIT, EDIT, EDIT

Make your letter factual, brief, and concise.

Fishwhacker/(Date)/page 2

I'm enclosing a 15 percent discount certificate for your use on any products you purchase before September 1. We look forward to serving you in the future.

Sincerely

Stan Swinebuckle
Customer Service

Delayed Shipment Due to Strike

(Date)

Nigel Redenbacker
President

Dear Mr. Redenbacker:

Thanks for your call today. I had just dictated a letter to you to keep you up-to-date on your shipment (order #4456) of April 14. The dockworkers' strike in New York persists; however, we have heard that a settlement is expected this week.

> **Identify the problem.**

In the meantime I'm enclosing pictures I took this morning of some great rugs we have in-house, which I can ship to you immediately if you need them to fill out your inventory for your upcoming sale. I am willing to offer you a 5 percent discount on the prices listed.

> **Explain your solution.**

The minute the strike is settled I will be in contact, and if you decide to order any of the rugs pictured, please give Gertrude a call: (617) 889-4321.

> **Close with a positive statement.**

Sincerely,

Hasan Raheeb
President

Negative Response to Request to Return Merchandise

(Date)

Mr. Charles Reeves

Dear Mr. Reeves:

Thank you for your letter of March 19. I was sorry to hear that sales of the custom-made hutches did not go as you expected. The question of returning the thirty-two remaining miniature hutches you have in stock is a difficult one. Since you ordered these sixteen months ago, and we had them made to your specifications and delivered them to your stores eleven months ago, any return policies have long expired.

I have checked with the manufacturer and with other retailers, and have been unable to locate other stores interested in purchasing them. Bill Hornblower at Country Way in Boston (617/ 788-9334) and Henry Hopewell at Repasts in Rhapsody (213/434-1290) both offered to discuss with you some ideas for selling them. Additionally, we have received infrequent calls from interior decorators in your area for

Reeves/(Date)/page 2

similar pieces: Ted Booker at Draper Designs (544-1010) and Hillary Groves at Design Works, Inc. (770-3000).

I hope this is helpful, and I look forward to serving you in the future.

Sincerely,

Sherman Taylor
Customer Accounts

Supplier Sent Wrong Product

(Date)
Vivian Waverly

Dear Ms. Waverly:

I was sorry to learn that an error was made and that you were sent the wrong fabric color on the sofa you ordered from us May 15. Our source at the factory has located your sofa, and it is being shipped to you tomorrow. It will arrive on Thursday, and someone will telephone you on Wednesday to arrange an exact delivery time. The delivery people will pick up the burgundy sofa at that time.

You have selected the finest sofa of the season, and I'm sure it will offer you great enjoyment. I am enclosing a brochure on a pair of chairs the manufacturer is showing with your sofa. If you wish to order these, we would be happy to offer you a 10 percent discount. Just show the salesperson this letter.

Sincerely,

Janice Placid
Customer Service

Replacement of Damaged Goods, Problem Unknown

(Date)
Arthur Knight

Dear Mr. Knight:

I am enclosing a check for $553.12, the amount you paid for the custom-made Wright suit. We are very sorry this unfortunate accident occurred.

My investigation did not turn up the exact source of the stains on the suit. Our laboratory determined they were made by an acid of the kind used in automobile batteries. Evidently something was spilled on the package during shipment. In eighteen years we have never had such an incident.

I am also enclosing a certificate for a 15 percent discount should you want to order another suit. We would be happy for the opportunity to serve you.

Sincerely,

Frank Fong
President

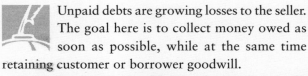

39
COLLECTION LETTER

Remember that time is money.

—BENJAMIN FRANKLIN

Unpaid debts are growing losses to the seller. The goal here is to collect money owed as soon as possible, while at the same time retaining customer or borrower goodwill.

Don't bypass the friendly reminder telephone call. This is often the first and best approach in collecting. In writing the first collection letter, use an indirect approach (see "Refusal," page 186) and write the letter in a persuasive tone. Collection letters to individuals should take an empathetic "you" attitude, and business-to-business letters should also ring with sensitivity to the reader.

Most organizations develop a series of four to six progressively stronger collection letters. They must be well-timed to be effective, and although the computer makes this process very easy, you must carefully monitor it.

The first-stage letter is usually a *reminder,* the next an *inquiry,* followed by an *appeal,* and finally a *demand.* The wording and timing depend on whether the customer is an individual or a business, the balance owed, your type of business, and a number of other financial and industry factors.

There are local, industry, state, and federal standards and regulations concerning collection practices. These must be carefully followed.

THINK ABOUT CONTENT

- Let the reader know in the first sentence that this is a collection letter.
- You can then ask him or her to act.
- Put the responsibility to communicate or explain on the reader. You may even ask the reader for an explanation on the back or bottom of the letter or statement.
- In each letter, state the total amounts owed, the original due date, suggest an alternative plan, and invite the reader to call and discuss it.
- Make it easy for the reader to respond. Enclose an envelope and provide a telephone contact name and number.
- Be flexible and as generous as possible in trying to work out terms for repayment, especially if the debtor expresses that difficult circumstances have caused nonpayment. This, of course, can be easily checked out.
- Use a polite tone in the first series of letters and gradually make it stronger.

Early or Reminder Letter

- Begin by identifying with the reader. Then remind the reader of the past-due bill.
- Include a statement that shows confidence the reader will pay.
- End with a goodwill comment or a statement about your future relationship.

Inquiry or Stronger Reminder Letter

Following the steps for the reminder, start with a neutral inquiry in an effort to start a dialogue, but make a stronger statement about the necessity of paying the overdue bill.

Middle or Appeal Letter

There may be a number of graduated letters in this stage, starting with ones with lots of goodwill statements to ones with fewer goodwill statements. In all these letters you should do the following:

- Begin with an attention-getting statement that sets up your appeal.
- State your appeal using the second-person ("you") viewpoint and persuasive language.
- Ask for payment.
- Optionally, repeat the appeal.

Develop a persuasive strategy that will appeal to your particular reader:

- The *pride* approach appeals to the reader's self-respect and desire for social acceptance.
- The *ethics* approach appeals to the reader's moral standards of honor, character, integrity, and "doing what's right."
- The *self-interest* appeal stresses the importance to the reader of keeping his or her credit rating and buying power.
- The *fear* approach is the flip side of self-interest: the consequences of not paying, such as legal action and not being able to buy on credit, etc.

Final or Demand Letters

- You must first consider any federal, state, and local laws governing collection procedures, business practices in your industry, and the image you wish to convey about your organization. Your objective is to get the debtor to take action and pay the delinquent account. It is not to harangue or demean.
- In most cases, you have three courses of action if payment is not made:
  1. Report the delinquent account to a credit inter-change group such as a credit bureau.
  2. Turn it over to a collection agency.
  3. Take the debtor to court.

  Deciding which alternative to take will, obviously, affect the content of your letter by dictating what you will write.

- Begin by stating which course of action you are taking and why.
- Explain the effects of this action matter-of-factly.
- Offer the reader one last chance to pay by setting a deadline and urging that it be met.
- Optionally, end with a statement that the reader can stop the action, or the reader will cause the action by his or her inaction.

ELIMINATE WRONG MESSAGES

- Never write an angry letter.
- Don't apologize.
- Do not use stilted language.
- Never repeat an appeal made in a previous letter.
- Never imply that your customer is not an honest person.
- Do not lapse into abuse or threats.
- Do not use inflammatory or demeaning words or phrases such as *demand, failure, repeated failure to respond,* or *failure to pay.*
- Don't use sanctimonious, coercive, or false reverse psychological terms or phrases in an effort to manipulate.
- Do not include any statements that could be considered libelous.
- Do not violate an individual's right to privacy.
- Do not send personal statements to his or her place of employment.

Initial Corporate Reminder Letter

(Date)

Antiqua Brookner
Accounts Payable

Dear Ms. Brookner:

Just a reminder that your account balance at Highlands Ranch is now overdue in the amount of $1,545.24. Please mail your payment today, or if your check has crossed this letter in the mail, please accept our thanks.

Yours truly,

Charles DeVoe
Accounting

Intensified Business-to-Business Reminder Letter

(Date)

Melissa Beale
Accounts Payable

Dear Ms. Beale:

This is a follow-up to our telephone conversation regarding your order #5443 of April 30 for seven chandeliers, totaling $7,540.76. We invoiced you on May 7, the day the chandeliers were shipped. They were received by you on May 15 (see copies attached).

We agreed that you would send a check for the chandeliers upon receipt, but that was sixty days ago. Please remit payment immediately so we can get this resolved and ship your present order sitting in our warehouse.

Sincerely,

Jeannie Dickson
Account Services

Initial Personal Reminder Letter

(Date)

Allyson Davis

Dear Ms. Davis:

This is a reminder that your payment of $2,540, due August 15, has not been received (see copy enclosed). If you will mail this today, you will avoid any interest charges.

Remind the reader, showing confidence he or she will pay.

I've enclosed our latest sales sheet covering this month's specials.

End with a goodwill statement.

Sincerely,

Jennifer Sharpe
Credit Manager

Appeal for Business Communication

(Date)

Delores Reviers
Accounts Payable

Dear Delores:

We have not received the check for $4,520 that Mr. Shikes said was sent on May 10 to pay our invoice #3554. Would you please check on this immediately and call me and let me know what has happened?

Sincerely,

Sarah Meeker
Accounts Receivable

Appeal for Further Business Communication

(Date)
Derek Dietz
Controller

Dear Derek:

Concerning your payment of our invoice #8990 for consulting services in the amount of $1,425 presented on April 17, I'm again asking you to call me or Eleanor Jeffries at 544-9550 to discuss any details you still have unresolved.

Perhaps if we talk, we can arrange an alternative payment schedule. Please call by Friday so we can get this settled.

Sincerely,

Sharron Decker
Accountant

Appeal for Business Communication

[faxed]
(Date)

Pearl Lacey
President

Dear Pearl:

I am surprised I haven't heard from you about the overdue balance of $1,450 for the speakers delivered on July 5. I've had no response from you or Jack to my earlier letters (copies attached).

Please let me hear from you by Wednesday about your plans for payment. Please respond on the bottom of this letter and fax it back, or give me a call at the office, 788-1020.

Regards,

Barbara Jackson
Customer Accounts

Demand Business Letter

(Date)

Grace Albertson
President

Dear Ms. Albertson:

This is the fourth and final request for payment of the 120-day overdue balance of $3,250 for your order #556, shipped to you on June 6.

I'm sure you will want to protect your credit rating, so please return your check in the enclosed envelope. We need to receive it before the first of the month, or we will have to turn your account over to the Bloodless Collection Agency.

Sincerely,

Arthur Knight
Controller

Appeal for Action to Customer with Financial Problems

[faxed]
(Date)

Mr. Kirk Foster
President

Dear Kirk:

We understand the trials and tribulations of a rotten season for retailers, but we still need to hear from you on the overdue payment of invoice #4559 for $4,650 (copy enclosed).

We'll work with you to reschedule payments so when things pick up in the next couple of months you won't be without a supplier.

Call me today. I'm going to be in Steamboat on Tuesday, and I'll stop by to resolve this.

Sincerely,

Joan Dickson
President

IX. SALES

40

DIRECT-MAIL

He profits most who serves best.

—ARTHUR R. SHELDON

Although it's true that nearly every letter you write has some sales message, the direct-mail sales letter is designed and written with the sole purpose of persuading the reader.

The term *direct-mail* means that the letter is sent out directly to the target market instead of being sent in response to an inquiry. It may promote a product, service, concept, or even a person.

In order to sell, the effective letter must (1) get the reader's attention, (2) appeal to the reader's needs or desires, (3) explain the product or service, and (4) motivate the reader to take the directed action.

First you must identify those things that are selling points of your product or service. With these in mind, you must select the right recipients. This can be scientifically done by combining and eliminating a variety of marketing data to select the names of the people most likely to be interested in what you're selling. A great number of firms do this. Or, with some work, you can develop your own lists.

Many products or services have more than one target audience. But each audience will need its own specially tailored sales letter. If you are selling a new product, your first mailing list is almost always made up of your present customers, the next of your current prospects. You have already established a positive rela-

tionship with the first, and are well on your way with the second.

To tailor your letter to these readers, learn as much about them as possible. If your mailing list hasn't designated it, learn the sex, age, marital status, vocation, income level, geographical location, interests, hobbies, etc., that will help define your readers in terms of your products or services.

Write your letter to fit this individual target audience, emphasizing how your product or service can benefit the reader. When possible, phrase these benefits in the second-person viewpoint. Remember to test your letter for any overstatement and check it against any possible liability statements.

Aim the closing at bringing the reader to the point of the desired action. In the case of big-ticket or complex concept sales, this will probably mean leaving the door open to make, or setting up, the next contact. So instead of ending with "Give me a call for more information," you will write, "I will call you on Friday morning about nine o'clock to give you the details."

In our electronic age of computer mail-merge, it is easy to "personalize" you letter's inside address and salutation.

DECIDE TO WRITE

Use this letter to

- Introduce a new product, service, or candidate
- Introduce other products after a sale
- Sell to known prospects
- Invite customers to a grand opening
- Announce a special sale or promotion
- Announce a business closing

THINK ABOUT CONTENT

Collect direct-mail sales letters. Test your own reaction to the messages. Examine what the writer did correctly and what he or she did poorly. Especially look at letters concerning the type of product or service you have to offer.

Direct mail has become so commonplace that only the very best will be read. Be sure to make yours as brief and complete as possible to give it the best chance. This includes having something unique to say, keeping paragraphs short, using white space to make the letter appear short and easy to read, and using visuals to attract attention.

Consider writing a series of letters. This will affect the letter content and approach.

Look at the length of the letters. It's best to keep your letter to a single page, if possible. There are certainly exceptions, but not many. If the letters are over one page, ask yourself if the sales process should have been broken into more steps. Maybe the letters should have had the goal of setting up a face-to-face meeting, participation in a seminar, or a personal sales call, rather than a "sales-in-one."

Get Your Reader's Attention

When you are ready to write, start with a statement to get the reader's attention and set up your strategy. Obviously many things can be used to gain the reader's attention. A heavily perfumed letter would do it, especially one scented with "Ode to a Skunk," which releases its essence when the reader follows the instructions to "Scratch this." But would this kind of attention prepare the reader to be receptive to your new marinara sauce? Probably not.

You must use your best creative efforts and think your lead all the way through to the follow-up sales letter and the final sale. An announcement letter telling the reader about a new-home loan interest rate of 6.7 percent in a 12 percent market, especially if the letter was mailed to a special list of targeted new-home shoppers, would get the reader's attention, preparing the reader for your loan message, your follow-up telephone call, and your sales presentation and closing statement.

A statement or question opening that introduces a need the reader has that the product will satisfy works well. These are based upon a rational appeal:

> "A Capital Loan can save you $125,000 in house payments."
> "You can qualify for a 6.1 percent home loan."

Or try a question:

> "Will you pay too much for your new home loan?"

Or your opening may be based on an emotional appeal, like this letter for aid to children:

> Pablo is seven years old today. As he sits inside the darkening hut that is his home, an old pot sits on the dirt floor beside him to catch rain dripping from the tin roof. He's very hungry. But he knows there will be no dinner tonight.

Select an approach appropriate to your product or service and your audience. Often there will be both rational and emotional elements in the same opening. The use of gimmicks in conjunction with the opening can work well if the gimmick supports the theme. Some that you have undoubtedly seen used effectively are coins or samples enclosed or adhered to the letter.

Select the Right Viewpoint

Use the second-person viewpoint (the "you" viewpoint) whenever possible to make the reader a participant in your appeal. This works well in the home-loan example above. The second example relies on the narrative, or "story," technique to draw the reader in. The second-person viewpoint or the reader-benefit approach helps focus the message and keep it direct and to the point.

Develop Your Strategy

After the "grabber" first sentence, you must make the transition to telling your reader how your product or service will fulfill his need or desire. This must logically follow, of course, from your opening statement. In the example of the home loan, you would follow this rational opening with, perhaps, a true example that your targeted reader can relate to: "Lynne and David Ross pay $1,457 each month on their home loan…"

Choose Your Voice

Make your writing conversational, fast paced, and assertive. The direct-mail sales letter is one of the most difficult letters you will write. You must gain and hold the reader's interest very quickly. This will require much writing and rewriting to perfect.

Select Your Words Carefully

Shades and nuances of words are very important. Strive for words that enliven your sentences. Check the difference in the effect of words:

HOT	sweltering, steaming, fiery, sizzling
COLD	freezing, frigid, frosty, cooling
DELICIOUS	sumptuous, delectable, feast, ambrosia

Very important here, too, is selecting positive words of persuasion. Negative words or statements are seldom the best choice:

Negative Wording	Positive Wording
Reduce downtime by 10 percent.	Increase your production by 10 percent.
Less than 2 percent of our clients do not get a new career.	We place over 98 percent of our clients in new careers.
Easy Press eliminates wrinkles.	You get a wrinkle-free shirt all day long.

Liven Up Your Text

Use visual techniques to add interest. Consider visual techniques like using boldfaced type of various sizes, italics, color, and graphics.

Give the Reader the Necessary Information

You must accomplish two things: (1) answer the reader's questions and overcome his or her objections, and (2) supply enough convincing information and facts to complete the sale. This requires a careful balancing act. You must include enough information without bogging the reader down. The fine details of most sales presentations require that you enclose supplementary collateral pieces. But again, this is a balancing act. Too many and the reader will toss the letter and the supplements into the wastebasket.

Keep supplemental materials to a minimum, and coordinate them with the letter by referencing them: "Price details are covered on page two of the enclosed brochure." Another good example of this might be a cruise with a whole variety of price possibilities. Your letter could include a statement like "… from $234" or "Prices begin at $234."

Close the Sale

There are several ways you can bring the reader to the point of taking action. Select the one consistent with your product, service, and audience, but be sure to make your close clear and specific, preferably with only one course to take. Here are the best ways to "close the sale":

- Call for action. If you offer an incentive to act now, this step makes sense:

  "…to get your free sample, mail in the enclosed card."

  "Order your GlowBright bulbs now, in time for Christmas."

  "Order your original print now, before they are gone."

- Complete the circle. Take the reader back to your opening. This is sometimes referred to as the payoff on your teaser lead: "Start saving $95 each month on your home mortgage payments now…"

In the case of the narrative story, end with the possible happy ending: "With your help Pablo can eat three meals a day, go to school…"

- Postscript punch. Sometimes overused, but often effective, is the added postscript (P.S.), which makes one last pitch for the reader to act. This should be short, punchy, and call for precise action:

    "Call now. Offer expires…"

    "Order Christmas gift subscriptions now for only $9.95."

    "To take advantage of this offer, place your call now."

Take the Final Steps

- Double-check your letter to be sure you have included all the information the reader needs in order to act and make sure it is easy for him or her to respond.
- Hand-address the envelopes and affix with stamps (make them commemorative). This is more appealing to readers than envelopes with address labels and metered postage marks.

ELIMINATE WRONG MESSAGES

- Avoid "hard-sell" techniques. Most readers find these a turnoff.
- Eliminate negative pitches unless they are the strongest.
- Do not give too much information or a fragmented message in your letter. Keep the information simple and straightforward. Use brochures to provide details, and tie the brochures and the letter together.
- Don't be too familiar. Many readers who are strangers don't want to be an instant "friend."

CONSIDER ALL YOUR MAIL-OUTS

- It is important to think of the direct-mail sales letter as part of all the letters you send to customers and clients. It is also important to think of the sales aspects of other letters you send.
- Create a complete family of letters. This is part of building an identity for your organization.
- Don't miss an opportunity to get the word out about your product or service. Think of everyone you do business with in terms of whether they can be customers.

SELECT A FORMAT

- Select a format consistent with the product and audience. The possibilities are limitless. Two-color embossed letterhead isn't the best choice for catalog sales, but it usually is for banking services, investments, and life insurance.
- Computer-generated letters make personalizing a simple task.

EDIT, EDIT, EDIT

Make sure the tone of your letter is friendly but not inappropriately familiar.

ALSO SEE "ANNOUNCEMENT," PAGE 23; "WELCOME," PAGE 43; "CONGRATULATIONS," PAGE 33; "PRESS RELEASE," PAGE 256; "INVITATIONS," PAGE 48; AND "APPRECIATION AND THANK-YOU" PAGE 55.

Direct-Mail Sales Letter

(Date)

Mr. Leo Payne
Chief Executive Officer

Dear Mr. Payne:

During the four years Marketing Communications served as Great Scott's public relations agency, that organization received 500 percent more positive press than it ever had in its history.

We would like the opportunity to make a presentation to you to serve as Main Deal's public relations agency to handle your entire marketing, public relations, and advertising programs. We feel sure we can offer you the same kind of representation that helped Great Scott become a leader in your industry. We have specialized in the real-estate industry in Chicago for over seventeen years.

I suggest we meet at your office next Wednesday at 2:00 P.M. Our presentation will take forty minutes.

Payne/(Date)/page 2

During our years as Great Scott's public relations agency, we worked with Dusty Parker, Monroe Shannon, and Elisa Banks of your company. I'm sure they can give you additional information on our qualifications, and you may want them to attend our presentation.

I will call your office to confirm a meeting time. We look forward to meeting with you.

Sincerely,

Montana Silver

41

FOLLOW-UP

If at first you don't succeed, try, try again.

—ANONYMOUS

A follow-up sales letter is any letter that follows an initial contact and has a sales motivation. A number of studies have shown that sending a follow-up sales letter to a prospective customer can get as good or better results than the initial sales letter (see "Direct-Mail," page 233).

In fact, the first sales letter or sales contact seldom produces enough results from readers to eliminate them from your follow-up sales list. Many organizations plan a series of sales letters, often four to six, as part of their total sales campaign.

Follow-up sales letters should contain some of the same vital information as the initial sales letter to build on the message already begun. Making this reference helps to build your sales effort.

A progressive number of follow-up letters—a sales-letter ladder—are actually required by some audiences. Probably some of the best examples are introducing ideas readers are initially opposed to, such as buying an insurance plan for an extended-care facility, or a product that uses brand-new technology.

Many follow-up sales letters also wear another label: *thank-you, congratulations, response, invitation,* and *request.*

DECIDE TO WRITE

Use this letter

- After an initial direct-sales letter has introduced a concept
- In response to an inquiry
- After a sales call
- As part of a planned, multicontact sales campaign
- After receiving a sales referral
- With new customers

THINK ABOUT CONTENT

- Reference how the reader has come to your attention. If he or she is a referral, name the person. If you are following up after a sales call or a telemarketing call, thank the reader for his or her time; if you met the reader at a meeting, say so. This information establishes a relationship and may increase the reader's receptivity to your message.
- Describe the product or service you are offering. Reference the first letter, if appropriate.
- Stress the customer benefits.
- Back up your lead with facts and information. Make statements that will overcome the reader's objections and answer needs and desires.

- Give new or additional information that may arouse the reader's interest.
- Make a strong close by tying a special offer or incentive to your lead.
- End by leaving an opening for your next contact.
- Following up also means thanking those who give you leads. Write a thank-you letter, and report your progress, if appropriate. As a point of courtesy, always let your referral source know if you make the sale.

ELIMINATE WRONG MESSAGES

Don't close the door to future contact. Close with a statement that you will make the next contact, if appropriate.

SELECT A FORMAT

Match or coordinate the look of this letter with any others you have sent the reader. You want to build recognition of your organization's name and products or services.

EDIT, EDIT, EDIT

Transforming your letter into an arresting, clear, and concise form is your challenge.

> ALSO SEE "DIRECT-MAIL," PAGE 233; "WELCOME," PAGE 43; "APPRECIATION AND THANK-YOU," PAGE 55; "REQUESTS AND INQUIRIES," PAGE 155; AND "RESPONSE," PAGE 171.

Follow-up to Sales Call

(Date)

Alexander and Elle Callan

Dear Alex and Elle:

It was a pleasure meeting you last evening. Thank you for the opportunity to introduce our insurance plan. I believe Plan D in the brochure is ideal for your first goal of sending Derek to college. And the other elements of the plan will meet your family protection, retirement income, and other education needs.

I will be conducting a luncheon workshop on Thursday for about twenty people. I'd like to invite you to attend because I will be covering the plan elements in depth. Alternatively, I would be happy to meet with you again on Thursday evening to answer any additional questions. I will call you on Tuesday evening to discuss which you would prefer.

Sincerely,

Charlie Sellwell
Insurance Manager

Follow-up Sales Letter

(Date)

Jonathan and Louise Kettering

Dear Jonathan and Louise:

Welcome to Tucson. Thank you for requesting our brochure from the Welcome Wagon. I've enclosed it along with several photos you requested in our telephone conversation. These are five of the homes we have landscaped in your area.

We have been giving homeowners the best of the desert Southwest for over twenty-five years. Please feel free to check with a few of those customers from the enclosed list.

We do have a small welcome gift for you that I will bring by after I call you next week to set up a time to give you a landscaping estimate.

Sincerely,

James Morningflower

Follow-up After Direct-Mail Letter

(Date)

Richard Munson
Photographer

Dear Mr. Munson:

I'm glad you and four of your staff are considering attending our Fifth Annual Shoot'em-Up Seminar October 20–22. We will cover advanced photo techniques and high-tech photographing in several hours of instruction on each of the three days. I have marked these sessions on the enclosed brochure.

International expert Flash Weasel will teach three of these sessions, and Edsel Redeye will teach the other three.

I've enclosed six applications for your use. If you return the completed applications with tuition payments before Friday, your staff will be assured of getting places and you will save $25 on each tuition fee. I will call you Wednesday to see if you have any additional questions.

Sincerely,

Miriam Foil
Program Coordinator

| Get the reader's attention. |

| Use the "you" viewpoint. |

| Close the sale. |

Follow-up to Set Sales Presentation Appointment

(Date)

Sybil Snidvider
Marketing Director

Dear Sybil:

It was a pleasure talking to you today. Yes, Marketing Communications is a full-service marketing, advertising, and public relations agency. We specialize in technical accounts and have been able to get great results for our clients using a personalized program emphasizing public relations. Enclosed is our capabilities statement and a list of some of our clients.

I will be in Orlando on the twenty-first and would like to talk with you about the possibility of LiveWire using us on a per-project basis. As I mentioned, you can call Roy Bender of B/PAA and discuss with him how we have helped that organization gain a 74-percent market share.

Your new energy products sound very exciting, and I'm already percolating some great, low-cost promotion ideas.

Snidvider/(Date)/page 2

Would you be able to give me thirty minutes at 1:30 P.M. on the twenty-first? I'll call your office on Friday to see if I can schedule that time.

Sincerely,

Eric Muskgrove
Account Manager

Sales Follow-up/Thank-You to New Customer

(Date)

Darrel Covey

Dear Mr. Covey:

Thank you for your order for the Bridgestone Model AS-34. I was happy to hear about your increase in production with this fine machine. As I mentioned to you on the telephone, I believe you will be interested in the two Bridgestone grinders, Model RE-34 and RE-50, to replace your present machines. I've enclosed the spec sheets for both.

I will be demonstrating these grinders during our open house on the fifteenth, and you could see all the benefits to your present operation with this hands-on opportunity. I will also have a complete sequence on machinery set up to demonstrate an operation similar to yours.

I'll call you later this week to see if I can sign you up for this session (it's free), or see exactly how I can help you with your next step.

Sincerely,

Frank Sharpe
Customer Sales

42

FUNDRAISING

*Cast your bread upon the water, and it may
come back with peanut butter and jelly.*

—ANONYMOUS

The fundraising letter is a sales letter with a heart tug. But it must be tempered with the kind of persuasive writing that brings results without broadcasting that it's selling the reader something.

Many charities are competing for the same dollars, and unsolicited direct mail has gone beyond the saturation point. Frustrated, people often toss requests for donations after only a cursory glance, or less. To be successful, a fundraising letter must be part of a larger campaign, which has established the cause as having worthy goals and demonstrated accountability for donations. It helps a great deal if the charity is immediately recognized as a good cause.

For economy, the letter recipients should be selected as persons who have demonstrated interest in the charity's work or who have track records of giving to other similar charities. Then the letter must deliver a simple, concise, and convincing message. All these factors make the fundraising letter very difficult to master.

DECIDE TO WRITE

You'll use this special communication to
- Elicit monetary or other contributions
- Request volunteers
- Invite contributors to a fundraising event (also see "Invitations," page 48)

THINK ABOUT CONTENT

- Grab the attention of the reader in the opening sentence.
- Identify the charity and its purpose.
- Convince the reader of the need to contribute.
- Define exactly how the reader's contribution will be used.
- Explain the benefits of the reader's contribution to charity recipients.
- Explain the benefits of giving to the reader.
- Make the act of contributing as easy as possible.
- Use language and a tone that expects the reader to help.
- Tune your message to your reader as closely as possible.
- Use positive, clear, and concise language. It works best. Rather than writing, "Jose Perez won't eat tonight unless you give," it is far better to say,

"Helping children like Jose Perez feels good," or "You can make sure Jose Perez eats tonight…"

- Define, specifically, your contribution request:

  There are several ways you can help:
  —Return a check for $15 or more.
  —Check the box that says, "I volunteer to be a telephone operator one hour a week."
  —Call this number, 455-2333, and tell the operator you have an item to be picked up Tuesday for the auction.

- Construct your letter using informal language, including contractions, some short sentences (but don't make it choppy or staccato), questions, and perhaps even acceptable slang to achieve a conversational tone. Contractions are useful: *isn't, don't, can't, won't, isn't,* and *we're.* But don't overdo it. Some short sentences that have been useful include "We're almost there!"; "Just $50,000 more and we'll start building."; "Can you believe it?"; "You've been wonderful!"; "And now for the final lap!"; and "We need your help."

- Include a mission statement. Briefly and exactly tell the reader what you want to accomplish: "In just three months we have raised $500,000 of the $1 million needed to build the new Lily Women's Center."

- Expect the reader to fulfill his or her commitment. If this is a letter in a series that follows a pledge on the part of the reader, you might say, "Your pledge is important to finishing the job."

- Remind the reader of his or her pledge, but don't let your letter slip into a harping, pressuring, or threatening tone.

- Use a postscript to attract additional attention. By placing a punchy point outside the body of the letter, you may create a strong emphasis.

- Remember your message should entice the reader to act now. Statistics indicate there's a dramatic drop in response if action is delayed by the reader: "Return your contribution in this envelope *now* to help."

ELIMINATE WRONG MESSAGES

- Don't let your letter take on negative, moralizing, or guilt-inducing tones. Givers want to feel their motivation is prompted by their own best intentions.

- Be sure your letter doesn't have a slick or patronizing tone. Test it on a number of readers to be sure it sounds genuine and sincere.

- Don't include more than two inserts. Including four or five inserts, such as background brochures, donor cards, and other pieces, dilutes and clutters your message, prompting the reader to classify your letter as junk mail.

- Avoid creating undue pressure, but make it easy for the reader to respond.

- Don't pressure contributors to give you the names of friends and associates.

CONSIDER SPECIAL SITUATIONS

- Target your letter to a specific audience. If a form letter is to be sent, be sure it is tailored to a carefully selected audience to increase your response. Then change it and tailor it to another audience.

- Computers make it possible to personalize form letters to the recipients. Use this approach, if possible.

- Successful direct-mail solicitation receives a 2.5-percent positive response. A 5-percent response is very good. This illustrates how important it is to be very selective about the people to whom you send fundraising letters. And it also makes a vital statement about the need to write an effective letter.

- It's important to have contributors feeling good about giving, even if it involves a dozen mailings.

- Enfranchise contributors, bringing them into the action. Make sure they feel a part of the fundraising: "We've almost met our goal."

- Fundraising requires a multifaceted approach to be successful. Appealing for contributions through direct mail is only a small part of it. Many other parts of your campaign, like effective public relations efforts, will be needed to help make your fundraising letters effective (see "Press Release," page 256; "Opinion Editorial," page 289; and "Announcement," page 23).

- Fundraising often involves functions like luncheons, gala events, dinners, dances, etc. Use the appropriate forms for mailing to contributors (see "Invitations," page 48).

SELECT A FORMAT

- Invite readership with an appealing letter layout. Your letter appears shorter and more inviting, for example, if you select a typeface that is easy to read and has space between the lines of type. Indenting also creates an attractive, open, easy-to-read impression.

- Individualize your letter, if possible, by using the reader's name in the inside address and salutation.

- Have the letter signed by the highest or most recognized official of the charity organization. Respected celebrity endorsements are sometimes helpful.

- Consider using a postscript to attract additional attention and get action.

WRITE STRONG SENTENCES

Start with an action verb and construct lean sentences with a strong message:

▶ Let's all work together to eliminate this devastating disease.

▶ Only $500,000 remains to be contributed before we can begin work.

▶ Your contribution can help send fifty underprivileged children to Cower's Camp for a week.

▶ Contributors of $5,000 or more will become listed in next year's programs under Patrons of the Library.

▶ Books are a wonderful thing to contribute!

BUILD EFFECTIVE PARAGRAPHS

▶ Let's eradicate this debilitating disease. Researchers believe one more year at a cost of $1,500,000 will produce the needed vaccine. We're that close to a solution. Won't you help with a contribution of $25 or more?

▶ You can help now in two ways:
—Write Senator Allen Dirkson and congressional representative Alice Schroeder and state your objection to the legislation.
—Return your check for $25 today.

▶ Operating Angel's Kitchen takes $3,500 and 400 volunteer hours each week. You can help by signing up to serve for one or more of the time slots indicated below, and by returning your contribution of $25, $50, or $75.

▶ The Sisters Against Crime meeting to organize for this year's campaign will be Tuesday, September 10, at 7:30 P.M., at Logan School in the auditorium. Please call Sarah Crimpton, *777-7879*, and tell her you'll be on hand to help.

▶ It's spring again and time to get our after-school program organized. With your volunteer efforts the children of Burton Township will have this enriching experience.

EDIT, EDIT, EDIT

Fine-tuning this communication will increase your response.

Community Fundraiser

(Date)

Dear Alice:

This Holiday Season we will again sponsor the Noel House Tour to benefit the Opera Society. Since last year's tour raised $150,000—which went directly and completely to the opera—we feel it was extremely profitable. And our contribution paid for the renovation of the Opera House. A complete breakdown of how the money was spent is itemized on the back of this sheet.

This year our goal is $175,000 for enlarging the stage area and providing two new sets. We believe we can meet this goal with all our members' help. Contributions from florists, designers, and interior decorators are already rolling in.

The tour committee is requesting that eight members of the Park Hill neighborhood volunteer their homes for the tour, 50 members volunteer to function as tour guides and receptionists, and 225 members volunteer to serve on the preparation subcommittees.

> Identify the charity and its purpose.

> Convince the reader to contribute.

Green/(Date)/page 2

We know you'll want to help. Please return the volunteer card indicating your choices.

Sincerely,

Roger Wagner

Alumni-Related Fundraiser

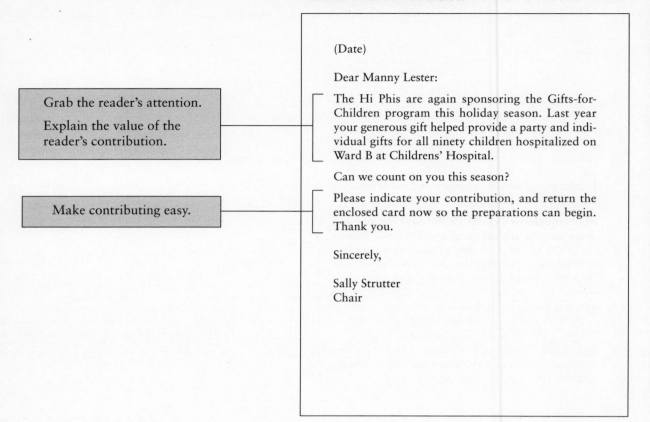

Grab the reader's attention.

Explain the value of the reader's contribution.

Make contributing easy.

(Date)

Dear Manny Lester:

The Hi Phis are again sponsoring the Gifts-for-Children program this holiday season. Last year your generous gift helped provide a party and individual gifts for all ninety children hospitalized on Ward B at Childrens' Hospital.

Can we count on you this season?

Please indicate your contribution, and return the enclosed card now so the preparations can begin. Thank you.

Sincerely,

Sally Strutter
Chair

Request for Volunteers and Money

(Date)

Dear Sally:

High Achievers has turned the lives of seventy-nine children around in just two years. The first year we sponsored the program, school officials reported that the twenty children who attended were at high risk for dropping out of school. The second year the number was fifty-nine children. And all seventy-nine are now performing far above average.

You can thank yourself and all the volunteers from Chambers Corporation who dedicated after-school hours to be tutors at Elbert Middle School.

This year we're taking on an even bigger challenge. In order to purchase needed supplies and operate a store where students can purchase things with their "achievement dollars," we are asking for money contributions. Chamber Corporation's President, Robert Elliot, has pledged a matching $15,000 for the program if we raise that amount and enlist volunteers for the needed 4,000 tutoring hours.

Johnson/(Date)/page 2

It's a great way to be involved in our community and to make a difference. Please put your commitment on the enclosed card and return it today.

Yours truly,

Angel Martin

P.S. Production has already pledged $2,000 and 600 tutoring hours. Can your department top that?

Fundraiser for Community Project

(Date)

Dear Neighbor:

Last year in Butler County 15,000 healthy cats and dogs, puppies and kittens, were destroyed. Why? Because our neighbors aren't having their pets spayed, and too many cute puppies and adorable kittens are adopted by families before they seriously consider the responsibility a pet brings.

Mistreated and abandoned pets are other horror stories.

The Humane Society deals with them all. But we need your help to educate children and adults about pet selection, responsibility, and care; to place pets with loving families; spay pets for a minimal charge; euthanize injured and unadoptable pets; and try to reunite lost pets with their families. This year these services will cost $342,000.

There are two ways you can help:

- Volunteer to serve at the shelter during the hours of 8:00 A.M. and 9:00 P.M. by calling 775-7600.
- Send your tax-deductible contribution in the enclosed envelope.

Humane Society/(Date)/page 2

Help us take better care of Butler County's pets.

Sincerely,

Winnie Wheatland

Special Invitation to Fundraising Event

(Date)

Dear Andrea:

The North Bay Arthritis Foundation counts on you. In fact, if it weren't for you and our other 500 members, the Foundation would have been unable to fund the Remus Research Project last year. Thanks to you we are closer to a solution to this debilitating disease.

Our goal for this year is to again fund the Remus Research Project (see the encouraging progress report enclosed). And we will all need to work together like last year—even harder—to achieve our goal of $230,000.

This year's art show, Contemporary Artists of America, will include 200 pieces of art by contemporary artists. It's the second largest show of its type in the country. A blind-drawing, fixed-price sale will be conducted at the opening gala at the Historical Society Hall on September 15. Works not sold that night will be available on a first-come basis starting the following day.

Simple/(Date)/page 2

Tickets for the gala will be $125. The fee will include a cocktail party, a souvenir medallion designed by Hugo Halsey of Santa Fe, admission to a private preview of the exhibit, and an art seminar at the downtown Chilcott on September 12.

Please call and order your group tickets today, 233-4550.

Sincerely,

Horatio Gailbladder

P.S. This year we will have seventy-five of the artists attending the gala.

Call for Time and Commitment Pledge

(Date)

Dear Jim:

Little League time is here! And we need to get organized. We already have enough kids to field fourteen teams. That means, of course, we will need another $3,500 for equipment and supplies and sixty coaching volunteers. At this moment we have $1,250 and ten head-coach volunteers.

The team families committee feels it can raise over $3,500 at the bake sale next weekend, so that leaves the coaching volunteers.

This promises to be Little League's best year ever. But we'll need your help. Please call Joe Baker at 322-3445 by March 15 to sign up.

Yours truly,

Sparky Henderson

P.S. The Jaguars are determined to take it all this year, Jim!

Plea for Food Contributions

(Date)

Dear Viewer:

Channel 4's fifth annual Holiday Basket drive starts Thursday, October 17.

Your help last year meant that 1,900 families throughout the metro area got holiday baskets. This year you and other captains requested we make our appeal to clubs, schools, and businesses too, setting our goal at baskets for 2,500 families.

Please list your club name and number of members on the enclosed card, selecting the type of participation you'd like to volunteer for.

Let's make this the city's brightest holiday season.

Sincerely,

Levitt Lighthorse

X. PUBLIC RELATIONS

43
PITCH LETTER

Writers are like baseball pitchers.
Both have their moments. The intervals
are the tough things.

—ROBERT FROST

Most editors, reporters, and interviewers will insist you send a letter explaining your idea or the subject you are requesting they cover for a feature. This letter, the pitch letter, must be designed to gain media interest in your idea.

A good pitch letter must not only suggest a newsworthy idea but it should also offer the reader background information, the opportunity to set up an interview, and, when appropriate, a product sample. Include all the ingredients that will make it easy for the reader to cover your story.

THINK ABOUT CONTENT
- Be sure you understand the subject or product, so you can explain newsworthy aspects well.
- Know the target media and appeal to their particular interests.
- Make sure you target the right editor.
- Call the editor, reporter, or interviewer and, if appropriate, make a verbal pitch, stating you will follow up with a letter.
- It may be necessary to offer an "exclusive" on the story. If there are competitive newspapers, for example, try to get one to do a feature by using this approach.

- Check the spelling of the recipient's name, title, and address.
- Personalize your letter to your reader, even offering a personal note or "slant" for his or her readership.
- Use an intriguing first sentence to hook the reader immediately. This "hook" can be a news angle or something the reader needs or wants.
- Use a professional but friendly tone.
- Keep your letter short, pithy, and full of information.
- When you wrap it up, take the initiative to make the next contact.
- Follow up exactly as you promised, to increase your credibility.

ELIMINATE WRONG MESSAGES
- Do not use a first name in the salutation unless the reader is a personal friend.
- Gimmicks are risky. Don't use them unless you've tested them on a substantial market sample and know they fit the reader well.
- Avoid overused adjectives like *unique, fantastic, greatest, incredible,* or *best.*

CONSIDER SPECIAL SITUATIONS

- If you are pitching a product, single out the most newsworthy and interesting aspect of the product and make that the first sentence.
- If you are pitching the results of a survey or a personality for an interview, use a provocative opening, maybe a question: "Over 97 percent of husbands are unfaithful," "Nine accidents will happen today within twenty-five feet of your desk," "The job market for sports editors is drying up," or "Did you know that 93 percent of today's editors will…?"
- Back up your first sentence with facts, an explanation, or an expansion on the lead.
- Put the meat in the middle of your pitch, but keep it short and snappy.
- Use bullets and indentations to make important points.
- Keep your purpose in mind: to get the reader to agree to do an interview, take a tour, or do whatever it takes in order to write a piece.

- Edit. Remember, your letter must be short, preferably no longer than a page. After you write, go back and eliminate any redundancies and nonessential information.
- Even if you will follow up with a telephone call, give information on who to contact, when, and how.
- Call newspaper editors and reporters of a morning newspaper between 10:00 A.M. and noon, since their deadlines are in the afternoon. Radio and television editors and producers have varying deadlines. Always ask, "Is this a good time to talk?" and don't call just before airtime.

SELECT A FORMAT

- Use 8½-by-11-inch letterhead.
- Use a standard business letter format. Some exceptions are required in special situations.

Magazine Pitch Letter

(Date)

April Meehan, Senior Editor

Dear April:

I suggest a feature story on Blanchard Banks of Detroit, who, at the age of sixty-four, has just read his first book ever to his granddaughter, Jasmine, age four. "It's a miracle," the silver-haired man explains.

Blanchard began life as a farmworker in Mississippi and migrated to Detroit as a young man in 1940. Working in a factory, he managed to get by without reading, by meticulously following instructions and occasionally asking someone to "clarify" written communications.

When Marks Industries, where Blanchard works, joined the fight for literacy, Blanchard signed up for the after-work tutoring program offered at his local library. In June he will graduate in a special program to be attended by several U.S. members of Congress.

Meehan/(Date)/page 2

In the Marks Industries program alone, fifty people have already been able to experience the joy of learning to read. It wasn't easy for Blanchard and the others to admit their reading deficiencies; it wasn't easy to overcome the obstacles of getting enough volunteer instructors and a suitable meeting place; but the Marks program is making a big difference. In fact there are now plans to expand it into a fifteen-state partnership with local community organizations.

I believe your readers would be inspired by Blanchard's story. There are great photo opportunities here. I'll give you a call in a few days to discuss your interest.

Sincerely,

Samantha Gerkins

*What the mind doesn't catch,
the mind grieves after.*

—JACQUES BARZUM

The media kit, or press kit, is a collection of written pieces in a folder used together to give editors, reporters, interviewers, and other media people background information on a subject. Usually the kits are made available to media people at large-scale, newsworthy events, and include

- New releases describing something that will be announced at the event
- Biographies of speakers
- Backgrounder, or organization, brochure
- Copy of speech delivered at the event
- Q&A
- Photo

At large trade shows, regional or national book fairs, political meetings, or sports events, there will usually be a central press room where all participants may make such information available to media people.

Keep the pieces to a few comprehensive ones to maximize impact. Don't clutter the media kit with nonessential items.

See the chapter for each of the elements that may be included in the press or media kit: "Press Release," page 256; "Backgrounder," page 271; "Bibliography," page 280; "Biography," page 268; "Fact Sheet," page 275; "Timeline," page 278; "Questions and Answers," page 264; and "Brochure," page 294.

John Templeton Foundation—The Mind/Body Medical Institute at Beth Israel Deaconess Medical Center—Harvard Medical School "Spirituality & Healing in Medicine II." Public Relations Society of America 1997 Silver Anvil Award–winning entry in the category of special events and observances.

Backgrounder Included in Media Kit

- At the time of discharge, hip-fracture patients who are religious walk longer distances and have less depression than non-religious patients do (Pressman et al 1990).

- Rel
  fast
  199

- If p
  198

- He
  reli

- Ho
  affi
  san
  reli

- Bla
  con

- Pat
  pai

- He
  stay

Religio
beliefs.
180:67

"Syste
epidem
792-79

"Throu
spirit i
practic
the pov
Healin

Clinical Study Data
Spirituality, Religion and Healing in Medicine and Health Care

Our growing understanding of the biological basis for disease and healing, combined with modern medications and procedures, have produced dramatic improvements in mortality and morbidity in the United States. Yet, our current state of knowledge does not fully account for the individual experience of many patients that mind-body interactions, and specifically, spirituality and religion have resulted in better health outcomes. Survey data suggest that most Americans and their physicians see this connection as viable (Time/CNN poll, Time Magazine, 1995; Templeton Foundation Family Physician survey, 1996. Both surveys by Yankelovich Partners).

The value of research on the impact of spirituality and healing can be seen as two-fold. First is the potential for more targeted and effective use of such interventions, with improved health and potential cost savings as the result. Second, many patients are intuitively aware of the power of spirituality and religion and desire validation of their natural inclination. For example:

- 40% of hospitalized patients say their religious faith is the most important factor that enables them to cope (Koenig, 1997). This has also been documented for patients with gynecologic cancer (Roberts et al 1997), other types of malignancies (Kaczorowski 1989), endstage renal disease (O'Brien 1982), open-heart surgery (Oxman et al 1995), cardiac transplantation (Harris et al 1995), Alzheimer's disease (Whitlatch et al 1992) and health problems related to aging (Conway 1985).

- A prospective, matched-control study of persons living in religious kibbutzim versus secular kibbutzim in Israel, demonstrated pervasive morbidity and mortality advantages to those who led religious lives, even in comparison with those in a tightly-knit community without religious focus (Kark et al 1996).

While the scientific literature on spirituality, religion and healing is growing and is highlighted below through both epidemiologic studies and clinical trials, ongoing work should produce more results over the next few years.

Studies that Demonstrate Clinical Effectiveness

- Patients are three times more likely to survive open-heart surgery if they depend on their religious faith (Oxman et al 1995).

- Over a 28-year study period, the risk of dying was almost 25% less (35% in women) for frequent religious service attendees, after controlling for health practices, social ties, and well being (Strawbridge et al 1997).

- Similarly, those who attend religious services, at least once per week, have been shown to have stronger immune system functioning (Koenig et al 1997a) and maintain their physical activity significantly longer (Idler & Kasl 1997), compared with less frequent attendees.

1

45

PRESS RELEASE

*A word to the wise is not sufficient
if it doesn't make any sense.*

—JAMES THURBER

The press release is a vital tool—the workhorse of any organization's public relations program. Used properly, it can raise your visibility in the public eye, help create a positive image, and assist in marketing your organization's services or products.

A press release should describe an event of importance: a personnel appointment or promotion, the release of a new product or service, a new business opening, major expansion, reorganization, or a change in management or philosophy.

Write releases in journalistic style, answering *who, what, when, where, why,* and *how.* Present the information in order from the most important to least important, from the central idea to specific facts. Imagine that an editor will take a pair of scissors and clip from the bottom of your release. Be sure that no vital information gets eliminated from your message until the scissors reach the top paragraph. Include all critical information in the first paragraph, the first sentence if possible.

The press release should be objective, clear, and easy to read, and it should not include extra words or superlatives. Photos, if used, should be carefully identified on the back or with a paper glued to the bottom. Attach the photo to the release with a paper clip,

taking care to use a clip that will not mark the photo.

No cover letter is necessary, and the format described in this chapter should be strictly adhered to.

THINK ABOUT CONTENT

- Determine what about your subject is *newsworthy*—new information. Ask yourself:
  1. Who will care?
  2. Will the release answer the questions it will undoubtedly raise?
  3. Will it advance my objectives?
  4. Have I gathered all the facts and double checked them for accuracy?
- Determine if the release is hard news (personnel appointments, new products, company openings, new services, events, research, or survey results), or soft or feature news (human-interest items, business trends, ongoing research or projects).
- Create an outline to ensure a logical and clear flow of information.
- The lead is all-important. It should read like the lead of a news story.

- The personnel appointment press release should focus first on the responsibilities of the appointee. Then it should give the appointee's background.
  1. State the appointee's title and credit the announcement to the proper organization official.
  2. Give the person to whom the appointee will report and the start date.
  3. State the appointee's responsibilities. (In this second paragraph, you may want to use a quote by the organization official.)
  4. Describe the appointee's professional experience and educational background. Social and personal information, such as marital status, professional affiliation, charity, or social affiliations, is sometimes included.
  5. State if the position is new. You may also want to give the name of the person being replaced if the circumstances are positive.
- Rewrite and edit for clarity, trying to keep your release to one or two pages. Make sure your copy is clear and concise.
- Define any technical terms.
- Quotations add interest and lend personal authority. Use some, if possible, but only those that provide relevant information. If you use a quotation—and be sure to quote the correct official or authority here—check it with that person for approval. If you obtained a direct quote in an interview, you should still get the person's approval before using.
- Samples, photos, and review copies (books, CDs, etc.) add interest to your release, so include them when it's practical. If not, make an event, press conference, or interview available to the editor.

CONSIDER SPECIAL SITUATIONS

- Send the press release to a specific person if possible. If you cannot, address the news release to a particular editor, for example, the business editor, social editor, or sports editor. It is worth calling major media such as daily newspapers or television stations to learn the correct person's name, title, department, and specific address (4th floor, Department 4-A). It's often worth a telephone call to that editor stating you are sending a press release.
- The official statement, for use in crisis situations or when controversial situations arise, should be developed and distributed to the press and internal organization representatives to help control rumors and eliminate misinformation.
- Use electronic distribution of releases—fax or e-mail—for updates when news is critical and fast-breaking, when time is critical for an upcoming event (this is usually after you have mailed the press release and you are reminding the editor), or when the editor or reporter requests that you fax or e-mail information.
- Check and note publicity policies. Some organizations do not welcome unsolicited e-mails, faxes, or other electronically transmitted information.
- Crisis news releases should be used when information in a crisis situation is changing rapidly. Frequency is the key to keeping the media informed, eliminating false reports, and preventing public anxiety caused by misinformation. It is extremely helpful to have a crisis public relations team ready to act in emergencies like a flood, fire, earthquake, or other disaster. This team should draw up and have in place a crisis plan. Preparations for disasters should allow you to create and send releases from another location on official letterhead.

Consider these additional factors in crisis situations:

- Estimate the audience scope and send releases to local, state, regional, national, and international media.
- Write in a brief, concise style, using bullets so the facts can be easily pulled out.

- Type in the time after the date on page one, and put the date and time on every page. (Exceptions to this rule are press releases that aren't time-sensitive, such as new-book press releases.)
- Add "Issued by: [person's name]," with a telephone number.
- Include a contact name and telephone number on a twenty-four-hour basis.
- Issue updates as frequently as new information is available.
- Get legal approval, if possible, before releasing.
- Keep a release log covering when, and to whom, releases were made.
- Use recorded telephone messages, and update them, if possible, for incoming calls.
- Set up a schedule of briefings.
- Make videotapes or live reports from the disaster scene, if possible.
- Use audiotaped official statements for radio, if possible.
- Have press kits with background information about the organization available, if possible.

USE THE CORRECT FORMAT

- All releases must be consistent, be sent on official letterhead, and look professional.
- Leave the top third of the first page blank for the editor to write his or her headline.
- All press releases must have six key elements. Follow the placement of these six elements as illustrated in the samples.
  1. A date indicating when the release was issued. Indicate when the information should be made public: "For Immediate Release" or "For Release On (or After) (date)_____" should be included, as illustrated in the samples.
  2. A press release should have a title. Type "NEWS RELEASE" in capitals at the center of the first page.
  3. A contact appears two lines below the title, type "CONTACT" flush left with the margin (or as illustrated in the samples). Include the name of the contact person for the release, with a telephone or fax number or both. The name of the organization may also be included.
  4. A headline (subject line) appears two lines below the contact, centered, and usually in caps. If possible, include the company's business and the subject of the release: GRAND OPENING OF DOODLE'S HAIR SALON.
     Try to catch the reader's attention. This is your chance to advertise your story to the editor so he or she will decide to print it. If the story is complicated, use a subhead as well: Free Styling on January 10 by New York's Best.
  5. The dateline appears two lines below the subject line and is indented two spaces. It is composed of the city (and, if necessary, the state, in caps). The date may appear in upper and lower case, followed by a double dash.
  6. Copy begins on the same line, immediately after the dateline.
- Typing should be done on a single side of an 8½-by-11-inch paper, double spaced with a minimum of one-inch margins all around. Exceptions to this rule do exist. In some industries, like publishing, an 8½-by-14-inch paper is sometimes used.
- If more than one page is required, center and type "(MORE)" or "(CONTINUED)" in capitals at the bottom of the page and begin the next page flush left on the margin with a one-word title and page number: "Doodles 2."
- Short paragraphs are best.
- Use capitalization sparingly.
- Be consistent.
- At the end of the news release, center one of the following to indicate the end: # # # or (END) or - 30 -.
- Use the active voice if possible.
- Write in an objective tone.
- Use simple, clear, and concise sentences.
- Edit. Eliminate all unnecessary words.

Press Release Announcing a Community Internship Program

We want you to feel welcome at every Mobil Friendly Serve station. Every time!

Mobil

FOR IMMEDIATE RELEASE

Contact: Jeanne O. Mitchell
Mobil Oil Corp.
(703) 846-2722
1(800) SKY-PAGE
PIN 5219855#
Paula Gifford
The Rowland Company
(212) 527-8818

MOBIL TO BENEFIT ORLANDO YOUTH WITH $10,000 IN SCHOLARSHIPS

Mobil Summer Intern Program Provides
Education, Employment and Scholarships for Orlando Youth

ORLANDO, May 1 -- The City of Orlando and Mobil Oil have joined forces to introduce the Mobil Friendly Serve Academy, an internship program providing service industry education and employment for Orlando young people. This City/corporate partnership to benefit local youth will offer classroom and on-the-job training for over 75 Orlando young people.

To further encourage the pursuit of careers in the service industry, Mobil Foundation, Inc. will contribute $10,000 in scholarship funds to the City of Orlando to establish the Mobil Friendly Serve Scholarship program. Through this grant, 19 scholarships of $500 will be awarded each to young people participating in the summer employment programs administered by the City's Department of Community and Youth Services and Orlando Fights Back, a grass-roots program to promote drug free communities. Remaining funds will be used toward graduation ceremonies and a celebration honoring program participants.

The summer internship and scholarship programs will be implemented through Orlando's13 Neighborhood Centers, which are dedicated to fulfilling the recreational and increasingly, the educational needs of city youth.

- more -

(cont.)

Mobil Corporation Friendly Serve Academy Announcement by Mobil Corporation with the Rowland Company. Public Relations Society of America 1996 Silver Anvil Award–winning community relations program.

Press Release (continued)

- 2 -

Through the Mobil Friendly Serve Academy, each intern will receive over 27 hours of classroom instruction by City, Neighborhood Center, and Mobil Oil representatives. Seminars include instruction in good citizenship, assertiveness training, financial planning, cultural diversity, and interviewing techniques.

From May through August, interns will put learning into action while working as Friendly Serve Attendants at 25 local Mobil Friendly Serve stations. On-the-job-training will include providing customers with consistent high-quality service -- from greeting customers with a smile at the self-serve islands to offering services like cleaning windshields, checking tire air pressure or picking up soda to go at the mart. Crest, The Uniform Company will donate specially designed uniform sets valued at $7,000 for the interns.

To help guide their progress throughout the program, Friendly Serve Academy interns will be assigned mentors from the Neighborhood Centers and from the City's "Joining Older and Younger" (JOY) program.

Mobil Oil's emphasis on superior customer service makes Mobil Friendly Serve stations an ideal training ground for young people interested in service industry careers. Mobil Friendly Serve uses an innovative approach to the gasoline buying experience. The Friendly Serve program, instituted at 80 stations in the Orlando area, promises to provide customers with speedy transactions in clean, well-lit stations, staffed by Friendly Serve Attendants -- 7 AM to 7 PM -- who appreciate their business.

"The Orlando community, like Mobil Oil, is acclaimed for the level of service it provides. We at Mobil partnered with the City of Orlando in creating the Mobil Friendly Serve Academy to help educate and train the City's next generation of service industry professionals," explains Ted Rullo, District Manager, Mobil Oil.

The Mobil Friendly Serve Academy program will culminate with a graduation ceremony on August 11. Interns will have the opportunity to continue employment with Mobil upon completion of the program.

Mobil is the third largest U.S. gasoline retailer with more than 8,000 gasoline outlets nationwide. The Mobil Friendly Serve initiative began in Orlando during January.

# # #

orl/med/r-fsa

Press Release Announcing a Medical Continuing Education Course

For Immediate Release

Sponsored by:

Harvard Medical School
Department of Continuing Education

The Mind/Body Medical Institute
CareGroup
Beth Israel Deaconess Medical Center

Supported in part by educational grants
from the John Templeton Foundation

Contacts: Liz Hall   Elizabeth Melone
202-944-5138 202-944-1923

GROWING NUMBER OF SCIENTIFIC STUDIES POINT TO ROLE OF SPIRITUALITY IN HEALING

Health Professionals and Religious Scholars at Harvard Medical School CME Course
Discuss Scientific Evidence Linking Medicine and Religion

Houston, March 23, 1998 – Over the next three days, physicians from Harvard, Duke, Dartmouth and Georgetown University medical schools will share with more than 600 physicians, nurses, social workers and psychologists data that suggests religion plays a role in their patients' ability to survive surgery, recover from depression and live longer. These data come from the increasing number of scientific studies that offer evidence of the clinical benefits of belief. The physician-researchers will discuss the key studies at a **12:30 press conference, Monday, March 23.**

These presentations are part of the 3-day *Spirituality & Healing in Medicine* continuing medical education course – the first held in Houston -- which examines the growing use of belief as a complement to traditional medical practices. Medical researchers and theologians will address questions such as: 'What are the scientific data that support the healing power of belief?' and 'What is the best way to tap a patient's belief system and apply the strength of their conviction to the healing process?'

Highlights of Clinical Studies:

- Patients are 12 times more likely to survive open-heart surgery if they have religious faith and social support. (Oxman et al, Dartmouth Medical School, 1995; <u>Psychosomatic Medicine</u>, 57:5-15)

- Over a 28-year study period, the risk of dying was almost 25% less (35% in women) for frequent religious service attendees, after controlling for health practices, social ties and well being (Strawbridge et al, University of California – Berkeley, 1997; <u>American Journal of Public Health,</u> 87:957-961)

- Similarly, those who attend religious services, at least once per week, have been shown to have stronger immune system functioning (Koenig et al, Duke University Medical Center, 1997 <u>International Journal of Psychiatry in Medicine</u>, 27:233-250). The investigators suspect that attending services counteracts stress, which is believed to play a role in immune function.

- In a study that will measure the financial impact, Koenig et al have begun a four-year study of the effect of religion and spirituality on the use of health services among sick, elderly patients. These patients typically are high-users of health services; e.g., re-hospitalization, nursing home use, etc.

The course's founder and director, Herbert Benson, M.D., hopes the scientific data and the cost-benefit analysis catches the eye of both physicians and health insurers. Many physicians are reluctant to broach matters of religion with patients, he said, and they often don't have the time to directly address their patients' support systems and stress levels.

John Templeton Foundation—The Mind/Body Medical Institute at Beth Israel Deaconess Medical Center—Harvard Medical School educational program. Public Relations Society of America 1997 Silver Anvil Award–winning community relations program.

Press Release (continued)

Science, Medicine and Religion, Page Two

"As a result," Dr. Benson said, "patients don't bring the full effect of their belief systems to bear on their illness." Dr. Benson, the Mind/Body Medical Institute Associate Professor at Harvard Medical School, has studied the relationship between stress, belief and healing for 30 years. He has long witnessed that prayer is a powerful means to elicit the "relaxation response," a quieting of the body which has been shown to decrease blood pressure, heart rate, and breathing and metabolic rates. He uses techniques that elicit the relaxation response in his patients as a complement, not an alternative, to traditional medicine.

"Modern medicine should pay attention to the beliefs of patients in order to take full advantage of the body's awesome healing power," Dr. Benson said. "There must be a balance," he said, between the use of medicines, surgery and procedures, and self-care methods like relaxation therapies, prayer or meditation.

Courses such as Dr. Benson's are evidence of a growing interest and acceptance by today's medical providers in the clinical effect of spirituality.

Two recent surveys of health professionals* found that 99% of family physicians, and 94% of HMO executives believe personal prayer, meditation or other spiritual practices can aid medical treatment and accelerate the healing process.

In fact, more than half of the physicians surveyed (55%) reported they currently incorporate relaxation and/or meditation -- common mind/body techniques -- as a complement to their patient's traditional medical treatment. And 80% of these doctors believe the techniques should be a standard part of formal medical training for healthcare professionals.

The growing awareness among health professionals of the healing power of prayer has prompted teaching programs on the topic in 30 of the nation's top medical schools, including Johns Hopkins, Georgetown, University of Chicago and Bowman-Gray. Susan Hobbins, a student at Harvard Medical School, will speak in Houston about the curriculum she, Dr. Benson and Dr. Gregory Fricchione are developing to offer future Harvard medical students.

"Medical professionals around the world acknowledge that spirituality helps the healing process," John Templeton, Jr., M.D., President of the John Templeton Foundation, said. "The best part about medicine's growing interest in the power of faith is that we will create a more holistic approach to health care, and a generation of doctors who understand and address their patients' spiritual needs," he said.

Harvard Medical School's Department of Continuing Medical Education and the Institute of Religion at the Texas Medical Center are presenting the March conference, *Spirituality and Healing in Medicine,* which is sponsored in part by an educational grant from the John Templeton Foundation.

The John Templeton Foundation was founded in 1987 by internationally renowned investment manager Sir John Templeton to encourage the pursuit of religious and scientific knowledge. The Foundation currently funds over 90 projects, studies, award programs and publications around the world, and its programs focus on five areas: spiritual information through science; spirituality and health; character development; free enterprise education; and the Templeton Prize for Progress in Religion. The John Templeton Foundation underwrites a program to expand the teaching of spirituality in medical schools as a complement to traditional medicine.

For more information about the John Templeton Foundation, see www.templeton.org.

# # #

* Sponsored by the John Templeton Foundation, the surveys were conducted by Yankelovich Partners at annual meetings of the American Association of Family Physicians (1996) and the American Association of Health Plans (1997).

Press Release Announcing Essay Contest Winners

Page 2

"Avon Kids Care" Essay Contest

"Av

Av
So
w
DB   w
e
for   R
th   f
av
ou

AVON'S
BREAST
CANCER
AWARENESS
CRUSADE

Contact: Patricia Sterling   Marjorie Walker/Nancy Rosenblum
           Avon Products, Inc.   PT&Co.
           212-282-5523   212-229-0500

"AVON KIDS CARE" ESSAY CONTEST AWARDS $800,000 IN GRANTS TO BREAST HEALTH PROGRAMS ON BEHALF OF STUDENT WINNERS

Sixteen Winners, Kindergarten to College, Also Receive $1,000 Savings Bonds

"I never want my mom out of my world. I am the guardian of her future."—Jake Close, 11

"...no matter how fit, you must have a happy heart to be truly healthy."—Becky Schneider, 14

NEW YORK (March 12, 1998) — These quotes typify the insight and sensitivity displayed in the essays of 16 **"Avon Kids Care"** winners who, in expressing why and how they would encourage a favorite female adult to take care of her health, helped 16 regional breast health programs receive $800,000 in grant money.

The winners range in age from six to 22 and express sentiments as diverse as "My grandma should stop smoking and I should stop sucking my thumb" (Hillary Hee, 6, of Colchester, Vermont), to "It is my responsibility to give my mother the same love and support that she has always given me" (Jacquelyn Coles, 22, of McDonald, Ohio). But the winning entries collectively choose love or admiration as a motivating force for encouraging the grown-up women in the children's lives to embrace healthful eating, exercise, regular check-ups and companionship as means to ensure healthy futures.

On behalf of these young health crusaders, Avon's Breast Cancer Awareness Crusade — the largest corporate supporter of breast health programs in America — has divided the $800,000 into sixteen $50,000 **"Avon Kids Care"** grants. These are being awarded to breast health programs selected by breast cancer experts through a competitive application process administered by Avon and its partner, the National Alliance of Breast Cancer Organizations (NABCO). The programs have been matched geographically to individual contest winners, in whose name each $50,000 grant will be presented.

-more-

Avon's Breast Cancer Awareness Crusade. Public Relations Society of America 1997 Silver Anvil Award–winning public service campaign.

46

QUESTIONS AND ANSWERS

*The more we proceed by plan, the more effec-
tively we may hit by accident.*

—FRIEDRICH DURRENMATT

The question and answer, or Q&A, promotes understanding of a topic. It anticipates questions editors may have, states them, and provides the answers or explanations. It most commonly accompanies a complicated press release and is also an effective tool for distribution within the organization to help personnel deal consistently with press questions.

In a number of forms—often just the questions—the Q&A is used to distribute to radio or television talk-show hosts or interviewers to interest them in interviewing a person, and to help direct the interview into comprehensive areas of public interest.

The key to an effective Q&A is doing the proper research to learn what your public wants to know.

DECIDE TO WRITE

Use this communication to

- Suggest questions of general interest to an interviewer
- Promote an author of a book, play, research paper, etc.
- Stimulate the reporters' interest
- Simplify and address common questions of a complicated news release

THINK ABOUT CONTENT

- Use a thought-provoking title to capture interest.
- Develop a list of the questions most likely to be asked about the topic. For an advanced personal computer, for example, the questions might include

*What advantages does it offer over other
    products now available?*
When will it be available for home use?
Where can it be purchased in our area?
How easy will it be to operate?
*What kind of setup, instruction, etc. will
    it require?*
What will the price be?
Who will buy it?
*Are other companies making a competitive
    product?*
*What are the company's first-year sales
    projections?*
How long did it take to develop this product?
How will this make consumers' lives better?

- Write short yet comprehensive answers to the questions for the people who will be interviewed.
- Be sure to have both the questions and answers approved by organization officials before you distribute them to the media.

ELIMINATE WRONG MESSAGES

- Do not include technical terms without defining them.
- Remove all jargon.

CONSIDER SPECIAL SITUATIONS

Be sure the people who will be interviewed are prepared. Rehearse with them.

SELECT A FORMAT

- If the Q&A is sent with a press release, the design of the two documents should look compatible. It should be on a matching or coordinating 8$\frac{1}{2}$-by-11-inch letterhead in the same format, with the same typeface.
- Many other formats may be used to create interest. Oversized postcards printed in glossy four-color ink might be used for a list of interview questions, for example.

Question and Answer Sheet

Questions and Answers

For questions that may be asked as you conduct media/community outreach.

Please note that these "answers" are not scripts to be read/recited. They include the key message points that can/should be presented in the responder's own language.

Q: Why is the APA launching this effort NOW?

A: Several reasons:

- With all of the change and flux that exist in the health care system today, and the ongoing debate and media coverage about proposals to further change the way health care is provided and funded, it's a very confusing time for consumers. With all of this change, it's a time when consumers really need to be educated about their options, their care and their coverage.

- Additionally, APA members are aware that their patients are facing increasingly stressful situations, especially related to the workplace and family issues.

- To assess the situation, the APA conducted a national survey — and found that there is definitely a need for public education. We found out that people understand the role/value of psychological health, and think it's okay to get help (which was a welcome surprise given past research on stigma), BUT at a time when they most need to be aware and educated, the public doesn't have the information they need.

Q: Isn't this just an effort to get more people to see psychologists?

A: First, our intention is to provide information to those people who NEED help. We have no interest in promoting inappropriate or overutilization of psychological services.

Second, our campaign promotes talking to "someone who can help," and our consumer information material notes that there are many types of mental health care providers, and tells consumers how to find names of and evaluate the qualifications of potential providers.

Third, the survey makes it quite clear that people really do need information. Because there has been a stigma in the past about seeking mental health care, people simply haven't talked about it and there isn't an overall public awareness of when and how to get help. That's a need that should be filled and our campaign is filling it. Imagine the situation if someone had a broken leg, but had no idea if he should get professional help, or how to go about getting help. We'd have a lot of people limping around in pain, just as today we have a lot of people dealing with extremely stressful lives, and no idea how they can help deal with that stress.

American Psychological Association with Pacific Visions Communications and Porter Novelli, "Talk to Someone Who Can Help," Public Relations Society of America 1997 Silver Anvil Award–winning institutional program.

Question and Answer Sheet (continued)

Q: Why are so many people confused about how to get help?

A: It's partially due to the stigma that used to be attached to needing or seeking mental health services. Because it was such an awkward situation, most people didn't talk freely about finding a professional to help; they didn't even acknowledge that they were in therapy.

Now, as the APA survey reveals, people are more aware of the value of mental health services, and more likely to at least understand that they can get help in coping with life stresses, emotional problems, etc.

But we've got a gap — because as a society we were silent for so long on the subject, most people really don't know exactly who to ask or how to go about finding help.

Q: Is life today REALLY that much more stressful?

A: Yes, it is in reality — and in terms of people's perceptions.

Stress related to jobs is at an all-time high, for real and perceptual reasons. The reality is that people are being laid off, downsized, displaced and all the other euphemisms. So those people are affected in reality. Then you've got the people who are still on the job — but doing the work of 2 people and worried about their

job security. According to national studies, corporations lose about 16 days annually in productivity per worker due to stress, anxiety and depression. Finally, due to the immediacy and pervasiveness of media coverage, we have an atmosphere of fear and anxiety that affects even people in situations where they may not be in any real jeopardy.

And job stress isn't the only problem facing Americans. Creating and maintaining a happy and stable family is much more of a challenge. From divorce to drugs in elementary schools, from how to care for elderly parents to teen suicides — it is increasingly difficult for families to cope. The reality is that there is simply much more for them — parents and children — to cope with.

And people's psychological health is definitely affecting their physical health. Studies have indicated that up to half of all visits to primary care physicians are due to conditions that are caused or exacerbated by emotional issues.

All of this comes at a time when both the hectic pace of life and the scattering of the extended family leave many people feeling like they have nowhere to turn, no one to talk to.

That's why this public education campaign is so important.

47
BIOGRAPHY

Let another man praise thee,
and not thine own mouth.

—PROVERBS 27:2

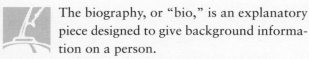 The biography, or "bio," is an explanatory piece designed to give background information on a person.

There are basically two forms to follow. The first is the newspaper or journalistic style. It is simple and comprehensive. The second form, a feature biography, gives information more as a personality profile.

Either piece may be accompanied by a fact sheet or timeline (see pages 275 and 278, respectively).

DECIDE TO WRITE

Use this piece:
- To get special media coverage
- As part of a media kit
- To give information to someone who will introduce the person for a speech
- With a book the person has authored

THINK ABOUT CONTENT
- Develop a logical outline.
- Write a commanding lead.
- Flesh out your ideas.
- Vary and simplify sentence structure and language.
- Make sure there's a logical flow and comprehensive coverage.
- Back up all your claims, and pay off on your lead.
- Include some human-interest facts.
- Check for consistency and tense.
- Edit, edit, edit.
- Proofread.

For the newspaper-style bio:
- Open by identifying the person by name, title, and achievements relevant to the point of the biography.
- Summarize the person's accomplishments, position, and activities.
- State the person's educational and professional background.
- Include or exclude personal information, such as marital status, children, and academic standing, depending on the audience.

For the feature-style bio:

- Use a more relaxed writing style, more like a magazine feature.
- Add human-interest details.
- Include quotes from the person.

ALSO SEE "ANNOUNCEMENT," PAGE 23; "PRESS RELEASE," PAGE 256; "BACKGROUNDER," PAGE 271; "TIMELINE," PAGE 278; "MEDIA KIT," PAGE 253; AND "PITCH LETTER," PAGE 251.

SELECT A FORMAT

Use 8½-by-11-inch letterhead and a typeface consistent with any other pieces in the mail-out.

Celebrity
2-2-2

CHAR
Coors
Berry
have

Da
of
in

Coors "Literacy. Pass It On."
311 Tenth Street, NH 420
Golden, Colorado
80401
1-800-525-0308

Coors "Literacy. Pass It On."
Celebrity Biographies

DANNY GLOVER -- Actor Danny Glover is the national celebrity spokesperson for Coors "Literacy. Pass It On." program. Known in Hollywood as the man who "...is always doing something for underprivileged people...," according to co-star and friend Mel Gibson, Glover has dedicated his life to helping others.

> **"The issue of family literacy is an important one to me personally. I have worked to inspire a love of reading within my own family,"** says Glover.

One of Hollywood's most versatile and respected actors, Glover has gained international star status for his box-office-busters *Lethal Weapon, Lethal Weapon 2, Lethal Weapon 3* and *Grand Canyon*. Glover is in the good company of Alec Baldwin, Hume Cronyn, Harrison Ford, Clint Black, Al Gore, Wayne Gretzky, Tom Hanks, Michael Jordan and Paul Newman as being named one of the top 10 sensitive men by Daphne Rose Kingma in her book *The Men We Never Knew.*

JOHN BERRY -- Singer/songwriter John Berry is joining Coors "Literacy. Pass It On." for its country music promotion. Berry, one of the most talked-about new stars in Nashville, is making a name for himself as he climbs the country music charts singing what he calls "romantic songs that are also a little tough."

Berry's rich trademark sound grips his listeners with his raw, Southern country blues. His songs are incisive, well-crafted yet spontaneous and gutsy. He looks for songs with a lot of range and movements and compares his singing style to Wynonna, saying "I don't think there are any other male singers that do the kind of stuff I do."

Berry was born in South Carolina and grew up in Atlanta, Georgia. He began playing the guitar at age 12 and by 17 he had become a serious songwriter.

Berry's self-penned songs include hit singles, "More Sorry Than You'll Ever Know," "Kiss Me In The Car," and the love-in-the-'90s "She's Got A Mind Of Her Own." His song "Your Love Amazes Me" off his self-titled album went #1 on Billboard and R&R charts in May. Five months later, in October the same self-titled album was named Recording Industry Artists Association (R.I.A.A.) certified gold.

(continued)

The Biography or Bio offers concise background information on a person, usually focused on his or her relationship to the organization, cause, or event being publicized.

48

BACKGROUNDER

Nothing is more simple than greatness; indeed, to be simple is to be great.

—RALPH WALDO EMERSON

The backgrounder gives pertinent and comprehensive information about products, places, and organizations (see "Biography," page 268, for people). This piece should be kept to one page.

DECIDE TO WRITE
Use this piece to enable readers to understand the subject.

THINK ABOUT CONTENT
- Vary language and sentence structure, but be consistent in tone and use the present tense. Make sure the information is complete.
- Construct information paragraphs as follows:
  —In paragraph 1, the lead, make an important statement, then back it up with substantiating information: "ICQ, the city's largest employer, now has 8,999 employees."
  —In paragraph 2, give the scope of the announcement, and back this up with facts.
  —In paragraph 3, give the history or background, and summarize the developmental steps, functions, size, structure, and operation.
  —In paragraph 4, cover the organization's philosophy, including objectives, goals, priorities, new areas, research, and development.
  —In paragraph 5, the conclusion, include boilerplate data like the number and location of branch offices.
- Edit.
- Proofread.

SELECT A FORMAT
Use 8½-by-11-inch letterhead.

Backgrounder

AVON'S
BREAST
CANCER
AWARENESS
CRUSADE

Avon's Breast Cancer Awareness Crusade

Background

Founding National Partners:

Federal Centers for Disease Control and Prevention (CDC)
Atlanta, GA

National Alliance of Breast Cancer Organizations (NABCO)
New York, NY

National Cancer Institute (NCI)
Bethesda, MD

YWCA of the U.S.A.
New York, NY

Avon Worldwide Fund for Women's Health

As a company dedicated to the total well-being of women everywhere, Avon has created The Avon Worldwide Fund for Women's Health. The goal of this global initiative is to improve the health of women around the world. Under this plan, Avon's operations and facilities worldwide are encouraged to develop programs that address a leading health-related problem faced by women locally.

Avon's Breast Cancer Awareness Crusade in the United States, founded in October 1993, is a program that exemplifies the goals of The Avon Worldwide Fund for Women's Health. Its mission is to provide women across the country, particularly those who are medically underserved, with access to a full range of breast cancer education and early detection screening services.

Partnerships/Collaborations

Avon's Crusade is able to offer these vital services through the formation of innovative private/non-profit/public partnerships. The organizations with whom Avon collaborates are: the YWCA of the U.S.A. and the National Alliance of Breast Cancer Organizations (NABCO), the Federal Centers for Disease Control and Prevention (CDC) and the National Cancer Institute (NCI).

YWCA of the U.S.A.'s ENCORE*plus* Program

Avon's partnership with the YWCA of the U.S.A. was established with assistance from the Federal Centers for Disease Control and Prevention (CDC), to create and fund ENCORE*plus*. This program is available to qualified YWCA Associations that want to offer women in the community a structured program of education, early detection and post-diagnosis services for breast and cervical cancer. ENCORE*plus* provides each Association (76 are currently participating in 30 states) with comprehensive training in outreach, health education and referral mechanisms for women, particularly those who are underserved, to medical services at little or no cost. Avon offers volunteer support to ENCORE*plus* programs from its national sales force of Representatives.

- more -

Avon's Breast Cancer Awareness Crusade. Public Relations Society of America 1997 Silver Anvil Award–winning public service campaign.

Avon's Crusade Background, p. 3

<u>Additional Projects and Programs</u>
Avon's Crusade encompasses numerous projects and programs, beyond those of
the YWCA of the U.S.A. and NABCO, to promote the importance of breast cancer
education and early detection as widely as possible.

The Avon Breast Cancer Leadership Awards
Avon's Breast Cancer Awareness Crusade awarded $1 million in October 1996
to ten individuals whose leadership of an organization made an outstanding
contribution to breast cancer education, outreach, patient advocacy, support services
and quality-of-life research. The Avon Breast Cancer Leadership Awards marked the
first time that excellence of this kind was recognized with funding. The event was
promoted in media nationwide last October during National Breast Cancer Awareness
Month.

The Avon Breast Cancer Screening Survey
Avon's Crusade commissioned a pioneering survey in the fall of 1996 to examine
factors that influence women's decisions about breast cancer early detection screening.
The results of the survey, the first of its kind ever conducted, were published in media
nationwide last October during National Breast Cancer Awareness Month.

Pink Ribbon Pin, Pen, Earrings and Mug
Avon's 450,000 Sales Representatives have raised over $25 million since 1993 for
Avon's Breast Cancer Awareness Crusade through the sales of products featuring the
pink ribbon. This symbol was chosen by the international breast cancer community to
represent awareness of and hope for women affected by the disease. Proceeds from the
sales of Avon's pink ribbon products are used to fund the programs supported by the
Crusade. All pink ribbon products are gift-boxed and accompanied by an educational
flyer about breast cancer and Avon's Crusade.

The Avon Pink Ribbon Pin sells for $2.00 and is available in two sizes. The larger
pin is crafted in goldtone metal with a pink enamel finish and a delicate goldtone rose.
The smaller version, suitable for men as well as women, is designed in a simpler style
without the rose. The Avon Pink Ribbon Pen, which bears the ribbon motif on its clip,
sells for $3.00.

In October 1996, Avon introduced Pink Ribbon Earrings that subtly reinterpret the
symbol in a heart-shaped design crafted of goldtone metal and pink enamel. The
earrings are available for $3.00 in clip-on style and with posts for pierced ears.

-more-

Backgrounder (continued)

Avon's Crusade Background, p. 5

Shopping Mall Events

Avon Sales Representatives donated their time on Saturday, October 7, 1995, at 67 shopping malls nationwide in partnership with Simon Property Group, one of America's leading shopping center developers and managers. The theme of the event was "Women Helping Women" and Avon Representatives did just that by attending each mall event and distributing educational materials, creating special displays, and selling the Crusade's pink ribbon fundraising products. Avon Representatives also encouraged women to use the Crusade's Pink Ribbon Pen to sign giant "Pledge Walls" and their own personal pledge cards, as gestures of commitment to take better care of their breast health.

PBS Television Special

In 1993, Avon underwrote *The Breast Care Test,* a PBS special produced by WQED of Pittsburgh that aired on most PBS stations on October 15, 1993.

Jane Pauley hosted this straightforward, woman-to-woman program about breast cancer. The late Erma Bombeck and other women who have had breast cancer shared their compelling stories. Susan Love, M.D., author of *Dr. Susan Love's Breast Book,* answered women's most-asked questions. The program also included step-by-step demonstrations of breast self-exams, and information about mammography and clinical breast exams.

A highlight of the one-hour program was a series of 10 questions, the answers to which began the empowering process of information-sharing and increased understanding about breast cancer. *The Breast Care Test* continues to be rebroadcast by PBS affiliated and non-affiliated stations across the country.

The Breast Care Test Project included community outreach activities with the American Cancer Society (ACS), the National Education Association (NEA) and the YWCA of the U.S.A., to encourage viewership and participation in on-going educational activities.

Spanish Television Special

Because the message of breast cancer early detection must be delivered in a way that reflects the unique culture and language of Hispanic women, PBS and Avon also developed an original videotape in Spanish for use by media and organizations serving Hispanic women. The program is called *Mujer a Mujer: Hablemos Sobre el Cancer del Seno,* and aired nationwide on the Telemundo Network on January 29, 1994.

- more -

49
FACT SHEET

Prove all things; hold fast that which is good.

—I THESSALONIANS 5:21

The fact sheet breaks down complicated or very involved information into related sections so editors, reporters, interviewers, and others can quickly find the information they want. It often accompanies a complicated news release or is part of a press kit distributed before a press conference.

DECIDE TO WRITE
Use the fact sheet
- As part of a press kit
- To accompany a complex news release

THINK ABOUT CONTENT
First develop a comprehensive outline. For a corporation, include name and description, address, number of employees, key officers, history, developmental changes, and locations. A fact sheet for international visitors to a city, for example, should include name and location, language, population, employment, government, climate, history, hotel accommodations, meeting and convention facilities, cultural attractions, sightseeing, and events. Also include notes about customs, dress, formalities, visas, and inoculation requirements. Make statements clear and concise.

Fact Sheet

FACTS

About the Mind/Body Medical Institute
at Beth Israel Deaconess Medical Center Care Group, and Harvard Medical School
www.feltco.com/hmscme

The Mind/Body Medical Institute is a non-profit scientific and educational organization dedicated to the study of behavioral medicine, including mind/body interactions and the relaxation response. Herbert Benson, MD, the Institute's founder and president, pioneered these approaches and the scientific study of the role they play in furthering better health and well-being.

The Institute's Programs:

- Conducting basic and clinical research, both independently and collaboratively.
- Quantifying the cost and benefits of mind/body and other behavioral medicine approaches.
- Scientifically evaluating complementary healing practices including the role of religious belief.
- Disseminating the results of its findings through medical and general publications, lectures, symposia, teaching and training programs.

The Institute's research team–comprised of scientists from Beth Israel Deaconess Medical Center, a Harvard Medical School teaching hospital–has pioneered research to determine the physiology and health benefits of mind/body interactions and their clinical applications. At the forefront of modern medicine, the Institute serves as a bridge between the mind and body, science and religion and Eastern and Western medical practices.

Areas of Research:

- Basic scientific research of the physiology, biochemistry and behavior of mind/body interactions.
- Clinical research applying mind/body interactions to the treatment and management of hypertension and cardiovascular diseases, cancer, chronic pain, insomnia and infertility as well as other medical conditions.
- Investigation of the cost effectiveness of behavioral medicine and mind/body treatments.
- Cross-cultural studies, including the continued scientific evaluation of the world's healing practices, meditation traditions and the importance of religious or spiritual belief in health and healing.
- Educational applications of mind/body relationships.

The Mind/Body Medical Institute is a subsidiary of Care Group, the parent company of the Beth Israel Deaconess Medical Center, which is affiliated with the Harvard Medical School. For more information contact:

Herbert Benson, MD
The Mind/Body Medical Institute
10 Francis Street, Suite 1A
Boston, MA 02215
617-632-9530

John Templeton Foundation—The Mind/Body Medical Institute at Beth Israel Deaconess Medical Center—Harvard Medical School "Spirituality & Healing in Medicine II." Public Relations Society of America 1997 Silver Anvil Award–winning entry in the category of special events and observances.

Fact Sheet

We want you to feel welcome at every Mobil Friendly Serve station. Every time!

Mobil

MOBIL FRIENDLY SERVE ACADEMY AND SCHOLARSHIP PROGRAM

FACT SHEET

Mobil Friendly Serve Academy

The Mobil Friendly Serve Academy is an innovative community service initiative by Mobil Oil to provide service industry education and employment for Orlando youth.

- Implemented by 13 Neighborhood Centers throughout Orlando, 50 student interns have enrolled in the program which will provide classroom education in career skills and on-the-job training at local Mobil Friendly Serve stations.

- Student interns will receive 22 hours of classroom training on topics including Good Citizenship, Assertiveness Training, Cultural Diversity, and Interviewing Techniques.

- Student interns will receive on-the-job training beginning in May at over 25 participating Mobil Friendly Serve stations throughout Orlando.

- The company's emphasis on superior customer service makes Mobil Friendly Serve stations an ideal training ground for young people interested in service industry careers.

- As Mobil Friendly Serve interns, students will greet customers and can offer services like cleaning the windshield, checking tire air pressure or picking up soda to go at the mart.

- The Mobil Friendly Serve internship will culminate with a graduation ceremony on August 11.

- Student interns will have the opportunity to continue employment with Mobil upon completion of the program.

- more -

Mobil Corporation Friendly Serve Academy Announcement, by Mobil Corporation with the Rowland Company. Public Relations Society of America 1996 Silver Anvil Award–winning community relations program.

50

TIMELINE

If the bugle gives an indistinct sound,

who will get ready for battle?

—CORINTHIANS 14:8

 When information lends itself to chronological organization, a timeline format allows for easy comprehension.

Timelines usually accompany complex news releases, and they are written so that editors and reporters can quickly grasp the sequence of events.

DECIDE TO WRITE
Use this communication
* To clarify when events happened
* As part of a press kit

THINK ABOUT CONTENT
* Line up important events or developments by time designation.
* Edit to the concise facts.

MOBIL FRIENDLY SERVE ACADEMY

MOBIL FRIENDLY SERVE SCHOLARSHIP PROGRAM
OFFICIAL SELECTION PROCESS AND TIMELINE

7/31

- Deadline for applications; assume last of the applications with proper postmark will arrive at City of Orlando Youth Services no later than 8/4

- As applications arrive they will be screened by a Community and Youth Serviced staffer who will verify that the applications meet all of the required criteria

8/4

- Selection Committee made up of Community and Youth Service staffers will receive quantities of applications to review

8/7

- Selection Committee will determine top 30 applicants and send those applications to members of the Awards Panel for review

- Awards Panel will be made up of members of the Community and Youth Services Advisory Board and the Neighborhood Centers Advisory Board

8/9

- Each member of the Awards Panel will select his or her choice for the 19 scholarship awards and submit those recommendations to Herb Washington

8/10

- Herb Washington will present the tally of those recommendations to the Awards Panel in a special session; determination will be made for the 19 scholarship recipients

- Notification will be sent to 19 recipients by overnight mail

- Community and Youth Services may also notify employer or volunteer project supervisor for each of the recipients so that employer or supervisor can personally notify student of award prior to arrival of notification letter

8/11

- Notification letters arrive at homes of 19 scholarship recipients

- Mobil Friendly Serve interns who are scholarship recipients will be recognized at the 8/11 graduation ceremony

8/26

- Scholarship recipients will be honored by the Mayor at the August 26 Orlando City Council Meeting

- Mobil representative will present certificates to each of the recipients at that time

Mobil Corporation Friendly Serve Academy Announcement, by Mobil Corporation with the Rowland Company.
Public Relations Society of America 1996 Silver Anvil Award–winning community relations program.

51

BIBLIOGRAPHY

Devise, wit; write, pen.

—WILLIAM SHAKESPEARE

A bibliography is a useful accompaniment to a biography (bio) or a backgrounder. A bibliography may list articles and books that have been published by or about the subject. When this piece is part of a press kit or is attached to a news release, the reporter, editor, or interviewer can quickly retrieve any additional information he or she needs.

DECIDE TO WRITE

Use this piece
- As part of a person's credentials or credits
- To accompany a resume
- As background information if a person is going to be introduced
- As part of a press kit

THINK ABOUT CONTENT
- Use a standard format such as one described in the *Chicago Manual of Style* for your listings.
- Be consistent throughout.

Also see "Press Release," page 256; "Biography," page 268; "Media Kit," page 253; "Backgrounder," page 271; "Timeline," page 278; and "Resume," page 74.

Bibliography

Annotated Bibliography

Azhar, M.Z., Varma, S.L., & Dharap, A.S. (1994). Religious psychotherapy in anxiety disorder patients. Acta Psychiatrica Scandinavica, 90, 1-3. Randomized 62 Muslim patients with generalized anxiety disorder to either traditional treatment (supportive psychotherapy and anxiolytic drugs) or traditional treatment plus religious psychotherapy. Religious psychotherapy involved use of prayer and reading verses of the Holy Koran specific to the person's situation. Patients receiving religious psychotherapy showed significantly more rapid improvement in anxiety symptoms than those receiving traditional therapy.

Bliss JR, McSherry E, Fassett J (1995). Chaplain intervention reduces costs in major DRGs: An experimental study. In Heffernan H, McSherry E, Fitzgerald R (eds), Proceedings NIH Clinical Center Conference on Spirituality and Health Care Outcomes, March 21, 1995. Randomized 331 open-heart surgery patients to either a chaplain intervention ("Modern Chaplain Care") or usual care. Patients in the intervention group had an average 2 day shorter post-op hospitalization, resulting in an overall cost savings of $4,200 per patient.

Byrd, R.C. (1988). Positive therapeutic effects of intercessory prayer in a coronary care unit population. Southern Medical Journal, 81, 826-829. Randomized 393 coronary care patients to either intercessory prayer or control groups. Patients didn't know they were being prayed for; doctors didn't know which patients were being prayed for; and the persons who were praying didn't know the patients they were praying for and had no contact with these patients. Compared with control patients, those who were prayed for had significantly less congestive heart failure, used fewer diuretics, and fewer cardiopulmonary arrests, had less pneumonia, used fewer antibiotics and were less frequently intubated.

Chu, C.C., & Klein, H.E. (1985). Psychosocial and environmental variables in outcome of black schizophrenics. Journal of the National Medical Association, 77, 793-796. Studying 128 Black schizophrenics and their families, investigators reported that Black urban patients were less likely to be re-hospitalized if their families encouraged them to continue religious worship while they were in the hospital (p.001).

Florell JL (1973). Crisis-intervention in orthopedic surgery: Empirical evidence of the effectiveness of a chaplain working with surgery patients. Bulletin of the American Protestant Hospital Association 37(2):29-36. Randomized patients either to a chaplain intervention which involved chaplain visits for 15 minutes/day per patient or to a control group ("business as usual"). The chaplain intervention reduced length of stay by 29% (p.001), patient-initiated call on RN time to one-third, and use of PRN pain medications to one-third.

3

John Templeton Foundation—The Mind/Body Medical Institute at Beth Israel Deaconess Medical Center—Harvard Medical School "Spirituality & Healing in Medicine II." Public Relations Society of America 1997 Silver Anvil Award–winning entry in the category of special events and observances.

52

SPEECH

I love a natural, simple and unaffected speech,
written as it is spoken and such upon the paper
as it is in the mouth, a pithy, sinewy, full,
strong, compendious and material speech.

—MONTAIGNE

Public speaking is an effective way to gain recognition and demonstrate leadership. It is also a powerful tool for informing, inspiring, persuading, helping to set policy, and initiating action. An effective speech is both provocative and memorable, but a speech must be easily understood to be effective. For that reason, each speech should be custom made to fit the audience, the speaker, and the occasion. And remember, the best speeches go beyond spoken words; they make a connection between the speaker and the audience.

In speech writing, the rules for written English must be replaced with the rules for spoken, conversational English.

THINK ABOUT CONTENT

- Before starting the actual writing process, consider the audience, its composition, number, needs, and educational background.
- Learn all you can about the time and setting for the speech.
- Focus on a single theme.
- Research the subject thoroughly.
- Rehearse—on site, if possible—and make adjustments and corrections as needed.

WRITE THE SPEECH

- Consider the audience and the speaker's relationship to it. How much background will audience members have? Will uninvolved spouses and friends attend? What will the age range be? What will be the audience's reference points, interests, and attitudes?
- If you are writing the speech for someone else, you will want to take some additional preparatory steps. Interview the person who will deliver the speech, acting like a reporter. Record the session and take notes. Pay attention to how the person speaks, his or her style, manner, range, pronunciation, and delivery. Note if he or she is aggressive, soft-spoken, loud, or mild-mannered. Listen for natural speech patterns, colloquialisms, expressions, and mannerisms.
- Select possible topics. Consider issues facing your industry, anecdotes, areas of expertise, and areas of special concern.

- Calculate the length of the speech. (A typewritten, double-spaced page takes between one minute to one-and-a-half minutes to deliver.)
- Interview the organizers of the event to learn every detail: the setting, time of day, other speeches and speakers, presentations, awards, and other activities. Ask what the audience will be doing during the speech: Will they be eating, drinking, standing, or sitting? If possible, visit the site and examine the setup.
- Select the topic of the speech. Now the speechwriter must be an ideas person. Review other speeches from other such events, perhaps from previous years if this is an annual event. Sometimes the event will dictate the speech topic and content.
- Present the ideas for approval, if necessary.
- Research the subject. Gather all the material you can, making sure your references are the most comprehensive and current. Use the library as well as any organization files. Interview organization officials and other experts. Create notecards as you proceed.
- Outline the speech. Within the basic format of introduction, body, and summary, carefully detail the points. Here, for example, is an outline for a speech for a corporation's annual sales meeting:

1. Opening remarks and welcome
   —Recognition of sales managers
   —Purpose of the meeting
2. How are we growing?
   —Last year's sales figures
   —This year's sales figures
   —Next year's sales projections
3. How are you growing as a salesperson?
   —Looking at the numbers
   —Great accomplishments
   —New goals
4. Conclusion
   —New challenges ahead
   —This is how we will DO IT!

- Write out the speech. Make it conversational. Include interesting details, anecdotes, and points of review. To be most effective, keep the speech simple, with logical points of progression.

The *lead* should get the audience's attention with a compelling statement, humorous anecdote (be careful using jokes), thought-provoking question, quotation, or human-interest story. The opening must lead into the theme and set up the message.

The *body* of the speech should be easy to follow, progress logically, and emphasize and review major points. It must also be personalized to the audience and contain emotional content that will get them involved and make them care.

The *conclusion* should reiterate the major points, summarize, and tie the end to the beginning—pay off on your lead. It's best to leave the audience optimistically challenged.

- Repetition can help make a speech successful by emphasizing important points.
- Use solid transitions to keep the audience's attention.
- Repeat nouns instead of using pronouns.
- Use parallel phrases for clarity and emphasis: "... a government *of* the people, *by* the people, *for* the people."
- Stick to simple words and simple declarative sentences.
- Construct sentences with the subject and verb together. Don't use a construction like "He, with fear and trepidation, crept..."; instead, use "He crept...," or "With fear and trepidation, he crept..."
- Limit subordinate phrases and clauses. These become tedious and will lose your audience.
- Build in as much flexibility as possible to allow for changes during the speech, if necessary.
- Incorporate visuals to add interest and keep the audience's attention. They should be keyed to the points of emphasis in the speech in order to reinforce and illustrate the message.
- Include cues in parentheses: (Slide #4. Pause.)
- Make sure your visuals will work well with the size and composition of the audience. Emphasize them with action words.
- Practice the speech in front of a mirror and, if possible, in the setting with the visuals that will be used. Practice until the delivery is smooth.
- Rehearse the speech and change any problem areas.

- Test the speech on an audience sample, if possible, at the speech site. Make sure all the details are in place. (Speeches have failed because of a bad electrical cord or a screeching microphone.)

ELIMINATE WRONG MESSAGES

- Do not try to include more than one central idea or theme in a speech. Be sure you can explain the speech in one sentence.
- Don't trust an outline if you are not a practiced speaker or if you are writing a speech for someone else. Type it out, double spaced, underlining points for emphasis. Some speakers like all capital letters.
- Do not exaggerate the facts or overdramatize.
- Do not wander into side issues.
- Do not include jokes unless they are germane to the audience, occasion, and subject. The same applies to quotes. Throwing in a famous quote or two doesn't necessarily strengthen a speech. It may weaken it.

- Do not plagiarize. If you use a quote, give full credit to the author and source.
- Watch out for homophones, which can be misunderstood by the audience: *scene* or *seen; sew, so,* or *sow;* etc.
- Eliminate things that don't work with your skill level or presentation manner, and limit any elements that are difficult for you to deliver, such as words ending in *s*.

CONSIDER SPECIAL SITUATIONS

- If the media will attend, make copies of the speech available.
- Recycle the speech by using excerpts for news releases, magazine articles, newsletters, and trade publications.

53

PUBLIC SERVICE ANNOUNCEMENT

Writing good sentences means no dependent clauses, no dangling things, no flashbacks, and keeping the subject near the predicate. We throw in as many fresh words as we can get away with. Simple, short sentences don't always work. You have to do tricks with pacing, alternate long sentences with short, to keep it vital and alive.

—THEODORE GEISEL (DR. SEUSS)

The public service announcement, or PSA, is to broadcast public relations what the press release is to print public relations. It's the basic tool used to get broadcast coverage of an event or product. The Federal Communications Commission (FCC) requires radio and television stations to serve the community and public interest. Part of their obligation is interpreted as broadcasting brief announcements of nonprofit events. Although these were historically events sponsored by nonprofit organizations, they are increasingly becoming nonprofit events sponsored by for-profit organizations.

PSAs range from ten to sixty seconds in length and may be written in either release or script form and produced in audiotape for radio or videotape for television. PSAs can lead to radio or television interviews of official representatives of the event or to coverage of the event in a special feature segment.

Some PSAs feature health information or safety tips. All kinds of PSAs are opportunities for positive publicity.

DECIDE TO WRITE

Use this vehicle to offer information on

- Public health discussions
- New health, safety, or product information
- Health, welfare, or enrichment services offered to the public

THINK ABOUT CONTENT

- Write as a news release, starting with an arresting lead, usually in the form of a teaser—a catchy phrase, question, or term—that gets the audience's attention.
- Use action verbs and short, declarative sentences.
- State the facts.
- List any photo opportunities, audiotapes, videotapes, or interviewing sessions that are available.
- List any authorities or celebrities available for interviews.
- In writing the broadcast script, you must write for the eye as well as the ear, and your script must include all the instructions of how to create the end product. Start with your idea, then visualize how it should appear.
- Topics must have general public interest, a consumer angle, or an element of current news.
- Events with a news angle, products with a release date (books, new telephone service, a charity

race, a new drug), human interest, or consumer topics are all possibilities.

- Hard news releases are based on factual current events, and soft news releases are based on entertainment topics and celebrities. Know which you are doing.
- It is often best to telephone a radio or television producer and very briefly pitch your idea first. Be sure you have it boiled down to a very interesting fifteen- to twenty-second statement or two to grab his or her attention. Present it in one of these media categories, and be sure to suggest the audiotape or videotape opportunities:
  1. Natural disaster or crisis
  2. Health, medical, safety, or well-being
  3. Economics that affect the public
  4. Good Samaritans—personal stories about people who have done something for the community
  5. Humor or special human-interest stories

CONSIDER SPECIAL SITUATIONS

- Suggest ways to make the information or event visually interesting.
- Suggest ideas for interviews, filming, or audio recording.
- Make videotapes and audiotapes available, if possible.
- Suggest writing the broadcast script, if necessary. If you write the script, use the standard abbreviations listed below.

Location information

EXT: exterior (outdoors), followed by precise location
INT: interior (indoors), followed by precise location
ANGLE: person or thing camera focuses on

Shot directions

CU	close-up shot
ECU	extremely close-up shot
MS	medium shot
CS	close shot
LS	long shot
ELS	extremely long shot

Camera instructions

SIL	silent film
B-roll	camera pans, includes ambient sounds
OC	on camera
dolly in/out	camera moves in a straight line toward or away from the subject
truck right/left	camera moves right or left parallel to the object
pan right/left	camera head moves right or left
tilt up/down	camera head moves vertically, up or down

Transitions

wipe	new picture
dissolve	gradual replacement of one image with another
fade	gradually fading to or from black at the beginning or end of a scene

Other visual directions

Super	print that appears over visual on the screen
CHYRON	text on screen

Audio directions

SOF	sound on film
SOT	sound on tape, means the sound is the audio track from a video- or audiotape
SIL	silent film
SFX	special effects
VO	voice-over or voice only
music under	music volume is lowered beneath narration
music up and out	usually means the end of the production

SELECT A FORMAT

- Use 8½-by-11-inch sheets. Type the title in caps at the top of page l. Under the title, center and list the script time.
- Divide the pages vertically, with video directions on the left-hand side and audio script on the right-hand side.

54

MEDIA ALERT AND PHOTO OPPORTUNITY ALERT

Be always sure you're right—then go ahead.

—DAVID CROCKETT

This communication—the media alert, tip sheet, or news advisory—often serves as a bare-bones, short-notice invitation, or as a follow-up to an invitation.

The photo opportunity alert or photo tip sheet is basically the same communication geared to television or photo coverage. Make this as appealing as possible by adding pizzazz to the staging of the event.

DECIDE TO WRITE

Use this piece to

- Get the television and print media interested in covering an event
- Follow up on an invitation for an event

THINK ABOUT CONTENT

- Include the information appropriate to an invitation.
- Answer the questions *who, what, where, when,* and *how.*
- Include a sentence or two of background information if it will fit on a single page.

Media Alert and Photo Opportunity Alert

FOR IMMEDIATE RELEASE   February 9, 1996

MEDIA ADVISORY

BREAST CANCER STUDY TO ASSESS NEW TREATMENT APPROACH INTEGRATING MENTAL AND PHYSICAL CARE

WHAT: **American Psychological Association and Blue Cross/Blue Shield of Massachusetts** announce **collaboration on a landmark study** to assess the benefits of integrating psychological services into medical treatment plans for women diagnosed with breast cancer. Key spokespeople from the American Psychological Association and Blue Cross/Blue Shield of Massachusetts will provide details of the study, which is expected to reveal a correlation between psychological treatment and improved physical health outcomes, and a possible link to immunological functioning, as well as long-term analysis of cancer recurrence and mortality.

WHEN: **Tuesday, February 13, 1996**
11:00 A.M.–News Conference

WHERE: **Swissôtel Boston**
Rockport Room
One Avenue de Lafayette
Boston, MA 02111
617.451.2600

WHO: Dr. Russ Newman, Ph.D., J.D.–Executive Director,
Practice Directorate, APA
Nancy Langman-Dorwart–Director of Mental Health
Blue Cross/Blue Shield of Massachusetts
Dr. Richard Cornell, M.D.–Medical Director
Blue Cross/Blue Shield of Massachusetts
Jan Planter–Executive Director
Massachusetts Breast Cancer Coalition

MEDIA: To register or to receive additional information, please contact Terri Hernandez or Sunu Sukumaran, Pacific Visions Communications, 310.274.8787, extension 103.

Avon's Breast Cancer Awareness Crusade. Public Relations Society of America 1997 Silver Anvil–award winning institutional program.

55

OPINION EDITORIAL

For they can conquer who believe they can.

—VIRGIL

The opinion editorial, op-ed, or guest editorial column is a mainstay of many newspapers and magazines, appearing, as the name suggests, on newspaper editorial pages opposite pieces written by the publication's reporters and editors. In magazines these usually appear in a special section called "mail," "from our readers," etc.

Pieces selected to appear here affect the personal viewpoint of readers and include letters to the editor, contributing editorials, and articles with bylines.

Although the op-ed by nature offers substantial latitude, it is important to study the particular publication you wish to write for and follow that specific publication's guidelines.

DECIDE TO WRITE

Use this venue to

- Influence public opinion about a major political issue, societal ill, crisis, or current event
- Respond to or correct incorrect or inaccurate information presented in the publication
- Promote a particular point of view
- Point out that relevant information was omitted from an article
- Congratulate the editor or author on a position or piece

THINK ABOUT CONTENT

- Inquire before writing. The policy of some publications is not to include a statement of error but only a statement of the corrected facts.
- Letters to the editor offer the opportunity for publicity and visibility. Keep that connection in mind when writing.
- Write to the specifications or guidelines of the particular publication.
- Be sure to get the approval of organization officials if your letter will represent your organization.
- Take a positive approach and upbeat tone whenever possible.
- If you are refuting an editorial, reference the editorial title and date. State your position and support it with hard data and facts, giving the source and authorities, but use only one or two sources. Stick to the point and be as clear, objective, and brief as possible. Be passionate, but don't make threats of litigation.
- In responding to mistakes or inaccuracies, refer to the publication date and page of the piece you are responding to. Quote the incorrect statement and then state the correct information. Make

sure you document your statement with one or two sources. Finally, sign your letter with your name and, if applicable, title.

- Keep letters or articles brief and to the point. Most publications allow a maximum of 500 to 800 words per piece. Check with the publication.

ELIMINATE WRONG MESSAGES

- Don't fire off an immediate response to a negative article without reflection. Carefully weigh the decision and try to determine if a response is likely to fuel more negative press.
- Stay away from inflammatory or derogatory remarks.
- Do not threaten legal action.
- Unless you are doing a humorous piece or parody, refrain from hyperbole.

SELECT A FORMAT

Use 8½-by-11-inch letterhead. Type your piece double spaced with a minimum of one-inch margins.

CONSIDER SPECIAL SITUATIONS

Use the correct name and title of the editor, and address your op-ed piece directly to that person.

56
NEWSLETTER

Your writing is both good and original; but the part that is good is not original, and the part that is original is not good.

—SAMUEL JOHNSON

A newsletter is a publication for a defined and specific audience. Most are written for an "in" group, such as employees, neighbors, club, and association members—people with a common interest. Newsletters are generally written in an informal journalistic style, as news or features.

STUDY TYPES OF NEWSLETTERS

* Employee newsletters are usually produced by the organization to help create a sense of community. They usually include a mix of employee information and organization news.
* Community newsletters are usually directed at geographical neighbors to create a unity by addressing common concerns and issues and disseminating information.
* Association, club, or group newsletters exist to keep members of an identified group in touch. For example, the Rotarians, Toastmasters, Book-of-the-Month Club, Mystery Writers of America, and all sorts of small common-interest groups use newsletters to inspire, inform, and create camaraderie among their members.
* Publicity newsletters exist to create their own publics. Hotels, vacation clubs, fan clubs,

and politicians create newsletters to promote themselves.

* Self-interest newsletters make a profit by offering common-interest information, advice, and solutions to problems for a fee. Such newsletters exist for financial investors, public relations personnel, public speakers, bargain shoppers, writers, and many other kinds and groups of people.

THINK ABOUT CONTENT

* As a basic step to effectively focusing the newsletter contents before writing, know the audience thoroughly.
* Use a journalistic style of writing. However, there is no need to write in the inverted pyramid style of putting all the facts in the first sentence or paragraph.
* Informal writing is best for most readers.
* Article length depends on the audience, although business-related newsletters tend to keep article length between 200 to 600 words.
* Create a mix of informational and entertaining pieces. Features should have a beginning, middle, and end. Make the lead a hook for the readers,

and follow it in logical order, explaining and elaborating on the lead.

- Give feature pieces more human interest than news pieces, and more color.

SELECTING A FORMAT

- Almost any size paper may be used. The major consideration here will be the cost of the paper you select. A standard finished size of $8^{1}/_{2}$-by-11-inch, often folded to that size from an 11-by-17-inch sheet of paper, is practical. An address label may be applied so the piece is a self-mailer.
- Word processors, computer-generated type, or typesetting may be used. A typeset banner on the front page and line art or photos will give the newsletter character, but keep it simple.

- Balance pages, taking care to not place all the photos or illustrations on one side of the page, or all in the center where they will seem to be falling into the fold.
- Place the most important items in the upper left-hand or lower right-hand positions on the page since the eye falls to these spots first.
- Use the white space to add interest and create an open, easy-and-quick-to-read feel.

Newsletter

Baylor Launches United Way Campaign

The 1995 United Way campaign at Baylor will begin September 28 with a goal of raising $130,000 to benefit hundreds of programs that will touch thousands of lives. The campaign will run through October 27.

Co-chairs of the campaign are William R. Brinkley, Ph.D., Vice President for Graduate Sciences and Dean of The Graduate School of Biomedical Sciences, and Carlos Vallbona, M.D., Chairman of Community Medicine.

"Historically, Baylor has demonstrated extensive and compassionate support for the many fine programs United Way represents," Brinkley said. "Without these programs, many people would have nowhere to turn for help."

Vallbona pointed out that in addition to research and education, Baylor's mission includes a commitment to public service. "Everyone at Baylor can express concern for others through a donation to the United Way," he said.

Department coordinators will distribute pledge cards and envelopes. Contributions can be made by payroll deduction or single payment. Pledge cards, which allow you to designate your donation for a particular United Way agency, should be returned to department coordinators by October 27.

The United Way of the Texas Gulf Coast provides community services through 78 agencies in Fort Bend, Harris, Montgomery, and Waller counties. Baylor President William T. Butler, M.D., serves on the Board of Trustees of the United Way of the Texas Gulf Coast, and United Way of the Texas Gulf Coast President Judith L. Craven, M.D. (BCM '74), is a Baylor Assistant Professor of Community Medicine. ◆

"Our goal . . . is to promote awareness of healthy life styles."

Wellness Month Activities Offer Free Information, Prizes, and More

Join the more than 1,000 Baylor employees who will learn more about healthy life style habits during Wellness Month '95, held in October. The Health Promotion Section of the Office of Public Affairs is sponsoring a month's worth of events that promise healthy information, food, activities, and prizes.

"People can't change their habits overnight, but they can change a little at a time," said Harriet Spain, Assistant Director of Health Promotion. "Our goal during Wellness Month is to promote awareness of all aspects of healthy life styles and to let people know about the resources available at Baylor and in the community."

Donning a '60s theme of "Wellness Month '95: 31 Days of Peace, Love, and Health," the event will feature the health challenge competition, where employees collect tokens for participating in healthy life style activities, such as ordering the Wellness Month special at the Baylor cafeteria, donating blood, doing volunteer work, and going to aerobics classes. At the end of the month, tokens will be turned in for prize drawings. Prizes include dining and entertainment gift certificates, and a special grand prize. Employees can sign up to participate in the health challenge, October 2-6, from noon to 1 p.m. in the Baylor Cafeteria. Tie-dyed Wellness

WELLNESS MONTH '95
BAYLOR COLLEGE OF MEDICINE
◆

Month T-shirts can be purchased at a reduced price at this time.

A highlight of Wellness Month will be the Health Fair on Thursday, October 26, from 10 a.m. to 2 p.m. Approximately 50 booths, staffed by Baylor and community professionals and volunteers, will offer free blood pressure and cholesterol screenings, as well as eye exams for glaucoma and a skin sun sensitivity test. Other activities during the Health Fair include a healthy food sampling, free information on various medical and health issues, and an aerobics demonstration by the Amateur Athletics Union, the national aerobics champions.

During all Wellness Month activities, drawings will be held for dining and entertainment gift certificates.

Each Baylor employee will receive a flyer explaining all of the Wellness Month activities. If you have questions after reading the flyer, contact Harriet Spain at 798-5770.

Wellness Month '95 Schedule of Activities

- **Tuesday, October 10**, noon until 1 p.m., "Herb Growing in Houston," DeBakey Building lobby.

- **Wednesday, October 11**, noon until 1 p.m., meditation workshop, Jaworski classroom.

- **Friday, October 13**, noon until 1 p.m., demonstration of healthy wok cooking by Dorothy Huang, a well-known local chef, DeBakey Building lobby.

- **October 16-19**, 11 a.m. until 2 p.m., free flu shots, DeBakey Building lobby.

- **Wednesday, October 18**, noon until 1 p.m., "Happy and Healthy Feet."

- **Thursday, October 19**, noon until 1 p.m., safe biking seminar sponsored by Planetary Cycles, DeBakey Building lobby.

- **Monday, October 23**, 10 a.m. until 2 p.m., mini massages offered on Massage Day, DeBakey Building lobby.

- **Thursday, October 26**, 10 a.m. until 2 p.m., Health Fair, DeBakey Building lobby. ◆

Residency Fair: American Medical Student Association (AMSA) members from Baylor and other medical schools learned about the residency programs in Arizona, Arkansas, Oklahoma, and Texas at a residency fair hosted by the College recently. The fair was part of a regional conference sponsored by Baylor's AMSA chapter and the American Medical Association/Texas Medical Association.

Inside Information, *the newsletter of the Baylor College of Medicine. Public Relations Society of America 1997 Bronze Anvil Award–winning newsletter.*

57

BROCHURE

The great artist is the simplifier.

—HENRI-FRÉDÉRIC AMIEL

A brochure is a sales piece used in sales efforts, promotion, and media kits. It should present a description of the organization, its capabilities, product line, and goals.

The brochure should answer the questions
- What is the organization?
- Where did it come from? (background)
- What does it have to offer? (product or service)

It should also tell the reader where the organization is located, its representatives, and why it is unique or special. Always give the reader a way to contact the organization.

THINK ABOUT CONTENT
- Research, review, and collect scores of brochures. Then note what you like or don't like about them. It's especially important to collect ones for competitive products or services and analyze them carefully.
- Decide what and how much you want to say.
- Identify the message in terms of features and benefits. Features are the nitty-gritty of the services or products; benefit statements describe what's in it for the reader.
- Be as economical with words as possible. The most effective brochures are often the shortest.
- Decide how you want your brochure to look. The visual appearance of your brochure must promote the message.
- Decide how many to produce, estimating what the shelf life of the brochure will be and how much you have to spend. You may want or need to get the professional help of a designer and printer to make these decisions.
- Write the copy, review it, and do any necessary rewriting.
- Select a typesetter, if you will be using one, or prepare to have the copy produced on a word processor or computer. If you use a typesetter, work with him or her to do the copyfitting.
- Edit the copy, collect any photos or artwork, and rough out a layout indicating the size and placement of the headings, graphics, and photos.
- Select a paper with the right look, feel, color, and durability. The cost of the stock may limit your choices, but select one that will work best with your type style, graphics, and color choices.

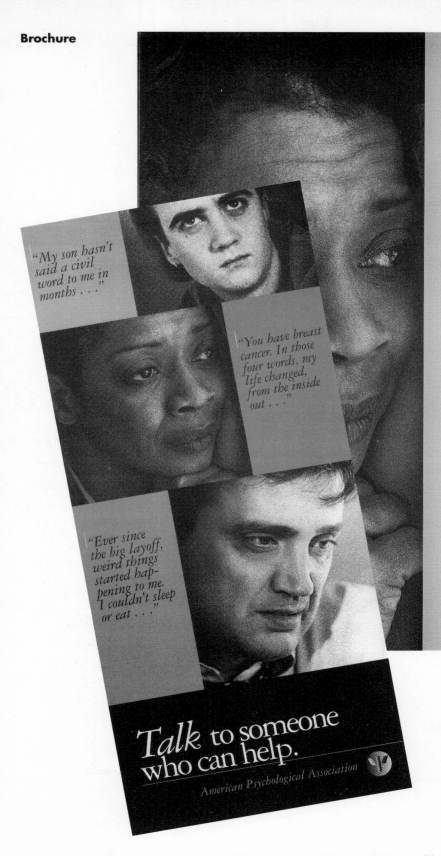

How does
"therapy" work?

Therapy works by helping you objectively look at behaviors, feelings and thoughts in situations which you find problematic. It helps you to learn more effective ways in dealing with those situations.

Therapy is a collaborative effort. You and your psychologist will identify your goals — what you want to have happen, and agree on how you'll know when you're making progress. Your psychologist will talk to you about the length of time it may take to help you see changes.

Progress, and change, can happen. Nine out of ten Americans surveyed by *Consumer Reports* said that psychotherapy had helped them. And in another recent major national study, half of the patients studied were making improvement after eight sessions of therapy, 75 percent after six months of therapy.

"My psychologist helped me to understand and deal with my feelings . . . Life is slowly getting back in balance."

"My son hasn't said a civil word to me in months . . ."

"You have breast cancer. In those four words, my life changed, from the inside out . . ."

"Ever since the big layoff, weird things started happening to me. I couldn't sleep or eat . . ."

Talk to someone who can help.

American Psychological Association

American Psychological Association's "Talk to Someone who Can Help." Public Relations Society of America 1997 Silver Anvil–award winning institutional program.

XI. ELECTRONIC COMMUNICATIONS

58

E-MAIL AND ONLINE COMMUNICATIONS

The more a man writes, the more he can write.

—WILLIAM HAZLITT

The revolution in electronic communications systems and tools requires that we have better writing skills and additional skills for these specialized modes of personal and business communication. The existence of electronic systems, evidence indicates, is resulting in more, not fewer, written communications. In fact, new problems have developed because of the proliferation of messages on electronic bulletin boards, the Internet, and e-mail.

The principles of writing clear, brief, timely, and precise communications are even more important here.

USE E-MAIL EFFICIENTLY

With e-mail, the writer can instantly send a message to one or more receivers and may attach electronic files to be sent along with the message.

E-mail may also be forwarded. If strict rules and procedures are not established and adhered to, however, users may constantly be overwhelmed with large numbers of redundant e-mail messages with attached files. These can clutter the system, use large amounts of memory, and slow message transmission.

THINK ABOUT CONTENT

- See "Memo," page 112, and use the general rules presented in that chapter.
- Know the organization's rules for use. If none are in place, create a well-thought-out policy. Begin by answering these questions: Are messages confidential and owned by the sender, or are they organization-owned, as part of the system? That is, is the sender the "custodian" or the "owner" of the e-mail messages he or she sends? May messages be forwarded without the original sender's permission or knowledge? Does the organization reserve the right to monitor, as owner of the system, all e-mail?
- Use organization dialect, etiquette, abbreviations, and symbols where they exist. Remember, correct capitalization and spelling are part of a proper message, and writing in all capitals equals a shout.
- Restrict messages to business topics, if appropriate.
- Restrict your message to one subject whenever possible. Multiple subjects impede the receiver's response and create a filing problem.
- State the subject up front, clearly, and precisely.

- Explicitly request that your message not be forwarded, if appropriate.
- Make messages not longer than one screen in length.

ELIMINATE WRONG MESSAGES

- Do not write confidential or sensitive messages that you do not want persons other than the intended recipient to read.
- Do not fire off messages without thoroughly thinking them through.

SELECT A FORMAT

- Create in two parts: the address and the body. Follow your organization's established format.
- Learn and use your organization's abbreviations and symbols.

USE BULLETIN BOARDS EFFECTIVELY

Electronic bulletin boards are worldwide, posted public messages on a wide variety of subjects. By using a computer, a telephone line, and a modem, people tune into this electronic dialogue of discussion and information.

THINK ABOUT CONTENT

- Learn the language and symbols.
- Evaluate your message before you send it to be sure it adds new information or ideas.
- Resist the urge to send "me-too" messages when you are participating with a group of e-mail participants. Limit your participation to new ideas and information.
- Don't e-mail back the entire message you're responding to; abbreviate a reference point, and send your concise message.
- Resist the urge to attach files.

USE INFORMATION SERVICES EFFECTIVELY

Electronic online databases provide a wide range of business news, indexes, and other kinds of information, including stock quotes, abstracts, and bibliographies on many subjects. These databases are accessible by using a computer and modem setup and include such sources as Standard & Poor's News (financial), Electronic Yellow Pages (lists of U.S. businesses and addresses), Bibliographic Retrieval System (BRS), Dunn & Bradstreet (information on businesses), Dow Jones News Retrieval Services (business and financial information), ABI/Inform (business journal article abstracts), LEXIS (legal references), and NEXIS (news references).

APPENDICES

APPENDIX I

FORMS OF ADDRESS

Person	Title for envelope / inside address	Salutation

Ambassador, American	The Honorable (Name)
	American Ambassador (in Canada and
	    Latin America, the Ambassador of
	    the United States of America)
	City, Country
		Sir/Madam:
		Dear Mr./Madam
		    Ambassador:

Ambassador, foreign	His/Her Excellency (Name)
	Ambassador of (Country)
	Washington, DC
		Excellency:
		Dear Mr./Madame
		    Ambassador:
		My dear Mr./Madame
		    (Name):

Archbishop, Roman Catholic	The Most Reverend (Name)
	Archbishop of (City)
	City, State
		Dear Archbishop
		    (Name):
		Most Reverend and
		    dear Sir:
		Your Excellency:
		Reverend Sir:

Bishop, Episcopal	The Right Reverend (Name) Bishop of (Diocese) City, State	Right Reverend Sir: Dear Bishop (Name):
Bishop, Methodist	Bishop (Name) City, State	Your Excellency: Dear Bishop (Name):
Bishop, Roman Catholic	The Most Reverend (Name) Bishop of (Diocese) City, State	Your Excellency: Most Reverend Sir: Dear Bishop (Name):
Brother	Brother (Name) Address City, State	Dear Brother (Name): Dear Brother:

Person	Title for envelope / inside address	Salutation
Cabinet member, United States	The Honorable (Name) The Secretary of (Dept.) Washington, DC	Sir/Madam: Dear Mr./Madam Secretary: Dear Mr./Mrs. (Name):
Cardinal, Roman Catholic	His Eminence (First Name) Cardinal (Last Name) Archbishop of (City) City, State	Your Eminence: My dear Cardinal: Dear Cardinal (Name):

Clergyman, Protestant (except Episcopal)	The Reverend (or with a doctorate,
	  Reverend Dr. (Name)
	Address
	City, State
		My dear Mr./Mrs./Ms.
		  (or Dr.):
		Dear Mr./Mrs./Ms.
		Dear Pastor (Name):

Consul	(Full Name), Esq.
	(Country) Consul
	City, State
		Sir/Madam (*Madame* if
		  foreign consul):
		Dear Mr./Mrs./Ms.
		  Consul:

Dean, college	Dean (or Dr.) (Name) College or University City, State	Sir/Madam: Dear Dean (Name): Dear Dr. (Name):
Doctor	Dr. (Name) or (Full Name), M.D. or Ph.D. or D.D. Address City, State	Dear Dr. (Name):
Governor	The Honorable (Name) Governor of (State) City, State	Sir/Madam: My dear Governor (Name): Dear Governor (Name):
Judge	The Honorable (Name) Name of Court City, State	Sir/Madam: My dear Judge (Name): Dear Judge (Name):
Legislator	The Honorable (Name) Name of Legislative Body City, State	Sir/Madam: Dear Senator (Name): My dear Mr./Ms./Mrs.: Dear Mr./Ms./Mrs.:
Mayor	The Honorable (Name) Mayor of (City) City, State	Sir/Madam: Dear Mayor (Name):

Person	Title for envelope / inside address	Salutation
Military officer	(Full or abbreviated rank) (Full Name), (Abbreviation for Service) Address City, State	Sir/Madam: Dear Major/Captain/ General/Admiral (Name):
Monsignor	The Reverend Monsignor (Name), or The Rev. Msgr. (Name) City, State	Dear Monsignor (Name): Monsignor (Name): Reverend and dear Monsignor (Name):
Nun	Sister (Name), (Initials of Order) Address City, State	Dear Sister (Name): Dear Sister:
Patriarch, Eastern Orthodox	His Beatitude the Patriarch of (Diocese) Address City, State	Most Reverend Lord: Your Beatitude:
The Pope	His Holiness Pope (name), or His Holiness the Pope Vatican City Rome, Italy	Your Holiness: Most Holy Father:
President, college or university	President (Full Name), or Dr. (Full Name) College or University City, State	Sir/Madam: Dear Dr. (Name): Dear President (Name):
President, Prime Minister (foreign country)	President (Name), or Prime Minister (Name) City, Country	Excellency: Dear Mr./Ms./Mrs. President: Madame Prime Minister:
President, United States	The President The White House Washington, DC 20500	Mr. President: Dear Mr./Ms./Mrs. President: Dear President (Name):
Priest, Roman Catholic, Episcopal	The Reverend (Dr.) (Name) Address City, State	Reverend Father: Dear Father (Name): Dear Father:

Person	Title for Envelope/Inside Address	Salutation
Professor	Prof. (Name) Department of (Subject) College or University City, State	Dear Sir/Madam: Dear Professor (Name): Dear Dr. (Name):
Rabbi	Rabbi (Name) Address City, State	Dear Rabbi (Name): Dear Dr. (Name):
Representative	The Honorable (Name) The House of Representatives Washington, DC 20515	Sir/Madam: Dear Mr./Ms./Mrs. (Name): Dear Representative (Name):
Secretary-General of the United Nations	His (Her) Excellency (Name) Secretary-General of the United Nations United Nations Plaza New York, NY 10017	Excellency: Dear Mr./Ms./Mrs. Secretary-General:
Senator	The Honorable (Name) United States Senate Washington, DC 20510	Sir/Madam: Dear Senator (Name):
Speaker of the House	The Honorable (Name) The House of Representatives Washington, DC 20515	Dear Mr./Madam Speaker:
Supreme Court Justice	The Honorable (Name), Associate (or Chief) Justice of the United States Supreme Court Washington, DC 20543	Sir/Madam: Dear Justice (Last Name): Dear Mr./Ms./Mrs. Justice (Last Name):
United Nations Representative	His/Her Excellency (Country) Representative to the United Nations United Nations New York, NY 10017	Excellency: Your Excellency: Ambassador: Sir/Madam (*Madame* if foreign): Mr./Ms./Mrs. (Name):

Person	Title for envelope / inside address	Salutation
Vice President, United States	Vice President of the United States, or The Vice President of the United States Washington, DC	Dear Mr./Ms./Mrs.: Dear Mr./(Madame) Vice President (Name):
Baron/Baroness	The Right Honorable Lord/Lady (Name)	My Lord/Lady: Dear Lord/Lady (Name):
Baronet	Sir (Name), Bt.	Dear Sir: Dear Sir (Name):
Wife of baronet	Lady (Name)	Dear Madame: Dear Lady (Name):
Duke/Duchess	His/Her Grace, the Duke/ Duchess of _____	My Lord Duke/Madame: Dear Duke of _____: Dear Duchess:
Earl/Countess	The Right Honorable the Earl/Countess of _____	My Lord/Madame: Dear Lord _____: Dear Countess:
Knight	Sir (Name)	Dear Sir: Dear Sir (Name):
Wife of knight	Lady (Name)	Dear Madame: Dear Lady (Name):
Marquess/ Marchioness	The Most Honorable the M_____ of _____	My Lord/Madame: Dear Lord/Lady ___:
Viscount/ Viscountess	The Right Honorable the V_____ of _____	My Lord/Lady: Dear Lord/Lady _____:
Other royalty	His/Her Royal Highness the Prince/Princess of _____	Your Royal Highness:

ABBREVIATING TITLES

Educational degrees, memberships, military or civil honors, and titles that follow a name include these:

Abbreviation	Title
A.A.	associate of arts
A.B.	bachelor of arts (artium baccalaureus)
A.M.	master of arts (artium magister)
B.A.	bachelor of arts
B.D.	bachelor of divinity
B.F.A.	bachelor of fine arts
B.S.	bachelor of science
CEO	chief executive officer
CFO	chief financial officer
CPA	certified public accountant
D.B.	bachelor of divinity (divinitatis baccalaureus)
D.D.	doctor of divinity (divinitatis doctor)
D.D.S.	doctor of dental surgery
D.O.	doctor of osteopathy
D.S.O.	Distinguished Service Order
D.V.M.	doctor of veterinary medicine
Esq.	esquire
F.R.S.	fellow of the Royal Society
Hon.	the honorable
J.D.	doctor of law (juris doctor)
J.P.	justice of the peace
Kt.	knight
L.H.D.	doctor of humanities (litterarum humaniorum doctor)
Litt.D.	doctor of letters (litterarum doctor)
LL.B.	bachelor of laws (legum baccalaureus)
LL.D.	doctor of laws (legum doctor)
L.P.N.	licensed practical nurse
M.A.	master of arts
M.B.A.	master of business administration
M.H.A.	master of hospital administration
M.D.	doctor of medicine (medicinae doctor)
M.P.	member of parliament
MP	military police
M.P.H.	master of public health
M.S.	master of science
M.S.W.	master of social work
Ph.B.	bachelor of philosophy (philosophiae baccalaureus)
Ph.D.	doctor of philosophy (philosophiae doctor)
Ph.G.	graduate in pharmacy
PM	prime minister
Psy.D.	doctor of psychology
R.N.	registered nurse
Rev.	reverend
S.B.	bachelor of science (scientiae baccalaureus)
S.J.	Society of Jesus
S.M.	master of science (scientiae magister)
S.T.B.	bachelor of sacred theology (sacrae theologiae baccalaureus)
VP	vice president

ABBREVIATING U.S. MILITARY BRANCHES

USAF	United States Air Force
USCG	United States Coast Guard
USMC	United States Marine Corps.
USN	United States Navy

APPENDIX II
AVOIDING DISCRIMINATORY WORDS

Eliminate discriminatory words from your writing. Because word usage changes over time, words fall out of favor, change in meaning, become outmoded, or even become offensive instead of accepted, or accepted instead of offensive.

Keep current. Know the present meaning of words and how to use them. Know which words are too harsh, which are regional and aren't understood by all your readers, which are redundant or fog your intended meaning, and, yes, which are offensive and should not be used at all.

Develop a sense for the proper, precise word. Choose every word carefully, and eliminate every one that isn't working, is unnecessary, carries the wrong meaning, or is too vague.

Here are some word guidelines.

AVOID SEXIST LANGUAGE
Treat all readers equally. That means addressing men and women as equals in your communications. Think about why you should use these words. Then test your choices by reviewing the following sections.

Instead of	Use	Why
Chairman	The chair is … The representative is … The leader is … The person responsible is … The moderator is … The convener is … The coordinator is … The presiding officer is … The head is …	Avoid gender-specific terms.
Manpower	employees, workforce, personnel, workers, staff	Select the most inclusive and descriptive non-gendered word.
The employee may select *his* benefit category	Employees may select benefit categories … Employees may select their benefit categories …	Use plural forms to avoid gender reference. (Eliminate *his* and *her*.)

Instead of	Use	Why

Dear Sir:
Gentlemen:
Madam:
	Dear Chairperson:
	Dear Editor:
	Dear Colleague:
	Dear Customer Service
	   Representative:
	Dear Service Manager:
	Dear Public Relations
	   Director:
		Use nongendered titles when gender is unknown.

Ms. C. Ross and Jim Burns ...	Ms. C. Ross and Mr. J. Burns ... Ross and Burns ... Cathy Ross and Jim Burns ...	Use parallel or equal construction for women and men.
The directress for the program ...	The director for the program ...	Eliminate gender connotation unless it is necessary to include it. (Don't use *poeess*, *priestess*, *deaconess*, or other words that imply the masculine form is standard and the feminine is exceptional.)
Mothering new employees ...	Nurturing new employees ...	Use inclusive, nonstereotypical terms.
Manhours worked ...	Hours worked ...	Rewrite to eliminate gender reference.

Hurricane Hilda did
   her worst damage ...
	Hurricane Hilda did
	   the worst damage ...
	The hurricane did
	   the worst damage ...
		Rewrite to avoid gender reference.

Since the beginning
   of mankind ...
	Since the beginning
	   of the human species ...
	Since the beginning
	   of humankind ...
	Since the first people ...
		Use an inclusive word.

Avoid the Generic *Man* Trap

When *man* denotes an adult male human, and that distinction is needed in your writing, use it, as in "The committee consisted of three women and one man." But don't use *man* when you mean both men and women. Here are four areas where you should be especially careful to use an inclusive term:

- Don't use *man* in general references to all people: "man of the hour" and "man for the job." Use an inclusive and correct word such as *person:* "*person of the hour,*" "*person for the job.*"
- Don't use *man* to refer to all humans: "mankind prefers," "all mankind." Use inclusive terms like *all people* and *humankind.*
- Don't use *man* as a prefix or suffix when there's a more inclusive word: *manhours, manmade, foreman.* Use inclusive and correct words like *time* or *work hours, synthetic,* and *supervisor.*
- Some male-sounding words containing *man* or *his* have nonsexist origins. They derive from the Latin *manus,* which means hand. Don't change these in error:

Don't Substitute This	For This
herufacture	manufacture
heragement	management
heripulate	manipulate
herual	manual
heruscript	manuscript
herage	manage

If the resulting *her* word or *person* word is silly, find another substitute, or use the old word.

Instead of	Use This
freshperson	freshman, first-year student
herstory	history
personhole	manhole

Avoid the *He/She* Pronouns

The word used to substitute for a noun is a pronoun, and although we have no difficulty with the first-person pronoun (*I, we, me, us, our,* and *ours*) or the second-person pronoun (*you, your,* and *yours*), the third-person pronoun (*he, she, they, him, her, hers, it, its, their,* and *theirs*) can create problems for writers.

Although it has been common practice to address both sexes of readers as *he,* it is best to change your writing to avoid this problem.

Option 1: Use Plural Pronouns
Change
If the **reader** has questions, **he** should call this office.
To
If **readers** have questions, **they** should call this office.

Option 2: Reword to Omit Pronouns
Change the same sentence to
Readers should call this office with questions.

Option 3: Reword to Use Second- or first-person Pronouns
If you elect to use second person or first person, be sure you are consistent throughout your communication and that first or second person works.
Use
If **you** have questions, call this office.
Or
Call this office if **you** have questions.
Or first person,
I will call the office if I have questions.

Option 4: Replace Pronouns with the
Change
The **employee** may use **his** vacation request form.
To
The **employee** may use **the** vacation request form.

Option 5: Repeat the Noun

This becomes tedious for the reader, so it should be used very sparingly.

Example:

The **employee** may use the **employee's** vacation request form.

Option 6: Restructure the Sentence to Passive Voice

Passive voice should be used very sparingly and only if it emphasizes what you want to emphasize or provides needed variety in your sentence structure. It usually results in longer and indirect writing.

Example:

The vacation request form should be used by the **employee.**

Option 7: Substitute *One* for Pronouns

This may result in a loss of the conversational tone you want in your writing.

Example:

The **employee** has three choices; **one** should select first, second, and third.

Option 8: Use *His* or *Her*

Use *his or her* very rarely because it distances you—the writer—from your reader and can make your writing very tedious. *He/she* and *his/her* are cumbersome and should be avoided in most writing.

Example:

The **employee** should list **his or her** first, second, and third vacation choices.

Or

The **employee** has three choices; **he/she** should select first, second, and third.

Avoid Feminine Words

Some English words that come from Latin or other language roots have hang-on feminine equivalents, or feminine prefixes or suffixes. (This is especially true of the Romance languages: Spanish, French, Italian, Portuguese, and Romanian.) The current trend is to make one form of these words:

Instead of	Use
actress	actor
adultress	adulterer
authoress	author
blonde	blond
comedienne	comedian
conductress	conductor
fiancée	fiancé
goddess	god
heiress	heir
majorette	major
masseuse	masseur
songstress	singer
waitress	waiter

There are some more in the listing in the next section.

Avoid Gendered Terms

Our American culture produced a language loaded with masculine words that are often used to refer to either sex. Take the sex out of your language by removing gender from occupations when possible.

Choose words that are inclusive of both sexes, easy to pronounce, and make logical sense. For most of your writing, you will want to include nongendered substitutions like the ones on the following pages.

Instead of	Use
actress	actor
adman	advertising writer, ad person, adsmith
administratrix	administrator
advanceman	advance agent, initiator
adventuress	adventurer
aircraftsman	aviator, aircraft engineer
airline stewardess	flight attendant
airman/woman	aviator, pilot, flier
airmanship	aviation skill, flying skill
alderman	public representative, council member/person
alumna/alumnus, alumnae/alumni	graduates, alums
ambassadress	ambassador
ancestress	ancestor
anchorman/woman	anchor
ape-man	prehuman
assemblyman	assemblyperson, assembly worker, line person
authoress	author
aviatrix	aviator
bachelor's degree	undergraduate degree
bagboy	bagger, assistant
barman/maid	bartender, waiter
baseman	base player
bastard	(eliminate)
bedfellow	associate, partner
bellboy, bellman	bellhop
benefactress	benefactor
blindman	blind person
blonde	blond
bondsman	bondsperson, guarantor, insurer
bookman	author, scholar, librarian
bossman/lady	boss, supervisor
brakeman (bobsled)	brake operator
brakeman (railroad)	railroad worker, guard
brakeman (train)	conductor's assistant
brethren	laity
brewmaster	brew director, chief brewer, head brewer
bridesmaid	bride's attendant
brotherhood	human kinship, camaraderie

Instead of	Use
brotherly	kind, helpful
brotherly love	charity, goodwill
brunette	brunet
bull session	talk-fest, get-together
busboy, busgirl	waiter's helper, waiter's assistant
businessman, businesswoman	business representative, business executive, businessperson
businessmen	businesspersons, businesspeople
busman	bus driver
cabin boy	crew member
cabman	cab driver, cabby
cameraman, camerawoman	camera operator, photographer
career woman	manager, supervisor (or name the job, profession, or title)
cattlemen	cattle breeders, cattle owners, cattle herders
cavemen	cave dwellers, cave people
chairman/woman	chairperson, chair, head, presider, presiding officer, convener, facilitator
chambermaid	housekeeper
choirgirl/boy	choir member
chorus girl/boy	member of the chorus, singer
churchman	lay officer
city fathers	city council, leaders, city officials
clansman	member of the clan
clergymen/women	ministers, clergy, clerics, pastors
coed	student
comedienne	comedian
committeemen	committee members
common man	commoner, average person
company man/woman	loyal employee, team player
concertmistress/master	concert leader, first violinist
conductress	conductor
confidante	confidant
confidence man	swindler
congressman	member of congress, representative

Instead of	Use
contact man	contact person, liaison
copyboy, copygirl	copy clerk, runner, carrier, messenger
copyman	copy editor, copy writer
councilman	council member
counterman/girl	clerk, waiter
countryman	compatriot, citizen, patriot
cowboy/girl	cowhand, rider
craftsman	artisan, crafter, craftsperson
creatrix	creator, maker
crewman	crew member
dairyman	dairy farmer, dairy worker
dayman	day worker, day laborer
deaconess	deacon, elder
debutante	debutant
deliveryman	deliverer, delivery clerk
directress	director, administrator
distaff	(eliminate in reference to women)
divorcée	divorcé
doorman	doorkeeper, doorkeep
draftsman	drafter
drum majorette	drum major, baton twirler
Dutchman	Dutch person
elder statesman	senior political leader
elderman	elder
emperor, empress	ruler, monarch, sovereign, commander, leader
enchantress	enchanter, sorcerer, magician, fascinating woman
engineman	engineer, engine driver
Englishman	the English, Englander, Briton
enlisted man	enlistee, member, recruit
equestrienne	equestrian, rider, horseback rider
executrix	executor
expressman	delivery person
fair sex	(eliminate)
fall guy	scapegoat, stand-in
family of man	humankind, the human family
farmeress, farmerette	farmer
fraternal twins	nonidentical twins

Instead of	Use
fatherland	homeland
favorite son	favorite candidate
feminine persuasion	female
feminine rhyme (poetry or music)	rhyme with an unstressed final syllable
fiancée	fiancé, betrothed
fighting man	fighter, soldier
filly	(eliminate in reference to girls or women)
fireman	firefighter, stoker (ships and trains)
fisherman	fisher, angler
five-man committee	five-person committee, five-member committee
flagman	flagger
floorman	floorwalker, person on duty
flyboy	aviator, pilot, flier
forefathers	ancestors, forebears, progenitors, foremothers and forefathers
foreman, forewoman (lady)	supervisor, boss, leader
forgotten man	(use specific noun: unemployed, poor, etc.)
founding father	founder, ancestor
Frenchmen	the French, French people
freshmen	first-year students, beginners
frogman	diver, sailor
front man	intermediary
frontiersman	pioneer, leader, settler
funnyman	comedian, humorist, comic
G-man	government employee
gagman	writer
gamesmanship	game playing, strategy
garbage man	garbage collector
gasman	gas deliverer, attendant
gateman	gate attendant
gentlemen's agreement	unwritten agreement, pact, agreement of honor
girl Friday, man Friday	aide, assistant, helper
goddess	god
governess	child caretaker, nurse
gownsman	gownsperson, academic person

Instead of	Use
grandfather clause	preexisting condition clause
guardsman	guard, soldier
guildsman	guild member, guildsperson
gunman	shooter, killer, assassin
hackman	hackie, cabdriver
handyman	fixer, face-of-all-trades
hardwareman	retailer
hat-check girl	hat checker, attendant
headman	boss, president
headmaster	principal
heiress	heir, inheritor
helmsman	coxswain, guider, steerer
henchman	right arm, enforcer
heroine	hero
history of man	history
hooker	prostitute
horseman/woman	rider, equestrian
hostess	host
hotelman	hotel operator, manager, hotel worker, desk clerk
housewife	homemaker
huntress	hunter
husbandman	farmer, husbander
idea man	idea person, creator
infantryman	infantry soldier, foot soldier
inner man	inner self, inner person, psyche, soul
inside man	accomplice, undercover agent, spy
inspectress	inspector
instructress	instructor, teacher
insurance man	insurance agent
Irishmen	Irish people
jack-of-all-trades	handy person
jazz man	jazz player, musician
John Q. Public	the public
johnny-come-lately	newcomer, new arrival
johnny-on-the-spot	prompt person
journeyman	experienced person, journey-level tradesperson
juryman	juror, member of the jury
key man	key person
king's ransom	valuable

Instead of	Use
king-size	huge, large
kinsmen	kin, kinfolk, relatives
laundress, laundryman	laundry worker
layman	layperson
laymen	laity, lay people
layout man	layout person
leadman	leader
learned man	learned person, scholar, sage
legman	runner, messenger
letterman	athlete of achievement, achiever
lighthouse man	lighthouse keeper
lineman	line repairer, technician, installer, football player
lioness (when referring to a person)	lion
longshoreman	stevedore, longshoreworker
lookout man	guard, sentry, lookout
lumberman, lumberjack	logger, woodcutter, forester
madam	(eliminate)
maid	house cleaner, house worker
maid of honor	honored attendant
maiden	first, untried, single
maiden name	family name, birth name
mailman	letter carrier, postal worker, mail carrier
maintenance man	janitor, repair person, caretaker
maitre d'	head waiter
majorette	major
makeup man	makeup person
male nurse	nurse
male/female hardware	couplings, plugs and sockets
man about town	(eliminate)
man among men	important person
man of action	human dynamo, go-getter
man of distinction	person of distinction
man of letters	literary person, writer, scholar, academic
man of the year	newsmaker of the year
man on horseback	dictator, tyrant

Instead of	Use
man on the street	average citizen, pedestrian, average person
man (verb)	operate, staff
man's best friend	dog
man's law	the law
man's work	work
man-of-war	armed warship
man-sized	large
man-to-man	face-to-face, person-to-person, one-on-one
manageress	manager
maneater	flesh eater, cannibal
manhandle	mishandle, rough up, maltreat
manhole	utility hole, maintenance access
manhours	time, work hours, labor time
manhunt	search
mankind	humankind, people, humanity
manlike	humanlike
manmade	handmade, hand-built, synthetic, manufactured, machine-made, simulated
manpower	workers, personnel, workforce
marked man	target, marked person
marksman	sharpshooter
masculine persuasion	male
masculine rhyme (poetry, music)	rhyme with stressed or strong final syllable
masseuse	masseur, massage
master	expert
master key	skeleton key, passkey
master plan	plan, blueprint, plan of action, working plan, design
masterful	skillful
masterpiece	great work of art
master's degree	graduate degree, graduate-level degree
matron of honor	honored attendant
mayoress	mayor
meatman	butcher, meat cutter
mechanical man	robot, machine, mechanical device
mediatress, mediatrix	mediator

Instead of	Use
medicine man	spirit healer, faith healer
men working	people working
meter maid	meter attendant, meter reader
middleman	go-between, contact person, negotiator, liaison, intermediary
midshipman	cadet
Miss	Ms.
modern man	people today, modern humans
mother country	homeland, native country
Mother Earth	earth, world
mother lode	main lode, pay lode
Mother Nature	nature
mother tongue	first language, native language
mother's son	parent's child
motherhood, fatherhood	parenthood
motorman	driver
Mrs.	Ms.
murderess	murderer
negress	black woman (only if necessary to distinguish)
newsboy	news deliverer, news carrier
newsman	reporter, newscaster
newspaperman	editor, reporter, journalist, writer
night watchman	guard, night guard, security guard, watcher
no-man's-land	desolate, uninhabited land
nobleman	nobleperson, member of nobility
Norseman	Norse person
number-one man	head, number one, chief
number-two man	second in command, chief
nurseryman	horticulturist, nursery
nymphomaniac	(eliminate)
oarsman	crew member, rower
odd man	extra person, eccentric
odd man out	person not included
office boy	messenger, clerk
oilman	oil executive, oil field worker
old wives' tale	superstition

Instead of	Use
ombudsman	representative, researcher, mediator
one-upsmanship	the art of one-upping
organization man	loyal employee, team player
outdoorsman	outdoors person
paperboy	paper carrier
patrolman, policeman	police officer
patroness	patron, benefactor, sponsor
penmanship	handwriting
pitchman	promoter, hawker
plainclothesman	police officer, detective
playboy/girl	pleasure seeker, carouser
poetess	poet
postman	letter carrier, postal worker
postmistress	postal official
prehistoric man	prehistoric people
pressman	press operator
priestess	priest
prioress	prior
procuress	procurer
prodigal son	prodigal child (except for Biblical reference)
prophetess	prophet
proprietress	proprietor, owner, manager
publicity man	publicist
queen's English	proper English
queenly	regal, noble
radioman	radio operator
ranchman	rancher
rangeman	range rider, ranger
reman	restaff
Renaissance man	Renaissance person
repairman	repairer
rewrite man	editor, reviser, rewriter
rifleman	shooter, soldier
right-hand man	assistant, right arm, chief assistant
salesman/woman/lady	sales agent, sales associate, salesperson
Scotsman	Scot, Scotlander
sculptress	sculptor
seaman	sailor, mariner, seafarer
seamstress	tailor, sewer, mender, needleworker

Instead of	Use
seductress	seducer
seeress	prophet, seer, clairvoyant
serviceman	sailor, soldier
shipmaster	commander, captain
showman	actor, director, producer
showmanship	showiness, stage presence
signalman	signal operator, signaler
sister ship	co-ship
snowman	snow creation
social man	social person
song-and-dance man	singer and dancer
songstress	singer
sorceress	sorcerer, enchanter
spaceman	astronaut, spacefarer, cosmonaut
spinster	(eliminate)
spokesman, spokeswoman	spokesperson, representative
sportsmanlike	sporting
sportsmanship	fair play, fairness
squaw	(eliminate)
starlet	young star, star in the theater
state policeman	state trooper, trooper
statesman	diplomat, mediator, leader (or a specific title)
statesmanlike	diplomatic
stewardess	flight attendant (aircraft), steward (ship, union shop)
straw man	straw, straw person
suffragette	suffragist
suffragettism	suffrage
suitor	pursuer
switchman	switch operator
taskmaster	supervisor, tyrant
temptress	tempter, enticer
testatrix	testator
tigress (when referring to a person)	tiger
timberman	timber worker, forester
to a man	to a person
toastmaster/mistress	speaker, toastmaker
Tom, Dick, and Harry	everyone, ordinary people

Instead of	Use
tomcat	(eliminate)
tragedienne	tragedian, actor who plays tragic roles
traitoress, traitress	traitor, betrayer, turncoat
trashman	trash collector
tribesman	member of the tribe
triggerman	assassin, hoodlum
trollop	(eliminate)
Uncle Sam	U.S. or United States
usherette	usher
villainess	villain, scoundrel
virginal	(eliminate in reference to women)
vixen	(eliminate in reference to women)
waitress	waiter, server
wardress	warden, prison warden
warhorse	(eliminate in reference to women)
watchman	guard, watch
weak sister	weakling, coward
weaker sex	(eliminate)
weatherman	weathercaster, forecaster, meteorologist
Welshman	Welsh person
wench	(eliminate in reference to women)
woman lawyer	lawyer
woman stockbroker	stockbroker
workman	worker
workmanlike	efficient, skillful
workmen's compensation	workers' compensation
yeoman	guard, attendant, assistant
yes-man	endorser, follower, supporter
yokefellow	companion, coworker
young man	youth, teenager

There are many more, of course. Make your own logical nonsexist substitutions, using the most precise word that describes the function.

Try Out *Person* Words and Phrases Before Using

Person substitutions—chair*person*, spokes*person*—are generally acceptable, but they are sometimes contrived and awkward. Try out *person* words before using. Better alternatives almost always exist. But don't make substitutions if the cure is worse than the disease.

Don't Use Female or Male Words That Lower a Person's Status

This occurs more often in female words than male:

Don't Use	When You Mean
my girl	secretary
the girls	women employees
gals	women
females	women
female	woman, girl
males	men
the boys	men
boy	man
manly	strong, vigorous, etc.
sissy	——
tomboy	——
man and wife	husband and wife
men and ladies	men and women
lady	woman
biddy	older woman
divorcée	woman who is divorced

AVOID WORDS THAT STEREOTYPE BY RACE OR NATIONALITY

Nationality and heritage word usage changes with time. Those used 100 years ago, or even 15 years ago, may not be acceptable today.

First, use the racial or ethnic background of people only when it is necessary and relevant. Then the term preferred by the people you are describing should be used, and it should be used with sensitivity. Remember the principles:

- Treat all people equally.
- Use the race or ethnic background of people *only* when it is a vital part of your message.
- Refer to race or nationality objectively.
- Be as specific as possible.

Make sure your writing reflects that you are in touch. Here are some present generally accepted usages:

- *African American* or *black* are the terms preferred by most Americans of African and Caribbean descent, and these terms are usually interchangeable. If writing about cultural heritages, however, use *African American*. Do not use black as a singular noun: A *black* was hired in Department B. Do use it to differentiate: There are fifteen black and thirteen white committee members. No longer preferred are the terms *negro, colored,* or *Afro-American*.
- *American* implies citizenship. If the person being written about is of Chinese heritage but isn't an American citizen, don't use Chinese American.
- If necessary, terms like *Irish American, Italian American,* and others may be used.
- *Native American* is the inclusive, preferred term for general reference to aboriginal people of the United States. This includes Alaska native groups like Inuit and Aleut peoples, and peoples of Hawaii and American Samoa. In reference to heritage, many native Americans prefer to be identified by their tribal affiliation of nation, such as Navajo, Hopi, Sioux, Arapaho, or Zuni.
- *American Indian* is not accurate, since Indians are from India. It was a name given by Europeans, and isn't usually preferred.
- *Asian American* is the preferred term for U.S. citizens of Asian descent but be more specific if possible. Asia is a vast area, and many people refer to be identified by their national heritage: *Korean American, Chinese American, Japanese American.*
- *Arab American* is acceptable, but select a more distinct national reference, if possible: Iraqis, Syrians, Omanis. It is important to remember that Iranians are not Arabs. Also, do not use Persian, except to refer to rugs, cats, or the Gulf.
- *Chinese* is preferred in referencing citizens of China. Do not use *Chinamen* or *Orientals*.
- *Russians* are citizens of Russia. There is no longer a Soviet Union, so there are no Soviets. Use the proper national term to describe people from this part of the world: Citizens of Ukraine are Ukrainians, citizens of Georgia are Georgians.
- *Jew* is used to describe a person descended from the ancient Hebrews with the ethnic heritage based on Judaism. Do not use the word as an adjective or a verb. The preferred term for a citizen of Israel is *Israeli,* and these citizens are descended from many heritages. Do not use *Jewess,* as it is both pejorative and patronizing.
- *Colored* or *Coloured* is used by South Africans to refer to other South Africans of mixed race. Do not use this term in referring to Americans of mixed race.
- *Illegal immigrants* is used to describe people who come to this country illegally, without a passport, visa, or other legal document that entitles them to visit, work, or live in the country. Be careful in using *illegal* or *alien,* because both are offensive and require certain knowledge of this fact. It is better to avoid these negative terms, but use *undocumented* or *without a passport,* when necessary.
- *Latino* and *Hispanic* are synonymous, inclusive ethnic names for groups in the United States who have a cultural Spanish heritage, including Mexicans, Cubans, Puerto Ricans, Central Americans, and South Americans. Latinos may be of any race, including white, black, Native American, Asian, etc. Some speak Spanish, others don't; some are immigrants, and others are U.S. born. It is important to remember that Spaniards are not Latinos.
- *Whites* is a racial designatation of people formerally referred to as the most inclusive definition of *Anglo*.

Don't Send Subtle Discriminatory Messages

Do not infer any of these untruths:

Jews are miserly.
Italians are members of the Mafia.
Hispanics are dishonest.
Chicanos are unkempt.
All blacks live in ghettos and are on welfare.
Puerto Ricans are lazy.
Germans are abrasive.
The English are bullheaded.
The French are arrogant.
The Chinese are not able to manage.
The Japanese are underhanded.

Discriminatory statements are often subtle. Take this example:

"This study encompasses two ghetto areas.
Our sample includes 300 black males … "

Or, statements may be discriminatory by implication:

"open-minded German"
"neatly dressed Chicano"
"generous Jew"
"an industrious Puerto Rican"
"Chinese manager"

Never Use Discriminatory Words of Race, Nationality, or Sexual Preference

Other unacceptable words that refer to race, nationality, and sexual preference include:

Before You Use	Think About This
abortionist	Offensive term; use the most correct term, e.g., *abortion doctor, abortion provider, abortion practitioner, gynecologist who performs abortions.*
acknowledged/ admitted/avowed homosexual	Offensive. Use *openly gay* or *gay.*
adopted child	Do not use to define a child's relationship to the parents.

Before You Use	Think About This
alcoholic	Use the term *recovering alcoholic* if the person has stopped drinking; *reformed alcoholic* is incorrect and offensive.
alien	Do not use to describe someone who has entered the country illegally.
Amerasian	Originated to describe the child of an Asian mother and American father. Use *Asian American* instead.
American Indian	Use Native American instead.
Anglo	Use *white* instead. May be used to identify a person of English Anglo-Saxon heritage.
Asian	Use the country of citizenship, e.g., India.
bi	Offensive. Use *bisexual.*
bitch	Offensive. Use *only* to refer to a female dog.
boy	Use only to describe a male person under 18 years of age.
braburner	Offensive term for feminist.
brave	Offensive term for Native American young men.
buck	Offensive term for black or Native American young men.
cabron	Offensively vulgar Spanish word for cuckold.
Canuck	Use Canadian or French Canadian.
chief	Use only in referring to the head of an official tribal government of Native Americans. Check first.
Chinese fire drill	Use another term to refer to mass confusion.
co-ed, coed	Do not use as a noun; use *student.*

Before You Use	Think About This	Before You Use	Think About This
Colored	Do not use to refer to Americans of mixed racial ancestry. May be used to refer to people of some African countries. Use the country of origin when possible. Capitalize when used.	hick	Offensive term for rural person.
		high yellow, high yeller	Offensive term for some black people.
		hillbilly	Offensive term for rural person.
companion	Generally preferred to describe a person in a homosexual relationship.	holy rollers	Offensive term for evangelical and charismatic Christians.
culo	Offensive Spanish word for ass.	homo	Offensive term for homosexual person.
dark continent	Do not use to refer to Africa.	homosexual lifestyle, gay lifestyle	Offensive and erroneous terms. There is no gay subculture single, gay, nongay, or heterosexual lifestyle.
Dutch courage	Do not use to refer to cowardice.		
Dutch treat	Do not use to refer to each person paying his or her own expenses.	illegal	Use only to describe a violation of the law. Often misused to mean a rule or contract agreement has been broken.
dyke	Offensive word for *lesbian*.		
Eastern Indians	Use *people of India* to distinguish from Native Americans.		
Eskimos	Use specific names such as *Inuits* or *Aleuts* whenever possible.	illegals, illegal aliens	Offensive terms to refer to people who have entered the country without a passport, visa, or other document that permits them to enter.
ethnic	Do not use as a noun. Use only if relevant, and then use nationality or race.		
fag	Offensive term for homosexual men.	illegitimate	Offensive term used to describe children of unmarried people.
gay	Use as a noun or adjective to describe homosexual men and sometimes women: *gay, gay men* and *lesbians*. Use the choice of your reader.	Indians	Use this term for citizens of India. Use *Native Americans* when referring to aboriginal peoples of North America.
		Injun	Offensive term for Native Americans.
ghetto	Offensive term for areas of a city where poor people live. Use the proper neighborhood name.	inner city	Use carefully to refer only to the center of the city. Do not use to refer to depict an area of the city inhabited by poor people. A better term is the neighborhood, district, or other appropriate name.
girl	Use only to describe a female person under 18 years of age.		
gringo	Offensive Spanish word for white Americans.		
guero	Offensive Spanish word for white Americans.	Jap	Offensive term that originated during World War II for Japanese people.
gyp/gypped/ gyp joint	Offensive words derived from *gypsy*.		

Before You Use	Think About This
JAP	Offensive term short for "Jewish American Princess"
joto	Offensive Spanish term for gay person.
kaffir	Offensive word used primarily in South Africa to refer to black people.
lesbian	Use as a noun when appropriate for a woman with same-sex orientation.
mayate	Offensive Spanish word for black person.
mestizo	Not a term of choice by most people of European and Indian heritage.
morocho	Offensive Spanish term for black person.
mulatto	Offensive word for people of African and European heritage.
natural parents	Use *biological parents,* or *birth parents* only if that term is accurate and necessary.
Negress	Offensive term for black woman.
Negro	Use only if chosen by the black people who are the subject and audience of your communication.
New World	Some Native Americans object to the use of this term for North America, since it does not recognize their existence on the continent prior to the landing of Christopher Columbus.
Oriental	Do not use in referring to persons or groups unless it is part of a proper name.
Persian	Do not use in reference to people. Refer instead to the correct country of citizenship.
powwow	Use only to properly refer to Native American spiritual or social celebrations.

Before You Use	Think About This
queer	Use only as an adjective when it is the preferred word of the subject and audience groups of your communiction to describe sociopolitical activists who want to integrate pro-gay attitudes into all aspects of American life.
racially diverse	Use to describe a group of people of different races.
racially mixed	Use to describe a person who has parents of different races.
real parents	Use *biological parents,* or *birth parents* only if those terms are accurate and necessary.
redskins	Offensive term for Native Americans.
sangron	Offensive Spanish term for a disagreeable person.
savages	Offensive term for Native Americans.
sexual orientation	Generally preferred over the terms *sexual preference* and *sexual persuasion.*
Spanish	Use only to refer to citizens of Spain. Do not use to describe Latinos.
Spanish speakers	Can be used to refer to any people who speak Spanish.
step-	Do not use in stereotypical slang expressions like *wicked step-mother.*
tribe	Use only as a proper noun in referring to ethnic groups, or African or Eastern European nations, or language groups. Native Americans tribal names are used by themselves: Navajo, Hopi, Sioux. Native Americans generally prefer *nation.*
undocumented immigrant	Use as a synonym for illegal immigrant.

Before You Use	Think About This
WASP	This acronym for White Anglo-Saxon Protestant is derogatory.
Welsh, welsher	Offensive term of uncertain origin, which was used to refer to going back on one's word.
wetbacks	Offensive term used to describe Mexican people who enter the United States illegally.
white trash	Offensive term that should not be used to refer to poor or socially deprived white people.
Whitey (Whitie, Whity)	Contemptuous term used by blacks to describe Caucasians. Do not use it.
wimp	Offensive term used to describe a weak or boring person.
wop	Offensive term for Italian or southern European people.
Yankee	May still be considered offensive by some when referring to people from the north and northeastern United States.
Yanqui	Offensive Spanish word for a white American.
zambo	Offensive Spanish word for a person of African or Indian heritage.

AVOID AGE DISCRIMINATION

Know your reader, and avoid age terms that might offend:

Before Using This	Consider
adolescents	young people
elderly	people over seventy
golden ager	person over sixty-two
middle-aged	people between forty-five and sixty
oldster	people over sixty-five
senior citizens	people over sixty-two
teenagers	young people
youngster	young person

AVOID BEHAVIOR STEREOTYPES

Avoid words that describe a very narrow type of behavior or wrongly characterize people.

Don't Use These

brat
feeble
forgetful
frilly
giggly
juvenile delinquent
loner
runaway
spry
superficial
truant

AVOID STEREOTYPING PEOPLE WITH DISABILITIES

Avoid derogatory, apologetic, or patronizing words:

Instead of	Use
attack	epilepsy (or appropriate)
birth defect	congenital disability
bobo (Spanish)	mental disabilities
crazy	(Use specific medical term, e.g., paranoid, manic-depressive, psychotic, etc.)
crippled	disabled
deaf	individual who cannot hear
deaf and dumb	hearing and speech disabled
deaf-mute	individual who cannot hear or speak
deformed	(Describe specific condition.)
disfigured	(Describe specific condition.)
fits	seizures
handicapped	disabled
idiota (Spanish)	mental disability
imbecil (Spanish)	mental disability
invalid	(Describe specific disability.)
lame	disabled (Or, use word for specific condition.)
mentally deranged	(Use specific term, e.g., neurotic, paranoid, etc.)
mongoloid	Down's syndrome
normal	(A trait, not a person, is normal.)
retarded	mentally disabled
special	(Use the correct term when referring to people with disabilities.)
spells	epilepsy (or appropriate)

APPENDIX III

SPELLING GUIDE

Many English words defy the best-learned rules of spelling. Others just seem to fall in that one-or-two-of-the-same-letter-category. Here's a list of commonly misspelled words.

A

a lot (not *alot*)
abbreviate
abhorrence
abruptly
absence
absurd
accede
acceleration
accept
acceptance
accessible
accessory
accidentally
accommodate
accompanied
accompanying
accordance
accrued
accumulate
accuracy
accustom
achieved
achievement
acknowledgment
acquaintance
acquainted
acquiesce
acquire
acquitted
across
adapt
address
adequate
adjourn
adjustment
admirable
advantageous
advertisement
advertising
advisable
advise
adviser
advisory
affect
affidavit
aggravate
agreeable
aisle
allot
allotment
allotted
allowable
allowance
almost
already
altar, alter
altogether
aluminum
alumnus
amateur
ambassador
amendment
among
analogous
analysis
analyze
angel
angle
announce
announcement
annoyance
annual
anticipate
anxiety
anxious
apocalypse
apologize
apparatus
apparel
apparent
appearance
appliance
applicable
applicant
appointment
appraisal
appreciable
appropriate
approximate
archaeology
archipelago
architect
Arctic
arguing
argument
arrangement
article
ascend
ascertain
assassin
assessment
assignment
assistance
associate
assured
athletic
attendance
attention
attorneys
auditor
authorize
auxiliary
available
awkward

B

baccalaureate
bachelor
bankruptcy
barbarous
bargain
baroque
beggar
beginning

beneficial
beneficiary
biennially
biscuit
bloc
bologna
bookkeeper
bouillon
boundary
boutonniere
brilliant
Britain
brochure
bruised
budget
bulletin
buoy
bureau
business

C

cafeteria
calendar
campaign
candidate
capital, capitol
carriage
casualty
catalog(ue)
chancellor
changeable
changing
characteristic
chauffeur
choice
choose
chose
clientele
clique
collateral
colonel
column
commission
commitment
committed

committee
commodity
comparable
comparative
comparatively
comparison
compel
compelled
competent
competitor
complement
compliment
compromise
concede
conceivable
conceive
concession
concur
concurred
congratulate
connoisseur
conscience
conscientious
conscious
consensus
consequence
contemptible
continuous
controversy
convenience
convenient
cordially
council
councilor
counsel
counselor
courteous
courtesy
creditor
crescendo
criticism
criticize
cruelty
cryptic
curiosity
cyanide

D

debater
debtor
deceit
deceive
deferred
deficient
deficit
definitely
delicatessen
demagogue
derivative
desperate
dialog(ue)
dictionary
dietitian
disappearance
disastrous
discipline
discrepancy
disk
disparate
dissatisfied
dissipate
drudgery
dungeon
dyeing, dying

E

ecclesiastical
ecstasy
effect
efficiency
eighth
eligible
emanate
embarrass
eminent
enthusiasm
envelop
environment
equipment
equipped
equivalent
especially

essential
etiquette
exaggerate
excellence
excessive
exhilarate
existence
experience
extraordinary
extremely

F

familiar
fascinate
February
fiery
financier
forcible
foreign
fortuitous
forty
fourth
freight
friend

G

generally
genuine
government
grammar
grievance
grievous
gruesome
guarantee
guerrilla
guidance
guitar

H

hallelujah
handkerchief
harangue
height
heinous

heiress
hesitancy
heterogeneous
hiccup
homemade
hors d'oeuvres
humorous
hundredths
hygiene
hyperbole
hypocrisy

I

icicle
identical
idiosyncrasy
immediately
immigration
imminent
imperiled
impromptu
incarcerate
incidentally
incredible
indebtedness
indict
indigestible
indispensable
individual
intelligible
investor
irrelevant
irresistible
itinerary
its, it's

J

jeopardize
judgment

K

khaki
kindergarten
kleptomaniac

knapsack
knead
knell
knotty

L

laid
lead
led
liaison
lightning
likable
likelihood
likely
loath
loneliness
loose
lose
losing
luncheon
lymph

M

maintenance
manufacturer
manuscript
marital
marriage
mathematics
maybe
medieval
memorandum
merchandise
messenger
mileage
miniature
miracle
miscellaneous
mischievous
misspell
monologue
mortgage
mysterious

N

necessary
negligible
negotiate
neighbor
neighborhood
neither
neurotic
niche
niece
ninety
ninth
notable
noticeable
nucleus

O

oblige
occasionally
occupant
occurred
occurrence
occurring
offense
offering
official
omission
omit
omitted
overrun

P

pageant
pamphlet
pantomime
parallel
paralyze
parliament
partial
pastime
peremptory
periphery
permissible
permitted

perseverance
persistent
perspiration
persuade
physically
physician
portentous
possess
possession
practically
precision
preferable
preference
prejudice
preliminary
premium
presence
prevalent
primitive
principal, principle
privilege
prodigy
pronunciation
prophecy
prosecute
psyche
psychiatrist
psychology

Q

qualm
quantity
quarrel
questionnaire
queue
quiet
quite
quizzes

R

raccoon
receipt
receive
referee

referred
religious
remember
reminisce
remittance
representative
reservoir
resistance
respectfully
respectively
responsibility
reticence
rhetoric
rhythm
ridiculous
route

S

sacrilegious
scenery
schedule
schism
science
secession
secretary
securities
seize
sentinel
separate
sergeant
serviceable

severely
shepherd
shriek
sieve
simultaneous
sincerity
soliloquy
sophomore
specimen
stationary, stationery
statistics
studying
subpoena
subsequent
subtle
suffrage
summarize
superintendent
supersede
supervisor
suppress
surprise
survey
syllable
symmetrical
symmetry

T

tariff
tendency
than, then

theater
their, there, they're
tipsy
to, too, two
tragedy
tremendous
twelfth
typically
tyranny

U

unbelievable
unfortunately
universally
unnecessary
utilize
utterance

V

vaccinate
vaccination
vaccine
vacillate
vacuum
vehicle
vengeance
vicinity
vigilance
villain
vitiate

W

weather
weird
whether
who's
wholly
whose
wrestle
writing
written

Y

yacht
yaw
yea
yield
you're
your

Z

zinc

INDEX

Sandra E. Lamb has worked as a technical writer, editor, ghostwriter, public relations consultant, account manager, and CEO. She co-authored the book *Equity Sharing* and has been a columnist for *The Rocky Mountain News* and *The Denver Post*. She writes for national magazines.